THE PROVERBS EPIGRAMS AND MISCELLANIES OF JOHN HEYWOOD

Early English Dramatists

The

Proverbs, Epigrams, and Miscellanies of

JOHN HEYWOOD

COMPRISING

A Dialogue of the Effectual Proverbs in the English Tongue concerning Marriages—First Hundred Epigrams—Three Hundred Epigrams on Three Hundred Proverbs—The Fifth Hundred Epigrams—A Sixth Hundred Epigrams—Miscellanies—Ballads—Note-Book and Word-List

EDITED BY

JOHN S. FARMER

This edition, published in 1966,
is a facsimile of the edition published by the
EARLY ENGLISH DRAMA SOCIETY, LONDON
in 1906

BARNES & NOBLE, Inc.
NEW YORK
PUBLISHERS AND BOOKSELLERS SINCE 1873

CONTENTS

John Heywoodes woorkes.

❧ A dialogue conteynyng the

number of the effectuall prouerbes in
the Englishe tounge, compact in
a matter concernynge
two maner of ma=
ryages.
With one hundred of Epigrammes : and
three hundred of Epigrammes
vpon three hundred pro=
uerbes : and a fifth
hundred of E=
pigrams.
Wherevnto are now newly added
a syxt hundred of Epigrams
by the sayde John
Heywood.

℈

LONDINI.

ANNO christi.

1562.

A DIALOGUE

CONTAINING THE NUMBER OF THE EFFECTUAL PROVERBS
IN THE ENGLISH TONGUE

PART I.   THE PREFACE

Among other things profiting in our tongue—
Those which much may profit both old and
    young,
Such as on their fruit will feed or take hold—
Are our common plain pithy proverbs old.
Some sense of some of which, being bare and
    rude,
Yet to fine and fruitful effect they allude.
And their sentences include so large a reach,
That almost in all things good lessons they
    teach.   [why?
This write I, not to teach, but to touch : for
Men know this as well or better than I.
But this, and this rest, I write for this,
Rememb'ring and considering what the pith
    is :
That, by remembrance of these, proverbs may
    grow.
In this tale, erst talked with a friend, I show
As many of them as we could fitly find
Falling to purpose, that might fall in mind ;
To th'intent that the reader readily may
Find them, and mind them, when he will
    alway.

Finis.

Chapter I.

Of mine acquaintance a certain young man
(Being a resorter to me now and than)
Resorted lately, showing himself to be
Desirous to talk at length alone with me.
And, as we for this a meet place had won,
With this old proverb this young man begun.
Whoso that knew what would be dear,
Should need be a merchant but one year.
Though it, (quoth he), thing impossible be
The full sequel of present things to foresee,
Yet doth this proverb provoke every man
Politically, (as man possible can),
In things to come after to cast eye before,
To cast out, or keep in, things for fore store;
As the provision may seem most profitable,
And the commodity most commendable.
Into this consideration I am wrought
By two things, which fortune to hands hath
        brought.
Two women I know, of which twain the tone
Is a maid of flowering age, a goodly one;
Th'other a widow, who so many years bears,
That all her whiteness lieth in her white hairs.
This maid hath friends rich, but riches hath
        she none,
Nor none can her hands get to live upon.
This widow is very rich, and her friends bare,
And both these, for love, to wed with me fond
        are.   [worse;
And both would I wed, the better and the
The tone for her person, the tother for her
        purse.   [woo.
They woo not my substance, but myself they
Goods have I none and small good can I do.

On this poor maid, her rich friends, I clearly
    know,   [bestow,
(So she wed where they will), great gifts will
But with them all I am so far from faver,
That she shall sure have no groat, if I have
    her.   [swear,
And I shall have as little, all my friends
Except I follow them, to wed elsewhere.
The poor friends of this rich widow bear no
    sway,
But wed her and win wealth, when I will I may.
Now which of these twain is like to be dearest?
In pain or pleasure to stick to me nearest?
The depth of all doubts with you to confither,
The sense of the said proverb sendeth me
    hither,   [scan'd,
The best bargain of both quickly to have
For one of them, think I, to make out of hand.

CHAPTER II.

Friend, (quoth I), welcome! and with right
    good will,
I will, as I can, your will herein fulfil.
And two things I see in you, that show you
    wise.
First, in wedding, ere ye wed to ask advice.
The second, your years being young it appears,
Ye regard yet good proverbs of old ferne years.
And, as ye ground your tale upon one of them,
Furnish we this tale with everychone of them,
Such as may fitly fall in mind to dispose.
Agreed, (quoth he). Then, (quoth I), first this
    disclose—   [maid,
Have you to this old widow, or this young
Any words of assurance ere this time said?

Nay, in good faith ! said he.   Well then, (said
    I),
I will be plain with you, and may honestly
And plainly too speak : I like you, (as I said),
In two foretold things; but a third have I
    weighed
Not so much to be liked, as I can deem;
Which is, in your wedding, your haste so
    extreme.
The best or worst thing to man, for this life,
Is good or ill choosing his good or ill wife.
I mean not only of body good or bad,
But of all things meet or unmeet to be had;
Such as at any time by any mean may,
Between man and wife, love increase or decay.
Where this ground in any head gravely
    grateth,
All fiery haste to wed, it soon rebateth.
Some things that provoke young men to wed
    in haste,
Show, after wedding, that *haste maketh waste.*
When *time hath turned white sugar to white*
    salt,   [*malt.*
Then such folk see, *soft fire maketh sweet*
And that deliberation doth men assist,
Before they wed, to *beware of Had I wist.*
And then, their timely wedding doth clear
    appear
That they were *early up, and never the near.*
And once their hasty heat a little controlled,
Then perceive they well, *hot love soon cold.*
And when hasty witless mirth is mated weele,
Good to be merry and wise, they think and
    feel.
Haste in wedding some man thinketh his own
    avail,

When haste proveth *a rod made for his own
    tail.*
And when he is well *beaten with his own rod,*
*Then seeth he haste and wisdom things far
    odd.*   [need,
And that in all, or most things, wisht at
Most times he seeth, *the more haste the less
    speed.*   [hasty man's foe,
In less things than wedding haste show'th
So that *the hasty man never wanteth woe.*
These sage said saws if ye take so profound,
As ye take that by which ye took your ground,
Then find ye grounded cause by these now here
    told,
In haste to wedding your haste to withhold.
And though they seem wives for you never so
    fit,   [wit
Yet let not harmful haste so far outrun your
But that ye hark to hear all the whole sum
That may please or displease you in time to
    come.   [cheap
Thus, by these lessons, ye may learn good
In wedding and all thing to *look or ye leap.*
Ye have even now well overlooked me, (quoth
    he),
And leapt very nigh me too. For, I agree
That these sage sayings do weightily weigh
Against haste in all thing, but I am at bay
By other parables, of like weighty weight,
Which haste me to wedding, as ye shall hear
    straight.

Chapter III.

He that will not when he may,
When he would he shall have nay.
Beauty or riches, the tone of the twain
Now may I choose, and which me list obtain.
And if we determine me this maid to take,
And then tract of time train her me to forsake,
Then *my beautiful marriage lieth in the dike*;
And never for beauty shall I wed the like.
Now if we award me this widow to wed,
And that I drive off time, till time she be dead,
Then farewell riches, *the fat is in the fire,*
And never shall I to like riches aspire.
And, a thousandfold would it grieve me more
That she, in my fault, should die one hour
        before   [voke,
Than one minute after; then haste must pro-
When the pig is proffered to hold up the poke.
When the sun shineth make hay; which is to
        say,   [away.
Take time when time cometh, lest time steal
And one good lesson to this purpose I pike
From the smith's forge, *when th'iron is hot,*
        strike!   [man;
The sure seaman seeth, *the tide tarrieth no*
And long delays or absence somewhat to scan,
Since that, *that one will not another will—*
Delays in wooers must needs their speed spill.
And touching absence, the full accompte who
        summeth
Shall see, *as fast as one goeth another cometh.*
Time is tickle; and, *out of sight, out of mind.*
Then catch and hold while I may: *fast bind,*
        fast find.   [bleared,
Blame me not to haste for fear mine eye be

And *thereby the fat clean flit from my beard.*
Where wooers hop in and out, long time may
    bring
Him that hoppeth best at last to have the ring.
I hopping without for a ring of a rush,
And *while I* at length debate and *beat the bush,*
There shall step in *other men* and *catch the*
    birds.
And by long time lost in many vain words,
Between these two wives make sloth speed
    confound;   [ground.
While, *between two stools, my tail go to*
By this, since we see sloth must breed a scab,
Best stick to the tone out of hand, *hab or nab.*
Thus, all your proverbs inveighing against
    haste,   [placed.
Be answered with proverbs plain and promptly
Whereby, to purpose all this no further fits,
But to show *so many heads so many wits.*
Which show, as surely in all that they all tell,
That in my wedding I may even as well
Tarry too long, and thereby come too late,
As come too soon by haste in any rate.
And prove this proverb, as the words thereof
    go—
Haste or sloth herein work nother wealth nor
Be it far or nigh, *wedding is destiny.*   [woe—
And hanging likewise, saith that proverb, said
    I.
Then wed or hang, (quoth he), what helpeth in
    the whole,
To haste or hang aloof, *happy man happy dole.*
Ye deal this dole, (quoth I), *out at a wrong*
    dur;
For destiny, in this case doth not so stir
Against man's endeavour, but man may direct

His will, for provision to work or neglect.
But, to show that quick wedding may bring
    good speed,   [deed.
Somewhat to purpose your proverbs prove in-
Howbeit, whether they counterpoise or out-
    weigh
The proverbs which I before them did lay,
The trial thereof we will *lay a water*
Till we try more. For trying of which matter
Declare all commodities ye can devise
That, by those two weddings, to you can rise.

Chapter IV.

I will, (quoth he), in both these cases straight
    show   [grow.
What things, (as I think), to me by them will
And, where my love began, there begin will I
With this maid, the piece peerless in mine eye;
Whom I so favour, and she so favoureth me,
That half a death to us ['tis] asunder to be.
Affection, each to other, doth us so move
That well nigh, without food, we could live by
    love.   [sight,
For, be I right sad, or right sick, from her
Her presence absenteth all maladies quite;
Which seen, and that the great ground in
    marriage
Standeth upon liking the parties personage,
And then of old proverbs, in opening the pack,
One sheweth me openly, *in love is no lack.*
No lack of liking, but lack of living
May lack in love, (quoth I), and breed ill
    chieving.
Well, as to that, (said he), hark this othing :
What time I lack not her, I lack nothing.

But though we have nought, nor nought we
    can geat,
God never sendeth mouth but he sendeth meat;
And *a hard beginning maketh a good ending;*
In space cometh grace, and this further amend-
    ing—
Seldom cometh the better, and *like will to like;*
God sendeth cold after clothes; and this I pike,
She, by lack of substance, seeming but a
    spark,
Steinth yet the stoutest: for *a leg of a lark*
Is better than is the body of a kite;
And *home is homely though it be poor* in sight.
These proverbs for this part show such a
    flourish,
And then this party doth delight so nourish;
That much is my bow bent to shoot at these
    marks,   [*have larks.*
And kill fear: *when the sky falleth we shall*
All perils that fall may, who feareth they fall
    shall,
Shall so fear all thing, that he shall let fall all;
And be *more fraid than hurt,* if the things were
    doone;   [*moon;*
Fear may force a man *to cast beyond the*
Who hopeth in God's help, his help cannot
    start:
Nothing is impossible to a willing heart.
And will may win my heart, herein to consent,
To take all things as it cometh, and be content.
And here is, (q'he), in marrying of this maid,
For courage and commodity all mine aid.
Well said, (said I), but awhile keep we in
    quench   [*wench.*
All this case, as touching this poor young
And now declare your whole consideration;

What manner things draw your imagination
Toward your wedding of this widow, rich and
    old?
That shall ye, (q'he), out of hand have told.

CHAPTER V.

This widow, being foul, and of favour ill,
In good behaviour can very good skill;
Pleasantly spoken, and a very good wit;
And, at her table, when we together sit,
I am well served—we fare of the best;
The meat good and wholesome, and whole-
    somely dressed;   [shift—
Sweet and soft lodging, and thereof great
This felt and seen; with all implements of
    thrift,   [coffers;
Of plate and money such cupboards and
And that without pain I may win these proffers.
Then covetise, bearing Venus's bargain back,
Praising this bargain saith, *better leave than
    lack.*
And greediness, to draw desire to her lore,
Saith, that the wise man saith, *store is no sore.*
*Who hath many peas may put the mo in the
    pot;*   [in lot.
Of two ills, choose the least, while choice lieth
Since lack is an ill, as ill as man may have,
To provide for the worst, while the best itself
    save.
Resty wealth willeth me this widow to win,
To *let the world wag,* and *take mine ease in
    mine inn*—   [chin;
He must needs swim, that is hold up by the
He laugheth that winneth. And this thread
    finer to spin,

Maister promotion saieth : make this substance
    sure ;
If riches bring once portly countenance in ure,
Then shalt thou *rule the roost* all round about;
And better to rule, than be ruled by the rout.
It is said : *be it better, be it worse,*
Do ye after him that beareth the purse.
Thus be I by this once le senior de graunde,
Many that commanded me I shall command.
And also I shall, to revenge former hurts,
Hold their noses to grindstone, and *sit on their*
    skirts
That erst sat on mine.   And riches may make
Friends many ways.   Thus, *better to give than*
And, to make carnal appetite content,   [*take.*
Reason laboureth will, to win will's consent,
To take lack of beauty but as *an eye fore,*
The fair and the foul by dark are like store;
When all candles be out all cats be grey;
All things are then of one colour, as who say.
And· this proverb saith, for quenching hot
    desire
Foul water as soon as fair will quench hot fire.
Where gifts be given freely—east, west, north
    or south—
No man ought to look a given horse in the
    mouth.   [*tail—*
And *though her mouth be foul she hath a fair*
I conster this text, as is most my avail.
In want of white teeth and yellow hairs to
    behold,
She flourisheth in white silver and yellow gold.
What though she be toothless, and *bald as a*
    coot?
Her substance is shoot anker, whereat I shoot.
Take a pain for a pleasure all wise men can—

What? *hungry dogs will eat dirty puddings,*
       man!
And here I conclude, (quoth he), all that I
       know
By this old widow, what good to me may grow.

Chapter VI.

Ye have, (quoth I), in these conclusions found
Sundry things, that very savourly sound;
And both these long cases, being well viewed,
In one short question we may well include;
Which is : whether best or worse be to be led
With riches, without love or beauty, to wed;
Or, with beauty without richesse, for love.
This question, (quoth he), inquireth all that I
       move.
It doth so, (said I), and is neerly couched,
But th'answer will not so briefly be touched;
And yourself, to length it, taketh direct trade.
For to all reasons that I have yet made,
Ye seem more to seek reasons how to contend,
Than to the counsel of mine to condescend.
And to be plain, as I must with my friend,
I perfectly feel, even *at my finger's end,*
So hard is your hand set on your halfpenny,
That my reasoning your reason setteth nought
But, reason for reason, ye so stiffly lay   [by.
By proverb for proverb, that with you do
       weigh,
That reason only shall herein nought move you
To hear more than speak; wherefore, I will
       prove you
With reason, assisted by experience,   [hence,
Which myself saw, not long since nor far
In a matter so like this fashioned in frame

That none can be liker—it seemeth even the
    same;
And in the same, as yourself shall espy,
Each sentence suited with a proverb well nigh;
And, at end of the same, ye shall clearly see
How this short question shortly answered may
    be.   [*prick;*
Yea, marry! (quoth he); now *ye shoot nigh the*
Practise in all, above all toucheth the quick.
Proof upon practise, must take hold more sure
Than any reasoning by guess can procure.
If ye *bring practise in place, without fabling,*
I will *banish both haste and busy babling.*
And yet, that promise to perform is mickle,
For in this case my tongue must oft tickle.
Ye know well *it is*, as telleth us this old tale,
Meet that a man be at his own bridal.   [were;
If he wive well, (quoth I), meet and good it
Or else as good for him another were there.
But for this your bridal, I mean not in it
That silence shall suspend your speech every
    whit.
But in these marriages, which ye here meve,
Since this tale containeth the counsel I can
    give,
I would see your ears attend with your tongue;
For advice in both these weddings, old and
    young.   [to talk,
In which hearing, time seen when and what
When your tongue tickleth, at will let it walk.
And in these bridals, to the reasons of ours,
Mark mine experience in this case of yours.

CHAPTER VII.

Within few years passed, from London no far
    way,   [lay,
Where I and my wife with our poor household
Two young men were abiding; whom to dis-
    crive
Were I, in portraying persons dead or alive,
As cunning and as quick, to touch them at full,
As in that feat I am ignorant and dull,
Never could I paint their pictures to allow
More lively than to paint the picture of you.
And as your three persons show one similitude,
So show you three one, in all things to be
    viewed.
Likewise a widow and a maid there did dwell;
Alike, like the widow and maid ye of tell,
The friends of them four, in every degree
Standing in state, as the friends of you three.
Those two men, each other so hasted or tarried,
That those two women on one day they
    married.   [stand,
Into two houses, which next my house did
The one on the right, th'other on the left hand,
Both bridegrooms bade me—I could do none
    other
But dine with the tone, and sup with the tother.
He that wedded this widow rich and old,
And also she, favoured me so that they wold
Make me dine or sup once or twice in a week.
This poor young man and his make, being to
    seek   [bad,
As oft where they might eat or drink, I them
Were I at home, to such pittance as I had.
Which common conference such confidence
    wrought

In them to me, that deed, word, ne well nigh
  thought
Chanced among them, whatever it were, [ear.
But one of the four brought it straight to mine
Whereby, between these twain, and their two
  wives, [lives.
Both for wealth and woe, I knew all their four
And since the matter is much intricate,
Between side and side, I shall here separate
All matters on both sides, and then sequestrate
Th'one side, while th'other be full rehearsed,
  in rate,
As for your understanding may best stand.
And this young poor couple shall come first in
  hand
Who, the day of wedding, and after a while,
Could not look each on other but they must
  smile;
As a whelp, for wantonness, in and out whips,
So played these twain, *as merry as three chips.*
Yea, there was God, (quoth he), when all is
  doone.
Abide ! (quoth I), it was yet but honey moon;
The black ox had not trod on his nor her foot.
But *ere this branch of bliss could reach any
  root,*
The flowers so *faded* that, in fifteen weeks
A man might espy the change in the cheeks,
Both of this poor wretch, and his wife, this
  poor wench— [*French.*
Their faces told toys, that *Tott'n'am was turned*
And all their light laughing turn'd and trans-
  lated
Into sad sighing; all mirth was amated.
And, one morning timely, he took in hand
To make, to my house, *a sleeveless errand;*

HEY. II.   C

Hawking upon me, his mind herein to break,
Which I would not see till he began to speak,
Praying me to hear him : and I said, I would ;
Wherewith this that followeth forthwith he
    told.

Chapter VIII.

I am now driven, (quoth he), for ease of my
    heart
To you, to utter part of mine inward smart.
And the matter concerneth my wife and me,
Whose fathers and mothers long since dead
    be ;
But uncles, with aunts and cousins, have we
Divers, rich on both sides ; so that we did see
If we had wedded, each where each kindred
    would,
Neither of us had lacked either silver or gold.
But never could suit, on either side, obtain
One penny to the one wedding of us twain.
And since our one *marrying, or marring* day,
Where any of them see us, they shrink away,
Solemnly swearing, such as may give ought,
While they and we live, of them we get right
    nought.   [get,
Nor nought have we, nor no way ought can we
Saving by borrowing till we be in debt
So far, that no man any more will us lend ;
Whereby, for lack, we both be at our wits'
    end.
Whereof, no wonder ; since the end of our
    good,
And beginning of our charge, together stood.
But *wit is never good till it be bought.*
Howbeit, when bought, wits to best price be
    brought ;

Yet *is one good forewit worth two after wits.*
This *payeth me home,* lo! and full mo folly
    hits;
For, had I looked afore, with indifferent eye,
Though haste had made me thirst never so dry,
Yet to drown this drought, this must I needs
    think:
As I would needs brew, so must I needs drink.
The drink of my bride cup I should have for-
    borne,
Till temperance had tempered the taste beforne.
I see now, and shall see while I am alive,
Who weddeth or he be wise shall die or he
    thrive.
I sing now in this fact, *factus est repente,*
Now mine eyes be open I do repent me:
He that will sell lawn before he can fold it,
He shall repent him before he have sold it.
Some bargains dear bought, good cheap would
    be sold;
No man loveth his fetters, be they made of
    gold;
Were I loose from the lovely links of my chain,
I would not dance in such fair fetters again.
In house to keep household, *when folks will*
    needs wed,   [bed.
Mo things belong than four bare legs in a
I reckoned my wedding a sugar-sweet spice;
But *reckoners without their host much reckon*
    twice.   [twain,
And, although it were sweet for a week or
Sweet meat will have sour sauce, I see now
Continual penury, which I must take,   [plain.
Telleth me: *better eye out than alway ache.*
Boldly and blindly I ventured on this;
Howbeit, *who so bold as blind Bayard is?*
                        C 2

And herein, to blame any man, then should I
　　rave
For I did it myself : and *self do, self have.*
But, *a day after fair* cometh this remorse
For relief : for, though *it be a good horse*
That never stumbleth, what praise can that
　　avouch　　　　　　　　　　　　　[touch?
To jades that break their necks at first trip or
And before this my first foil or breakneck fall,
Subtilly like a sheep, thought I, I shall
Cut my coat after my cloth when I have her.
But *now I can smell, nothing hath no savour* ;
I am taught to know, in more haste than good
How Judicare came into the Creed.　　[*speed,*
My careful wife in one corner weepeth in care, .
And I in another ; the purse is threadbare.
This corner of our care, (quoth he), I you tell,
To crave therein your comfortable counsel.

CHAPTER IX.

I am sorry, (quoth I), of your poverty ;
And more sorry that I cannot succour ye ;
If ye stir your need mine alms to stir,
Then of truth *ye beg at a wrong man's dur.*
There is nothing more vain, as yourself tell can,
Than to beg a breech of a bare-arsed man.
I come to beg nothing of you, (quoth he),
Save your advice, which may my best way be ;
How to win present salve for this present sore.
I am like th'ill surgeon, (said I), without store
Of good plasters.　Howbeit, such as they are,
Ye shall have the best I have.　But first declare
Where your and your wife's rich kinfolk do
　　dwell.　　　　　　　　　　　　　[well,
Environed about us, (quoth he), which showeth

The nearer to the church, the farther from God.
Most part of them dwell within a thousand rod;
And yet shall we *catch a hare with a taber*
As soon as catch aught of them, and rather.
Ye play cole-prophet, (quoth I), who taketh in
    hand
To know his answer before he do his errand.
What should I to them, (quoth he), fling or flit?
An unbidden guest knoweth not where to sit.
I am *cast at cart's arse,* some folk in lack
Cannot prease : *a broken sleeve holdeth th'arm
    back ;*
And shame holdeth me back, being thus for-
    saken.
Tush, man ! (quoth I), *shame is as it is taken ;*
And shame take him that shame thinketh ye
    think none.
Unminded, unmoaned, go *make your moan ;*
Till meat fall in your mouth, will ye lie in bed?
Or sit still? nay, *he that gapeth till he be fed*
May fortune to fast and famish for hunger.
Set forward, ye shall never labour younger.
Well, (quoth he), if I shall needs this viage
    make
*With as good will as a bear goeth to the
    stake,*
I will straight weigh anchor, and hoist up sail ;
And thitherward hie me *in haste like a snail ;*
And home again hitherward *quick as a bee :*
Now, for good luck, *cast an old shoe after me.*
And first to mine uncle, brother to my father,
By suit I will assay to win some favour.
Who brought me up, and till my wedding was
    done
Loved me, not as his nephew, but as his son ;
And his heir had I been, had not this chanced,

Of lands and goods which should me much
    avanced.   [bones
Trudge, (quoth I), to him, and on your mary-
Crouch to the ground, and not so oft as once
Speak any one word him to contrary.
I cannot tell that, (quoth he), by Saint Mary!
One ill word axeth another, as folks spake.
Well! (quoth I), *better is to bow than break—*
It hurteth not the tongue to give fair words;
The rough net is not the best catcher of birds.
Since ye can nought win, if ye cannot please,
Best is to suffer : *for of sufferance cometh ease.*
Cause causeth, (quoth he), and as cause causeth
    me,
So will I do : and with this away went he.
Yet, whether his wife should go with him or no,
He sent her to me to know ere he would go.
Whereto I said, I thought best he went alone.
And you, (quoth I), to go straight as he is
    gone,
Among your kinsfolk likewise, if they dwell
    nigh.
Yes, (quoth she), all round about, even here
    by.
Namely, an aunt, my mother's sister, who well,
(Since my mother died), brought me up from
    the shell,
And much would have given me, had my
    wedding grown
Upon her fancy, as it grew upon mine own.
And, in likewise, mine uncle, her husband, was
A father to me.   Well, (quoth I), let pass;
And, if your husband will his assent grant,
Go, he to his uncle, and you to your aunt.
Yes, this assent he granteth before, (quoth
    she),

For he, ere this, thought this the best way
    to be.   [none
But of these two things he would determine
Without aid : for *two heads are better than one.*
With this we departed, she to her husband,
And I to dinner to them on th'other hand.

Chapter X.

When dinner was done I came home again
To attend on the return of these twain.
And ere three hours to end were fully tried,
Home came she first : welcome, (quoth I), and
    well hied !
Yea, *a short horse is soon curried,* (quoth she);
But *the weaker hath the worse* we all day see.
After our last parting, my husband and I
Departed, each to place agreed formerly.
Mine uncle and aunt on me did lower and
    glome ;   [welcome.
Both bade me God speed, but none bade me
Their folks glomed on me too, by which it
    appeareth :
The young cock croweth, as he the old heareth.
At dinner they were, and made, (for manners'
    sake),
A kinswoman of ours me to table take ;
A false flatt'ring filth ; and, if that be good,
None better *to bear two faces in one hood.*
She speaketh as she would creep into your
    bosom ;   [bottom
And, when the meal-mouth hath won the
Of your stomach, then will the pickthank it tell
To your most enemies, you *to buy and sell.*
To tell tales out of school, that is her great
    lust ;

Look what she knoweth, *blab it wist, and out it
    must.*
There is no mo such titifils in England's ground,
*To hold with the hare, and run with the hound.
Fire in the tone hand, and water in the tother,*
The makebate beareth between brother and
    brother.
She can wink on the ewe and worry the lamb;
She maketh earnest matters of every flimflam.
She must *have an oar in every man's barge;*
And *no man may chat ought in ought of her
    charge.
Coll under canstick, she can play on both
    hands;*
Dissimulation well she understands.
She is *lost with an apple, and won with a nut;*
Her *tongue is no edge tool, but yet it will cut.*
Her cheeks are purple ruddy like a horse plum;
And *the big part of her body is her bum.*
But *little tit-all-tail,* I have heard ere this,
As high as two horse-loaves her person is.
For privy nips or casts overthwart the shins,
He shall lese the mastery that with her begins.
She is, to turn love to hate, or joy to grief,
A pattern *as meet as a rope for a thief.*
Her promise of friendship for any avail,
Is *as sure to hold as an eel by the tail.*
She is *nother fish, nor flesh, nor good red
    herring.*
She is a ringleader there; and I, fearing
She would spit her venom, thought it not evil
*To set up a candle before the devil.
I clawed her by the back,* in way of a charm
To do me, not the more good, but the less
    harm;
Praying her, in her ear, on my side to hold;

She thereto swearing, by her false faith, she
    would.
Straight after dinner mine aunt had no choice,
But other burst, or *burst out in Pilate's voice:*
Ye huswife, what wind bloweth ye hither this
    night?   *[is light.*
Ye might have knocked ere ye came in; *leave*
Better unborn than untaught, I have heard
    say;
But be ye *better fed than taught,* far away;
Not very fat fed, said this flebergebet;   *[jet.*
But *need hath no law;* need maketh her hither
She cometh, niece Alice, (quoth she), for that
    is her name,   *[shame.*
More for need than for kindness, pain of
Howbeit, she cannot lack, for *he findeth that*
    seeks;
Lovers live by love, yea, *as larks live by leeks,*
Said this Alice, much more than half in mock-
    age.
Tush! (quoth mine aunt), these lovers in dot-
    age   *[courage*
Think the ground bear them not, but wed of
They must in all haste; though *a leaf of borage*
Might buy all the substance that they can sell.
Well, aunt, (quoth Alice), *all is well that ends*
    well.   *[end;*
Yea, Alice, *of a good beginning cometh a good*
Not so good to borrow, as be able to lend.
Nay indeed, aunt, (quoth she), it is sure so;
She must needs grant she hath wrought her
    own woe.   *[stone,*
She thought, Alice, she had *seen far in a mill-*
When she gat a husband, and namely such one,
As they by wedding could not only nought win,
But lose both living and love of all their kin.

Good aunt, (quoth I), humbly I beseech ye,
My trespass done to you forgive it me.
I know, and knowledge I have wrought mine
     own pain;
But *things past my hands, I cannot call again.*
True, (quoth Alice), *things done cannot be un-
     done,*
Be they done in due time, too late, or too soon;
But *better late than never* to repent this.
Too late, (quoth mine aunt), this repentance
     showed is:
When the steed is stolen shut the stable durre.
I took her for a rose, but she breedeth a burr;
She cometh to stick to me now in her lack;
Rather *to rent off my clothes fro my back,*
Than to do me one farthing worth of good.
I see day at this little hole. For *this bood
Showeth what fruit will follow.* In good faith,
     I said,
In way of petition I sue for your aid.
Ah, well! (quoth she), now I well understand
*The walking staff hath caught warmth in your
     hand.*
A clean-fingered huswife, and an idle, folk say,
And will be lime-fingered, I fear, by my fay!
It is *as tender as a parson's leman*—   [than?
Nought can she do, and what can she have
As sober as she seemeth, few days come about
But she will once *wash her face in an ale clout.*
And then between her and the rest of the rout,
*I proud, and thou proud, who shall bear
     th'ashes out?*   [breathe,
She may not bear a feather, but she must
She maketh so much of her painted sheath.
She thinketh her farthing good silver, I tell
    you;

But, *for a farthing, whoever did sell you*
Might boast you to be better sold than bought.
And yet, though she be worth nought, nor have
    nought,
Her gown is gayer and better than mine.
At her gay gown, (quoth Alice), ye may repine,
Howbeit, *as we may, we love to go gay all.*
Well, well! (quoth mine aunt), *pride will have*
    a fall;   [*after.*
For pride goeth before, and shame cometh
Sure, (said Alice), in manner of mocking
    laughter,   [*worse*
There is nothing in this world that agreeth
Than doth a lady's heart and a beggar's purse.
But pride she showeth none, her look reason
    alloweth,   [*mouth.*
She looketh as butter would not melt in her
Well, *the still sow eats up all the draf,* Alice;
All is not gold that glitters, by told tales.
In youth she was toward and without evil:
But *soon ripe, soon rotten; young saint, old*
    devil—   [*horns.*
Howbeit, Lo God *sendeth the shrewd cow short*
While she was in this house *she sat upon*
    thorns,
Each one day was three till liberty was borrow,
For one month's joy to bring her whole life's
    sorrow.   [well;
It were pity, (quoth Alice), but she should do
For beauty and stature *she beareth the bell.*
Ill weed groweth fast, Alice: whereby the corn
    is lorne;
For surely the weed overgroweth the corn.
Ye praise the wine before ye taste of the grape;
But *she can no more harm than can a she ape.*
It is a good body, her property preves

She lacketh but even a new pair of sleeves.
If I may, (as they say), tell truth without sin,
Of truth she is *a wolf in a lamb's skin.*
Her heart is full high when her eye is full low—
A guest as good lost as found, for all this show—
But *many a good cow hath an evil calf.*
I speak this, daughter, in thy mother's behalf,
My sister, (God rest her soul!) whom, though I boast,
Was called the flower of honesty in this coast.
Aunt, (quoth I), I take for father and mother
Mine uncle and you, above all other.
When we would, ye would not be our child, (quoth she),   [we;
Wherefore now when ye would, now will not
Since thou wouldst needs cast away thyself thus,
Thou shalt sure sink in thine own sin for us.
Aunt, (quoth I), *after a doting or drunken deed,*
Let submission obtain some mercy or meed.
He that killeth a man when he is drunk, (quoth she),
Shall be hanged when he is sober; and *he,*
Whom in itching no scratching will forbear,
He must bear the smarting that shall follow there.
And thou, being borne very nigh of my stock,
Though nigh be my kirtle, yet near is my smock—
I have one of mine own whom I must look to.
Yea, aunt, (quoth Alice), that thing must ye needs do;
Nature compelleth you to set your own first up;
For I have heard say, *it is a dear collop*

That is cut out of th'own flesh. But yet, aunt,
So small may her request be, that ye may
    grant
To satisfy the same, which may do her good,
And you no harm in th'avancing your own
    blood.   [crave,
And cousin, (quoth she to me), what ye would
Declare, that our aunt may know what ye
    would have.
Nay, (quoth I), be they winners or losers,
Folk say alway *beggars should be no*
    choosers.   [please;
With thanks I shall take whatever mine aunt
Where nothing is, a little thing doth ease;
Hunger maketh hard beans sweet; where
    saddles lack,   [back.
Better ride on a pad than on the horse bare
And by this proverb appeareth this o'thing :
That alway *somewhat is better than nothing.*
Hold fast when ye have it, (quoth she), by my
    life !   [wife,
The boy thy husband, and thou the girl, his
Shall not consume that I have laboured for.
Thou art young enough, and I can work no
    more.
Kit Callot, my cousin, saw this thus far on,
And in mine aunt's ear she whispereth anon,
Roundly these words, to make this matter
    whole :
Aunt, *let them that be a-cold blow at the coal.*
They shall for me, Alice, (quoth she), by God's
    blist !
She and I have shaken hands : farewell, un-
    kissed !
And thus, with a beck as good as a dieu gard,
She flang fro me, and I from her hitherward.

Begging of her booteth *not the worth of a
          bean;*   [*mean.*
Little knoweth the fat sow what the lean doth
Forsooth! (quoth I), ye have bestirred ye
          well—   [fell?
But where was your uncle while all this fray
Asleep by, (quoth she), routing like a hog;
And *it is evil waking of a sleeping dog.*
The bitch and her whelp might have been
          asleep too,
For ought they in waking to me would do.
Fare ye well! (quoth she); I will now home
          straight,   [wait.
And at my husband's hands for better news

Chapter XI.

He came home to me the next day before noon:
What tidings now, (quoth I), how have ye
          doon?
Upon our departing, (quoth he), yesterday,
Toward mine uncle's, somewhat more than
          midway,
I overtook a man, a servant of his,
And a friend of mine; who guessed straight
          with this
What mine errand was, offering in the same
To do his best for me; and so, in God's name
Thither we went; nobody being within
But mine uncle, mine aunt, and one of our
          kin—
A mad knave, as it were a railing jester,
Not a more gaggling gander hence to Chester.
At sight of me he asked, who have we there?
I have seen this gentleman, if I wist where;
Howbeit, lo! *seldom seen, soon forgotten.*

He was, (as he will be), somewhat cupshotten :
Six days in the week, beside the market day,
Malt is above wheat with him, market men say.
But forasmuch as I saw the same taunt
Contented well mine uncle and mine aunt,
And that *I came to fall in and not to fall out,*
I forbear ; or else his drunken red snout
I would have made *as oft change from hue
 to hue*
As doth the cocks of Ind ; for this is true :
It is a small hop on my thumb ; and Christ wot,
It is wood at a word—*little pot soon hot.*
Now *merry as a cricket,* and by and by
Angry as a wasp, though in both no cause why.
But he was at home there, he might speak his
 will :
Every cock is proud on his own dunghill.
I shall be even with him herein when I can.
But he, having done, thus mine uncle began :
Ye merchant ! what attempteth you to attempt
 us,
To come on us *before the messenger* thus?
Roaming in and out, I hear tell how ye toss ;
But son, *the rolling stone never gathereth
 moss.*
Like a pickpurse pilgrim ye pry and ye prowl
At rovers, *to rob Peter and pay Poule.*
Iwys, I know, or any more be told,
That *draf is your errand, but drink ye wolde.*
Uncle, (quoth I), of the cause for which I
 come
I pray you patiently hear the whole sum.
In faith ! (quoth he), without any more
 summing,
I know to beg of me is thy coming.
Forsooth ! (quoth his man), it is so, indeed ;

And I dare boldly boast, if ye knew his need,
Ye would of pity yet fet him in some stay.
Son, *better be envied than pitied*, folk say;
And for his cause of pity, (had he had grace),
He might this day have been *clear out of the
case;*   [*frog—*
But now *he hath well fished and caught a
Where nought is to wed with, wise men flee the
clog.*
Where I, (quoth I), did not as ye willed or bad,
That repent I oft, and as oft wish I had.
Son, (quoth he), as I have heard of mine olders,
*Wishers and woulders be no good house-
holders:*
This proverb for a lesson, with such other.
Not like, (as who sayeth), the son of my
brother,
But like mine own son, I oft before told thee
To cast her quite off; but it would not hold thee
When I willed thee any other where to go—
Tush! there was *no mo maids but malkin*
though
Ye had been lost to lack your lust when ye list,
By two miles trudging twice a week to be
kissed.
I would ye had kissed—well I will no more stir:
It is good to have a hatch before the dur.
But *who will, in time present, pleasure refrain
Shall, in time to come, the more pleasure
obtain.*
*Follow pleasure, and then will pleasure flee;
Flee pleasure, and pleasure will follow thee.*
And how is my saying come to pass now?
How oft did I prophesy this between you
And your ginifinee nycebecetur?   [*petre?*
When sweet sugar should turn to sour salt-

Whereby ye should in saying that ye never
    saw,
Think that you never thought yourself a daw.
But that time ye thought me a daw, so that I
Did no good in all my words then, save only
Approved this proverb plain and true matter :
A man may well bring a horse to the water,
But he cannot make him drink without he will.
Colts, (quoth his man), *may prove well with*
    tatches ill,
For *of a ragged colt there cometh a good*
    horse—
If he be good *n*ow of his ill past no force. [he),
Well, he that hangeth himself a Sunday, (said
Shall hang still uncut down a Monday for me.
I have hanged up my hatchet, God speed him
    well !   [tell :
A wonder thing what things these old things
Cat after kind good mouse hunt; and also
Men say, *kind will creep where it may not go.*
Commonly all thing showeth fro whence it
    came ;
The litter is like to the fire and the dam;
How can the foal amble if the horse and mare
    trot?
These sentences are assigned unto thy lot,
By conditions of thy father and mother,
My sister-in-law, and mine own said brother.
Thou followest their steps *as right as a line.*
For when provender prickt them a little tyne,
They did as thy wife and thou did, both dote
Each one on other; and being not worth a
    groat,   [last,
They went (witless) to wedding; whereby, at
They both went a-begging. And even the like
    cast

HEY. II.   **D**

Hast thou; *thou wilt beg or steal ere thou
die—*
Take heed, friend, *I have seen as far come as
nigh.*
If ye seek to *find things ere they be lost,*
Ye shall find one day *you come to your cost.*
This do I but repeat, for this I told thee;
And more I say; but I could not then hold thee;
Nor will not hold thee now; nor such folly feel,
To set at my heart that thou settest at thy heel.
And as of my good ere I one groat give,
I will see how my wife and myself may live.
Thou goest a-gleaning ere the cart have carried;
But ere thou glean ought, since thou wouldst
be married,   [then?
Shall I make thee laugh now, and myself weep
Nay, good child! *better children weep than old
men.*   [upon fools;
Men should not prease much to spend much
Fish is cast away that is cast in dry pools.
To flee charge, and find ease, ye would now
here host—
It is easy *to cry ble* at other men's cost.
But, *a bow long bent, at length must wear
weak:*   [break.
Long bent I toward you, but *that bent I will*
Farewell, and feed full, that love ye well to do;
But you lust not to do that longeth thereto.
*The cat would eat fish and would not wet her
feet;*   [in heat.
They must hunger in frost that will not work
And *he that will thrive must ask leave of his
wife;*   [life,
But your wife will give none: by your and her
It is hard to wive and thrive both in a year.
Thus, by thy wiving, thriving doth so appear,

That thou art past thrift before thrift begin.
But lo! *will will have will,* though will woe
    win;
Will is a good son, and will is a shrewd boy;
And wilful shrewd will hath wrought thee this
    toy.
A gentle white spur, and at need a sure spear;
He standeth now as he had *a flea in his ear.*
Howbeit, for any great courtesy he doth make,
It seemeth the gentle man *hath eaten a steak.*
He beareth a dagger in his sleeve, trust me,
To kill all that he meeteth prouder than he.
He will perk: I here say he *must have the*
    bench—   [*French.*
Jack would be a gentleman if he could speak
He thinketh his feet be where his head shall
    never come;
He would fain flee, but he wanteth feathers,
    some.
Sir, (quoth his man), he will no fault defend,
But *hard is for any man all faults to mend*—
He is lifeless, that is faultless, old folks
    thought.   [*nought.*
He hath, (quoth he), *but one fault, he is*
Well, (quoth his man), *the best cart may over-*
    throw.   [*though.*
Carts well driven, (quoth he), *go long upright,*
But, for my reward, let him be no longer tarrier,
I will send it him by John Long the carrier.
O! help him, sir, (said he), since ye easily may.
Shameful craving, (quoth he), *must have*
    shameful nay.   [*one yea.*
Ye may, sir, (quoth he), *mend three nays with*
Two false knaves need no broker, men say,
    (said he).
Some say also, *it is merry when knaves meet;*

But *the mo knaves, the worse company to
        greet;*   [*craveth.*
The *one knave now croucheth while th'other*
But to show what shall be his relevavith,
Either after my death, if my will be kept,
Or during my life : had I this hall hept   [*eat*
With gold, *he may his part on Good Friday*
And fast never the worse, for ought he shall
        geat.   [*son :*
These former lessons conned, take for this,
*Tell thy cards, and then tell me what thou hast
        won.*

Now, here is the door, and there is the way;
And so, (quoth he), *farewell, gentle Geoffrey!*
Thus parted I from him, being much dismayed,
Which his man saw, and (to comfort me) said :
What, man, pluck up your heart, be of good
        cheer !
After clouds black, we shall have weather clear.
What, should your face thus again the wool
        be shorn
For one fall? What, man, *all this wind shakes
        no corn!*
Let this wind overblow; a time I will spy
To take wind and tide with me, and speed
        thereby.   [*small roast*
I thank you, (quoth I), but *great boast and*
Maketh unsavoury mouths, wherever men host.
And this boast very unfavourly serveth;
For *while the grass groweth the horse sterveth;*
Better one bird in hand than ten in the wood.
Rome was not built in one day, (quoth he), and
        yet stood
Till it was finished, as some say, full fair.
Your heart is in your hose, all in despair;
But, as every man sayeth, *a dog hath a day—*

Should you, a man, despair then any day?
    nay !
Ye have many strings to the bow, for ye know,
Though I, *having the bent of your* uncle's *bow,*
Can no way bring your bolt in the butt to stand ;
Yet have ye other marks to rove at hand.
The keys hang not all by one man's girdle,
    man ;   [can
Though nought will be won here, I say, yet ye
Taste other kinsmen ; of whom ye may geat
Here some, and there some : *many small make*
    a great.   [curses,
For come light winnings with blessings or
Evermore *light gains make heavy purses.*
Children learn to creep ere they can learn to
    go ;
And, little and little, ye must learn even so.
Throw no gift again at the giver's head ;
For, *better is half a loaf than no bread.*
I may beg my bread, (quoth I), for my kin all
That dwelleth nigh. Well, yet, (quoth he),
    and the worst fall,
Ye may to your kinsman, hence nine or ten
    mile,
Rich without charge, whom ye saw not of long
    while.
That benchwhistler, (quoth I), is a pinchpenny,
As free of gift as a poor man of his eye.
I shall get a fart of a dead man as soon
As a farthing of him ; his dole is soon done.
He is so *high in th'instep,* and *so straight-*
    laced,
That pride and covetise withdraweth all repast,
Ye know what he hath been, (quoth he), but
    i-wis,
Absence sayeth plainly, *ye know not what he is.*

Men know, (quoth I), I have heard now and
    then,
How the market goeth by the market men.
Further it is said, who that saying weigheth,
It must needs be true that every man sayeth.
Men say also : *children and fools cannot lie*—
And both man and child sayeth, he is a heinsby.
And myself knoweth him, I dare boldly brag,
Even *as well as the beggar knoweth his bag.*
And I knew him not worth a grey groat;
He was at an ebb, though he be now afloat,
Poor as the poorest. And now nought he
    setteth
By poor folk, For *the parish priest forgetteth
That ever he hath been holy water clerk.*
By ought I can now hear, or ever could mark,
Of no man hath he pity or compassion.
Well, (quoth he), every man after his fashion ;
He may yet pity you, for ought doth appear,
*It happeth in one hour that happeth not in
    seven year.*
Forspeak not your fortune, nor hide not your
    need ;
*Nought venture, nought have; spare to speak,
    spare to speed;*
Unknown, unkissed; it is lost that is unsought.
As good seek nought, (quoth I), *as seek and
    find nought.*
It is, (quoth he), *ill fishing before the net.*
But though we get little, *dear bought and far
    fet*
Are dainties for ladies. Go we both two;
I have for my master thereby to do.
I may break a dish there; and sure I shall
Set all at six and seven, to win some windfall.
And I will *hang the bell about the cat's neck,*

For I will first break and jeopard the first
    check.   [mine,
And for to win this prey, though the cost be
Let us present him with a bottle of wine.
What should we, (quoth I), grease the fat sow
    in th'arse,
We may do much ill, ere we do much wars.
It is, to give him, as much alms or need,
As cast water in Thames, or as good a deed
As it is *to help a dog over a stile.*   [while.
Then go we, (quoth he), we lese time all this
To follow his fancy we went together, [thither,
And toward night yesternight when we came
She was within, but he was yet abroad. [toad,
And straight as she saw me she swelled like a
Pattering the devil's Pater noster to herself :
God never made a more crabbed elf !
She bade him welcome, but the worse for me ;
This knave cometh a-begging by me, thought
    she.   [wind ;
I smelled her out, and *had her straight in the*
She may abide no beggars of any kind.
They be both greedy guts all given to get
They care not how : *all is fish that cometh to*
    net.   [ning
They know no end of their good; nor begin-
Of any goodness : such is wretched winning.
Hunger droppeth even out of both their noses.
She goeth with broken shoon and torn hoses ;
But *who is worse shod than the shoemaker's*
    wife,
With shops full of new shoes all her life?
Or *who will do less than they that may do*
    most?
And namely of her I can no way make boast.
She is *one of them to whom God bade ho ;*

She will all have, and will right nought forego;
She will not part with the paring of her nails;
She toileth continually for avails;
Which life she hath so long now kept in ure,
That for no life she would make change, be
    sure.
But this lesson learned I, ere I was years seven:
They that be in hell ween there is none other
    heaven.
She is nothing fair, but she is ill favoured;
And no more uncleanly than unsweet favoured;
But hackney men say at mangy hackney's
    hire,   [*squire.*
A scald horse is good enough for a scabbed
He is a knucklebone-yard, very meet
To match a minion nother fair nor sweet.
He winketh with the tone eye and looketh with
    the tother;
I will not trust him though he were my brother.
He hath a poison wit, and all his delight
To give taunts and checks of most spiteful
    spite.
In that house commonly, such is the cast,
A man shall as soon break his neck as his fast;
And yet, now such a gid did her head take,
That more for my mate's than for manner's
    sake,
We had bread and drink, and a cheese very
    great;
But *the greatest crabs be not all the best meat.*
For her crabbed cheese, with all the greatness,
Might well abide the fineness, or sweetness.
Anon he came in; and when he us saw,
To my companion kindly he did draw;
And a well favoured welcome to him he yields,
Bidding me welcome strangely over the fields

With these words : Ah, young man ! I know
    your matter ;
By my faith ! you come to look in my water ;
And for my comfort to your consolation,
Ye would buy my purse—give me a purgation !
But I am laxative enough there otherwise.
This, (quoth this young man), contrary doth
    rise ;
For *he is purse-sick, and lacketh a physician ;*
And hopeth upon you in some condition,
Not by purgation, but by restorative,
To strength his weakness to keep him alive.
I cannot, (quoth he), for though it be my lot
To have speculation, yet I practise not.
I see much, but I say little, and do less
In this kind of physic—and what would ye
    guess :
Shall I consume myself to restore him now?
Nay, *backare ! (quoth Mortimer to his sow) ;*
He can, before this time, no time assign,
In which he hath laid down one penny by mine,
That ever might either make me bite or sup.
And by'r lady, friend ! *nought lay down, nought*
    take up ;
Ka me, ka thee ; one good turn asketh another ;
Nought won by the tone, nought won by the
    tother.   [miles
To put me to cost, thou camest half a score
Out of thine own nest, to seek me in these out
    isles :
Where thou wilt not step over a straw, I think,
To win me the worth of one draught of drink,
No more than I have won of all thy whole
    stock.
I have been common Jack to all that whole
    flock ;

When ought was to do I was common
    hackney—
Folk call on the horse that will carry alway—
But evermore *the common horse is worst shod.*
Desert and reward be ofttimes things far odd;
At end *I might put my winning in mine eye,*
And see never the worse, for ought I wan
    them by.   [end,
And now, without them I live here at stave's
Where I need not borrow, nor I will not lend.
It is good to beware by other men's harms;
But thy taking of thine halter in thine arms
Teacheth other to beware of their harms by
    thine :
Thou hast stricken the ball under the line.
I pray you, (quoth I), pity me, a poor man,
With somewhat till I may work as I can.
Toward your working, (quoth he), ye make
    such tastings,
As approve you to be *none of the hastings.*
Ye run to work in haste as nine men held ye;
But whensoever ye to work must yield ye,
If your meet-mate and you meet together,
Then shall we see two men bear a feather;
Recompensing former loitering life loose,
As did *the pure penitent that stale a goose*
And stack down a feather. And, where old
    folk tell
That *evil gotten good never proveth well;*
Ye will truly get, and true getting well keep
Till time ye be *as rich as a new shorn sheep.*
Howbeit, *when thrift and you fell first at a*
    fray,   [*away.*
You played the man, for ye made thrift run
So help me God ! in my poor opinion,
A man might make a play of this minion,

And fain no ground, but take tales of his own
    friends :
I suck not this out of my own fingers' ends.
And since ye were wed, although I nought gave
    you,   [you !
Yet pray I for you, God and Saint Luke save
And here is all : for what should I further
    wade?
I was neither of court nor of council made;
And it is, as I have learned in listening,
A poor dog that is not worth the whistling.
A day ere I was wed, I bade you, (quoth I).
Scarb'rough warning I had, (quoth he), where-
I kept me thence, to serve thee according. [by
And now, if this night's lodging and boarding
May ease thee, and rid me from any more
    charge,   [large.
Then welcome ! or else get thee straight at
For of further reward, mark how I boast me,
In case as ye shall yield me as ye cost me,
So shall ye cost me as ye yield me likewise;
Which is, a thing of nought rightly to surmise.
Herewithal, his wife, *to make up my mouth,*
Not only her husband's taunting tale avoweth,
But thereto deviseth to cast in my teeth
Checks and choking oysters. And when she
    seeth
Her time to take up, to show my fare at best :
Ye see your fare, (said she), *set your heart at
    rest.*
Fare ye well! (quoth I), *however I fare* now;
And well mote ye fare both when I dine with
    you.
Come, go we hence, friend ! (quoth I to my
    mate)—
And *now will I make a cross on this gate.*

And *I*, (quoth he), *cross thee quite out of my
    book*
*Since thou art cross failed; avail, unhappy
    hook!*
By hook or crook nought could I win there;
    men say :
*He that cometh every day, shall have a
    cockney;*   [*hen.*
He that cometh now and then, shall have a fat
But *I gat not so much* in coming seeld when,
As a good hen's feather, or a poor eggshell:
As good play for nought as work for nought,
    folk tell.
Well, well! (quoth he), we be but where we
    were ;
Come what come would, I thought ere we came
    there,
That *if the worst fell, we could have but a nay.*
There is no harm done, man, *in all this fray;*
Neither pot broken, nor water spilt.
Farewell, he! (quoth I), I will as soon be hilt
As *wait again for the moonshine in the water.*
But is not this a pretty piked matter?
To disdain me, who muck of the world
    hoardeth not,
As he doeth; *it may rhyme but it accordeth not.*
She *foameth like a boar,* the beast should seem
    bold ;
For she is *as fierce as a Lion of Cotsolde.*
She frieth in her own grease, but as for my
    part,
If she be angry, beshrew her angry heart!
Friend, (quoth he), he may show wisdom at
    will,   [*still :*
That with angry heart can hold his tongue
Let patience grow in your garden alway.

Some loose or odd end will come, man, *some
    one day*
From some friend, either in life or at death.
Death! (quoth I), *take we that time to take
    a breath?*
Then graft we a green graft on a rotten root:
*Who waiteth for dead men shoes shall go long
    barefoot.*
Let pass, (quoth he), and let us be trudging
Where some noppy ale is, and soft sweet
    lodging.
Be it, (quoth I), but I would very fain eat;
At breakfast and dinner I eat little meat,
And *two hungry meals make the third a glutton.*
We went where we had boiled beef and bake
Whereof I fed me *as full as a tun;*   [mutton,
And a-bed were we ere the clock had nine run.
Early we rose, in haste to get away;
And to the hostler this morning, by day,
This fellow called, What ho! fellow, thou
    knave!
I pray thee let me and my fellow have
A hair of the dog that bit us last night—
And *bitten* were we both *to the brain* aright.
We saw each other drunk in the good ale glass,
And so did each one each other, that there was,
Save one; but old men say that are skilled:
*A hard foughten field where no man scapeth
    unkilled.*   [the shot;
The reckoning reckoned, he needs would pay
And needs he must for me, for I had it not.
This done we shook hands, and parted in fine;
He into his way, and I into mine.
But this journey was quite out of my way:
Many kinsfolk and few friends, some folk say;
But I find many kinsfolk, and friend not one.

Folk say—it hath been said many years since
    gone—   [deed,
Prove thy friend ere thou have need; but, in-
A friend is never known till a man have need.
Before I had need, my most present foes [goes :
Seemed my most friends; but thus the world
Every man basteth the fat hog we see;
But the lean shall burn ere he basted be.
As sayeth this sentence, oft and long said
    before :
He that hath plenty of goods shall have more;
He that hath but a little, he shall have less;
He that hath right nought, right nought shall
    possess.   [what obtain,
Thus, having right nought, and would some-
With right nought, (quoth he), I am returned
    again.

CHAPTER XII.

Surely, (quoth I), ye have in this time, thus
    worn,
Made *a long harvest for a little corn!*
Howbeit, comfort yourself with this old text,
That telleth us, *when bale is hekst, boot is*
    next;
Though every man may not sit in the chair,
Yet alway the grace of God is worth a fair.
Take no thought in no case, *God is where he*
    was.
But put case, in poverty all your life pass,
Yet poverty and poor degree, taken well,
Feedeth on this : *he that never climbed, never*
    fell.   [somewhere,
And some case, at some time, showeth prefe
That *riches bringeth oft harm, and ever fear,*

Where poverty passeth without grudge of grief.
What, man! *the beggar may sing before the*
And *who can sing so merry a note*   [*thief;*
As may he that cannot change a groat?
Yea, (quoth he), *beggars may sing before*
      thieves.   [*greeves.*
And weep before true men, lamenting their
Some say, and I feel, *hunger pierceth stone*
      wall;
Meat, nor yet money to buy meat withal,
Have I not so much as may hunger defend
Fro my wife and me.   Well! (quoth I), God
      will send   [*see.*
Time to provide for time, right well ye shall
God send that provision in time! (said he.)
And thus, seeming well-nigh weary of his life,
The poor wretch went to his like poor wretched
      wife :   [their knees ;
From wantonness to wretchedness, brought on
Their hearts full heavy, *their heads be full of*
      bees.
And after this a month, or somewhat less,
Their landlord came to their house to take a
      stress
For rent ; *to have kept Bayard in the stable—*
But that to win, any power was unable.
For, though *it be ill playing with short daggers,*
Which meaneth, that every wise man staggers,
In earnest or boord to be busy or bold
With his biggers or betters, yet this is told :
Whereas nothing is, the king must lose his
      right.   [*quight.*
And thus, king or keyser, must have set them
But warning to depart thence they needed none ;
For, ere the next day, *the birds were flown,*
      each one

To seek service; of which, where the man was
    sped,
The wife could not speed; but, maugre her
    head,   [nigh,
She must seek elsewhere, for either there or
Service for any suit she none could espy.
All folk thought them, not only too lither
To linger both in one house together;
But also, dwelling nigh under their wings,
Under their noses they might convey things—
Such as were neither too heavy nor too hot—
More in a month than they their master got
In a whole year.   Whereto folk further weigh-
    ing,
Receive each of other in their conveying,
Might be worst of all; for this proverb preeves:
Where be no receivers, there be no thieves.
Such hap here hapt, that common dread of such
    gyles
Drove them and keepeth them asunder many
    miles.
Thus, *though love decree departure death to be,*
Yet *poverty parteth fellowship, we see;*
And doth those two true lovers so dissever,
That meet shall they seeld when, or haply never.
And thus by love, without regard of living,
These twain have wrought each other's ill
    chieving;   [friends,
And love hath so lost them the love of their
That I think them lost; and thus this tale ends.

CHAPTER XIII.

Ah, sir ! (said my friend), *when men will needs
    marry,*
I see now, how *wisdom and haste may vary:*
Namely, where they wed for love altogether.
I would for no good, but I had come hither.
Sweet beauty with sour beggary ! nay, I am
    gone
To the wealthy withered widow, by Saint John !
What ! yet in all haste, (quoth I)?   Yea ! (q. he);
For she hath substance enough; and ye see
That lack is the loss of these two young fools.
Know ye not, (quoth I), that, after wise men's
    schools,
A man should hear all parts ere he judge any?
Why axe ye that (quoth he)?   For this, (quoth
    I):
I told you, when I this began, that I would
Tell you of two couples; and I, having told
But of the tone, ye be straight starting away,
As I of the tother had right nought to say;
Or, as yourself of them right nought would
    hear.   [clear
Nay, not all so, (quoth he), but since I think
There can no way appear so painful a life
Between your young neighbour and his old
    rich wife,
As this tale in this young poor couple doth
    show;
And that the most good or least ill ye know
To take at end, I was at beginning bent,
With thanks for this and your more pain to
    prevent,
Without any more matter now revolved,

I take this matter here clearly resolved;
And that ye herein award me to forsake
Beggarly beauty, and rivalled riches take.
That's just, if the half shall judge the whole,
    (quoth I);   [try.
But yet, hear the whole, the whole wholly to
To it (quoth he) then, I pray you, by and by.
We will dine first, (quoth I), it is noon high.
We may as well, (quoth he), dine when this
    is done;
The longer forenoon, the shorter afternoon—
All cometh to one, and thereby men have
    guessed,
Alway the longer east, the shorter west.
We have had, (quoth I), before ye came, and
    syne,
Weather meet to set paddocks abroad in:
Rain more than enough; and *when all shrews
    have dined,*
Change from foul weather to fair is oft inclined.
And all the shrews in this part, saving one wife
That must dine with us, have dined, pair of
    my life !   [ing
Now, if good change of ill weather be depend-
Upon her diet, what were mine offending
To keep the woman any longer fasting?
If ye, (quoth he), fet all this far casting
For common wealth, as it appeareth a clear
    case,   [place.
Reason would your will should, and shall take

THUS ENDETH THE FIRST PART.

PART II

Chapter I.

Diners cannot be long where dainties want;
Where coin is not common, commons must be
 scant.
In post pace we passed from potage to cheese,
And yet this man cried: Alas, what time we
 lese !
He would not let us pause after our repast;
But apart he plucked me straight, and in all
 haste,   [maid,
As I of this poor young man, and poor young
Or more poor young wife, the foresaid words
 had said,
So prayeth he me now the process may be told,
Between th'other young man, and rich widow
 old.
If ye lack that, (quoth I), away ye must wind,
With your whole errand, and half th'answer
 behind.   [you loth,
Which thing to do, since haste thereto showeth
And to haste your going, the day away goeth;
And that time lost, again we cannot win :
Without more loss of time, this tale I begin.
In this late old widow, and then old new wife,
Age and appetite fell at a strong strife:
Her lust was as young as her limbs were old.

The day of her wedding, like one to be sold,
She set out herself in fine apparel.
She was made like a beer pot, or a barrel;
A crooked hooked nose, beetle browed, blear
    eyed.
Many men wished, for beautifying that bride,
Her waist to be gird in, and for a bon grace,
Some well favoured visor on her ill favoured
But with visorlike visage, such as it was, [face.
She smirked, and she smiled, but so lisped this
    lass,   [alone
That folk might have thought it done only
Of wantonness, had not her teeth been gone.
Upright as a candle standeth in a socket
Stood she that day, so *simper-de-cocket.*
Of ancient fathers she took no cure nor care,
She was to them *as coy as a croker's mare.*
She took th'entertainment of the young men
All in dalliance, *as nice as a nun's hen.*
I suppose that day *her ears might well glow,*
For all the town talked of her, high and low.
One said, a well favoured old woman she is;
The devil she is, said another; and to this,
In came the third, with his five eggs, and said,
Fifty year ago I knew her a trim maid.
Whatever she were then, (said one), she is now
To become a bride, *as meet as a sow*
To bear a saddle.   She is, in this marriage,
As comely as is a cow in a cage.
Gup! with a galled back Gill, come up to
    supper!   [crupper!
What? *mine old mare would have a new*
And now *mine old hat must have a new band!*
Well, (quoth one), glad is he that hath her in
A goodly marriage she is, I hear say.   [hand;
She is so, (quoth one), *were the woman away.*

Well, (quoth another), fortune this moveth;
And in this case *every man as he loveth*
Quoth the good man when that he kissed his
*   cow.*   [a vow!
That kiss, (quoth one), doth well here, by God
But *how can she give a kiss, sour or sweet?—*
Her chin and her nose within half an inch
God is no botcher, sir! said another;   [meet.
He shapeth all parts as each part may fit
*   other.*   [scanning;
Well, (quoth one), wisely, let us leave this
God speed them! *be as be may is no banning.*
That shall be, shall be; and with God's grace
    they shall
Do well, and that they so may, wish we all.
This wonder, (as wonders last), *lasted nine*
*   days;*   [their ways,
Which done, and all guests of this feast gone
Ordinary household this man straight began
Very sumptuously, which he might well do
    than.   [was set
What he would have, he might have; his wife
In such dotage of him, that fair words did fet
Gromwell-seed plenty; and pleasure to prefer,
She made much of him, and he mocked much
    of her.
I was, (as I said), much there, and most of all
The first month; in which time such kindness
    did fall
Between these two counterfeit turtle birds;
To see his sweet looks, and hear her sweet
    words,   [ure,
And to think wherefore they both put both in
It would have made a horse break his halter
    sure.   [taught
All the first fortnight their ticking might have

Any young couple their love ticks to have
    wrought.   [*is green.*
Some laughed, and said: *all thing is gay that*
Some thereto said: *the green new broom*
    sweepeth clean.
But since *all thing is the worse for the wearing*,
Decay of clean sweeping folk had in fearing.
And indeed, ere two months away were crept,
And her biggest bags into his bosom swept,
Where love had appeared in him to her alway
Hot as a toast, it grew *cold as a kay.*
He at meat carving her, and none else before,
Now carved he to all but her, and her no more.
Where her words seemed honey, by his smil-
    ing cheer,   [hear.
Now are they mustard, he frowneth them to
And when she saw sweet sauce began to wax
    sour,
She waxed as sour as he, and as well could
    lower.
So turned they their tippets by way of ex-
    change,   [range
From laughing to lowering, and taunts did so
That in plain terms, plain truth to you to utter,
They two agreed like two cats in a gutter.
Marry, sir ! (quoth he), *by scratching and*
    biting   [citing.
Cats and dogs come together, by folks re-
Together by the ears they come, (quoth I),
    cheerly;
Howbeit those words are not void here clearly.
For, in one state they twain could not yet
    settle,
But wavering as the wind : *in dock, out nettle.*
Now in, now out; now here, now there; now
    sad,

Now merry; now high, now low; now good,
  now bad.
In which unsteady sturdy storms strainable,
To know how they both were irrefrainable,
Mark how *they fell out, and* how *they fell in :*
At end of a supper she did thus begin.

Chapter II.

Husband, (quoth she), I would we were in our
  nest;   [*rest.*
When the belly is full, the bones would be at
So soon upon supper, (said he), no question
Sleep maketh ill and unwholesome digestion :
By that diet a great disease once I gat.   [that.
And *burnt child fire dreadeth ;* I will beware of
What, a post of physic, (said she)?   Yea, a
  post ;
And *from post to pillar,* wife, I have been tossed
By that surfeit.   And I feel a little fit
Even now, by former attempting of it.
Whereby, except I shall seem to leave my wit
Before it leave me, I must now leave it.
I thank God, (quoth she), I never yet felt pain
To go to bed timely; but rising again,
Too soon in the morning, hath me displeased.
And I, (quoth he), have been more diseased
By early lying down, than by early rising.
But thus differ folk, lo ! in exercising :
That *one may not, another may.*
Use maketh maistry; and men many times say
*That one loveth not, another doth ; which hath
  sped*
All meats to be eaten, and all maids to be wed.
Haste ye to bed now, and rise ye as ye rate;

While I rise early, and come to bed late.
Long lying warm in bed is wholesome, (quoth
    she);   [(quoth he).
While the leg warmeth, the boot harmeth,
Well, (quoth she), *he that doeth as most men do,*
Shall be least wondered on; and take any two
That be man and wife, in all this whole town,
And most part together they rise and lie down.
When birds shall roost, (quoth he), at eight,
    nine, or ten,   [hen?
Who shall appoint their hour—the cock, or the
The hen, (quoth she); the cock, (quoth he);
    just, (quoth she),   [(quoth he).
As Germans lips. It shall prove more just,
Then prove I, (quoth she), the more fool far
    away;
But *there is no fool to the old fool,* folk say.
Ye are wise enough, (quoth he), if ye keep ye
    warm.
To be kept warm, and for none other harm,
Nor for much more good, I took you to wed.
I took not you, (quoth he), night and day to
    bed.
Her carrain carcase, (said he), is so cold
Because she is aged, and somewhat too old,
That she killeth me: I do but *roast a stone*
In warming her. And shall not I save one,
As she would save another? Yes, by Saint
    John!
Ah, sir! (quoth she), marry! this gear is alone.
Who that worst may shall hold the candle; I
    see   [me.
I must warm bed for him should warm it for
This medicine thus ministered is sharp and
    cold;   [told.
But *all thing that is sharp is short,* folk have

This trade is now begun, but if it hold on,
Then *farewell my good days! they will be soon
        gone.*   [break.
Gospel in thy mouth, (quoth he), this strife to
Howbeit, *all is not gospel that thou dost speak.*
But what need we lump out love, at once lash-
        ing   [for dashing?
As we should now shake hands? what! soft
The fair lasteth all the year; we be new knit,
And *so late met that I fear we part not yet,*
Quoth the baker to the pillory. Which thing,
From distemperate fonding, temperance may
        bring;   [strong,
And this reason to aid, and make it more
Old wise folk say : *love me little, love me long.*
I say little, (said she), but I think more;
Thought is free. Ye lean, (quoth he), *to the
        wrong shore.*
Brawling booted not, he was not that night bent
To play the bridegroom : alone to bed she went.
This was their beginning of jar.   Howbeit,
For a beginning, this was a feat fit,
And but a fleabiting to that did ensue—
The worst is behind; we come not where it
        grew.
How say you, (said he to me), by my wife?
The devil hath cast a bone, (said I), to *set strife*
Between you; but it were *a folly* for me
To put my hand between the bark and the tree;
Or *to put my finger too far in the fire*
Between you, and lay my credence in the mire.
To meddle little for me it is best;
For of little meddling cometh great rest.
Yes, ye may meddle, (quoth he), to make her
        wise,
Without taking harm, in giving your advice.

She knoweth me not yet; but if she wax too
     wild   [*child.*
I shall make her know *an old knave is no*
Slugging in bed with her is worse than watch-
     ing;   [*ing.*
I promise you *an old sack axeth much patch-*
Well, (quoth I), to-morrow I will to my beads
To pray, that as ye both will, so ache your
     heads;
And in meantime, my aching head to ease,
I will couch a hogshead. Quoth he, when ye
     please.
We parted; and this, within a day or twain,
Was raked up in th'ashes, and covered again.

CHAPTER III.

These two days past, he said to me, when ye
     will   [*have Jill.*
Come chat at home; all is well—*Jack shall*
Who had the worst end of the staff, (quoth I),
     now?   [*you?*
Shall the master wear a breech, or none? say
I trust the sow will no more so deep root.
But if she do, (quoth he), you must set in foot:
And whom ye see out of the way, or shoot
     wide,
Over-shoot not yourself any side to hide;
But shoot out some words, if she be too hot.
She may say, (quoth I), *a fool's bolt soon shot.*
Ye will me to a thankless office hear;
And a busy officer I may appear;
And, *Jack out of office,* she may bid me walk;
And think me *as wise as Waltham's calf,* to
     talk

Or chat of her charge, having therein nought
  to do.
Howbeit, if I see need, as my part cometh too,
Gladly between you I will do my best.
I bid you to dinner, (quoth he), as no guest,
And bring your poor neighbours on your other
  side.
I did so.   And straight as th'old wife us espied,
She bade us welcome, and merrily toward me :
Green rushes for this stranger, straw here,
  (quoth she).
With this, apart she pulled me by the sleeve,
Saying in few words : my mind to you to
  meve,
So it is, that all our great fray, the last night,
Is *forgiven and forgotten* between us quite ;
And all frays by this I trust have taken end,
For I fully hope my husband will amend.
Well amended, (thought I), when ye both
  relent,   [ment.
Not to your own, but each to other's mend-
Now, if hope fail, (quoth she), and chance
  bring about
Any such breach, whereby we fall again out,
I pray you tell him he's pars vers, now and
  than,
And wink on me.   Also hardly, if ye can
Take me in any trip.   Quoth I, I am loth
To meddle commonly.   For as this tale go'th,
*Who meddleth in all thing may shoe the
  gosling.*   [bring
Well ! (quoth she), your meddling herein may
The wind calm between us, when it else might
  rage.
I will, with good will, (quoth I), ill winds to
  swage,

Spend some wind at need, though I waste wind
   in vain.
To table we sat where fine fare did remain;
Merry we were *as cup and can could hold;*
Each one with each other homely and bold.
And she for her part, made us cheer heaven
   high—
The first part of dinner *merry as a pie:*
But *a scald head is soon broken;* and so they,
As ye shall straight hear, fell at a new fray.

Chapter IV.

Husband, (quoth she), ye study, be merry now;
And even as ye think now, so come to you.
Nay, not so, (quoth he), for my thought to tell
   right,
I think how ye lay groaning wife, all last night.
Husband! *a groaning horse, and a groaning
   wife,*   [life.
Never fail their master, (quoth she), for my
No, wife! *a woman hath nine lives like a cat.*
Well, my lamb! (quoth she), ye may pick out
   of that,
As soon goeth the young lamskin to the market
As th' old ewe's. God forbid, wife! ye shall
   first jet.
I will not jet yet, (quoth she), put no doubting:
It is a bad sack that will abide no clouting.
And, as we oft see, *the lothe stake standeth
   long,*
So is it an ill stake, I have heard among,
That cannot stand one year in a hedge.
I drink! (quoth she). Quoth he, *I will not
   pledge.*

What need all this? *a man may love his house*
    well
Though he ride not on the ridge, I have heard
    tell.   *[stinketh;*
What? I ween, (quoth she), *proffered service*
But *somewhat it is,* I see, *when the cat*
    winketh,   [shun;
And both her eyne out; but further strife to
Let the cat wink, and let the mouse run.
This passed, and he cheered us all, but most
    cheer
On his part, to this fair young wife did appear.
And as he to her cast oft a loving eye,
So cast her husband like eye to his plate by;
Wherewith in a great musing he was brought.
Friend! (quoth the good man), *a penny for*
    your thought.   [dish.
For my thought, (quoth he); that is a goodly
But of truth I thought: *better to have than*
    wish.   [(quoth he)?
What! a goodly young wife, as you have,
Nay, (quoth he), goodly gilt goblets, as here
    be.   [show,
By'r lady, friends! (quoth I), this maketh a
To show you more unnatural than the crow:
The crow thinketh her own birds fairest in the
    wood.   [stood),
But, by your words, (except I wrong under-
Each other's birds or jewels, ye do weigh
Above your own.   True, (quoth the old wife),
    ye say!
But my neighbour's desire rightly to measure,
Cometh of need, and not of corrupt pleasure;
And my husband's more of pleasure, than of
    need.   [*best feed;*
Old fish and young flesh, (quoth he), *doth men*

And some say, *change of pasture maketh fat
    calves.*
As for that, reason, (quoth she), *runneth to
    halves :*
As well for the cow calf as for the bull.
And though your pasture look barrenly and
    dull,
Yet *look not on the meat, but look on the man ;*
And whoso looketh on you, shall shortly skan.
*Ye may write to your friends that ye are in
    health ;*
But all thing may be suffered saving wealth.
An old said saw : *itch and ease can no man
    please ;*
Plenty is no dainty ; ye see not your own ease.
I see, *ye cannot see the wood for trees.*   [sees
Your lips hang in your light ; but this poor man
Both how blindly *ye stand in your own light ;*
And that *you rose on your right side* here right ;
And might *have gone further and have faren
    worse.*
I wot well I might, (quoth he), for the purse ;
But ye be *a baby of Belsabub's bower.*   [sour ;
Content ye, (quoth she) ! *take the sweet with the
Fancy may bolt bran and make ye take it flour.*
It will not be, (quoth he), should I die this
    hour,   [eye.
While this fair flower flourisheth thus in mine
Yes, it might, (quoth she), and hear this reason
    why :

Snow is white,	} *And every man lets it lie.*
And lieth in the dike.	
Pepper is black,	} *And every man doth it*
And hath a good smack.	*buy.*
Milk, (q' he), *is white,*	} *But all men know it*
And lieth not in the dike.	*good meat.*

Ink is all black, } *No man will it drink*
And hath an ill smack. } *nor eat.*
Thy rhyme, (quoth he), is much older than
    mine;
But mine, being *newer, is truer* than thine.
Thou likenest now, for a vain advantage, [age,
White snow to fair youth, black pepper to foul
Which are placed out of place here, by rood!
Black ink is as ill meat, as black pepper is
    good;   [is ill—
And white milk as good meat, as white snow
But a milk snow-white, smooth, young skin,
    who change will   [face?
For a pepper ink-black, rough, old withered
Though *change be no robbery* for the changed
    case,   [wit.
Yet shall that change rob the changer of his
For, who this case searcheth, shall soon see in
    it,
That as well agreeeth thy comparison in these,
As alike *to compare in taste, chalk and cheese;*
Or *alike in colour to deem ink and chalk.*
Walk, drab, walk! Nay, (quoth she), *walk,*
    knave, walk!
Sayeth that term. Howbeit, sir, I say not so;
And best we lay a straw here, and even there,
    ho!
Or else this gear will *breed a pad in the straw;*
If ye haul this way, I will another way draw.
Here is God in th'ambry (quoth I)! Quoth he,
    Nay!
Here is *the devil in th'orologe*, ye may say.
Since this, (quoth I), *rather bringeth bale than*
    boot,
Wrap it in the cloth, and tread it under foot.
Ye harp on the string that giveth no melody;

Your tongues run before your wits, by Saint
    Antony !   [(quoth he);
Mark ye, how she *hitteth me on the thumbs,*
And ye taunt me tit over thumb, (quoth she).
Since *tit for tat,* (quoth I), on even hand is set,
Set the hare's head against the goose giblet.
She is, (quoth he), bent to force you, perforce
To know that *the grey mare is the better horse.*
She choppeth logic, to *put me to my clargy:*
She hath *one point of a good hawk; she is
    hardy.*
But wife, *the first point of hawking is hold fast.*
And hold ye fast, I rede you, lest ye be cast
In your own turn.   Nay, she *will turn the leaf;*
And rather, (quoth I), take as falleth in the
    sheaf   [too bold.
At your hands; and let fall her hold, than be
Nay, I will spit in my hands, and take better
    hold.
He, (quoth she), *that will be angry without
    cause,*
Must be at one, without amends; by sage saws.
*Tread a worm on the tail, and it must turn
    again.*
He taketh pepper in the nose, that I complain
Upon his faults, myself being faultless;
But *that shall not stop my mouth,* ye may well
    guess.   [good;
Well, (quoth I), too much of one thing is not
Leave off this ! Be it ! (quoth he), fall we to
    our food ;
But *sufferance is no quittance* in this daiment.
No, (quoth she), nor *misreckoning is no pay-
    ment.*   [friend;
But *even reckoning maketh long friends,* my
For *alway own is own at the reckoning's end.*

This reckoning thus reckoned, and dinner once
    done,
We three from them twain departed very soon.

CHAPTER V.

This old woman, the next day after this night,
Stale home to me, secretly as she might,
    To talk with me; in secret counsel, (she said),
    Of things which in no wise might be bewrayed.
We twain are one too many, (quoth I), for men
    say:
Three may a-keep counsel, if two be away.
But all that ye speak, unmeet again to tell,
I will say nought but mum, and mum is counsel.
Well then, (quoth she), herein avoiding all
    fears,   [*ears.*
Avoid your children: *small pitchers have wide*
Which done, (she said), I have a husband, ye
    know,   [*show.*
Whom I made of nought, as the thing self doth
And for these two causes only, him I took—
First, that for my love, he should lovingly look
In all kind of cause, that love engender might
To love and cherish me by day and by night;
Secondly, the substance, which I to him
    brought,   [*nought.*
He rather should augment, than bring to
But now my good, shall both be spent, ye shall
    see,
And it in spending sole instrument shall be
Of my destruction, by spending it on such
As shall make him destroy me; I fear this
    much.   [*hoop;*
He maketh havoc, and *setteth cock on the*

He is so lavish, the stock beginneth to droop;
And as for *gain is dead and laid in tomb,*
When he should get aught, each finger is a
       thumb;
Each of his joints against other justles,
As handsomely as a bear picketh muscles.
Flattering knaves and flearing queans being the
       mark,   [*wark.*
Hang on his sleeve: *many hands make light*
He hath his hawks in the mew; but, make ye
       sure,
With empty hands men may no hawks allure.
There is a nest of chickens, which he doth
       brood,   [*hood.*
That will sure make his hair grow through his
They can curryfavel; and make fair weather
While *they cut large thongs of other men's*
       leather.
He maketh his marts with merchants likely
To bring a shilling to sixpence quickly.
If he hold on awhile as he begins,
We shall see him prove a merchant of eel-
       skins—
A merchant without either money or ware.
But all be bug's words, that I speak to spare.
Better spare at brim than at bottom, say I.
Ever spare and ever bare, (saith he), by and by.
Spend, and God shall send, (sayeth he), saith
       th' old ballet,
What sendeth he, (say I), a staff and a wallet?
Then up goeth his staff, to send me aloof;
He is at three words up in the house roof.
And herein to grow, (quoth she), to conclusion,
I pray your aid, to avoid this confusion;
And for counsel herein, I thought to have gone
To that cunning man, our curate, Sir John.

But this kept me back : I have heard, now and
    then,
The greatest clerks be not the wisest men.
I think, (quoth I), whoever that term began,
Was neither great clerk, nor the greatest wise
    man.
In your running from him to me, ye run
Out of God's blessing into the warm sun.
Where the blind leadeth the blind, both fall in
    the dike ;
And, blind be we both, if we think us his like.
Folk show much folly, when things should be
    sped,
To run to the foot that may go to the head.
Since he best can, and most ought, to do it,
I fear not, but he will, if ye will woo it.
There is one let, (quoth she), mo than I spake
    on :
My husband and he be so great, that *the ton*
Cannot piss but the tother must let a fart.
Choose we him aparty, then farewell my part ;
We shall so part stake, that I shall lese the
    whole.   [*sole.*
Folk say of old : *the shoe will hold with the*
Shall I trust him, then? nay, *in trust is treason.*
But I trust you, and come to you this season
To hear me, and tell me, what way ye think
    best
To hem in my husband, and set me in rest.
If ye mind, (quoth I), a conquest to make
Over your husband, no man may undertake
To bring you to ease, nor the matter amend
Except ye bring him *to wear a cock's comb* at
    end.
For, take that your husband were, as ye take
    him,

As I take him not, as your tale would make
  him,
Yet were contention like to do nought in this
But keep him nought, and make him worse
    than he is.   [clear,
But, in this complaint for counsel quick and
A few proverbs for principles, let us hear :
*Who that may not as they would, will as they
    may ;*   [obey.
And this to this : *they that are bound must*
Folly it is to spurn against a prick ;
To strive against the stream, to winch or kick
Against the hard wall.   By this ye may see,
Being bound to obedience, as ye be,
And also overmatched, *sufferance is your dance.*
He may overmatch me, (quoth she), perchance
In strength of body, but my tongue is a limb
To match and to vex every vein of him.
Tongue breaketh bone, itself having none,
    (quoth I) ;   [awry.
If the wind stand in that door, it standeth
The peril of prating out of tune by note,
Telleth us that *a good bestill is worth a groat ;*
In being your own foe, you spin a fair thread.
Advise ye well, for *here doth all lie and bleed ;*
Flee th'attempting of extremities all.
Folk say : *better sit still than rise and fall.*
For little more or less no debate make ;
At every dog's bark seem not to awake.
And where the small with the great cannot
    agree,
The weaker goeth to the pot, we all day see.
So that *alway the bigger eateth the bean—*
Ye can nought win, by any wayward mean.
Where the hedge is lowest men may soonest
    over :

Be silent! let not your tongue run at rover;
Since by strife ye may lose, and cannot win,
Suffer! *it is good sleeping in a whole skin.*
If he chide, *keep you bill under wing mute;*
Chatting to chiding is not worth a chut.
We see many times, *might overcometh right—*
Were not you *as good then to say the crow is*
    white?
And so, rather let *fair words make fools fain,*
Than be plain without pleats, and plant your
    own pain.
For, were ye *as plain as Dunstable highway,*
Yet should ye that way rather break a love day,
Than make one thus; though ye perfectly knew
All that ye conjecture to be proved true.
Yet better dissemble it, and shake it off,
Than to broid him with it in earnest or scoff.
If he play *falsehed in fellowship,* play ye
See me and see me not; the worst part to flee.
Why, think ye me so white-livered, (quoth
    she),   [ye
That I will be tongue-tied?   Nay, I warrant
They that will be afraid of every fart
Must go far to piss.   Well, (quoth I), your
    part
Is to suffer (I say); for ye shall preeve
Taunts   appease   not   things;   they   rather
    agrieve.
But for ill company, or expense extreme,
I here no man doubt, so far as ye deem;
And there is *no fire without some smoke,* we
    see.   [she);
Well, well! *make no fire, raise no smoke,* (said
What *cloak for the rain* soever ye bring me,
Myself can tell best where my shoe doth wring
    me.

But as ye say : *where fire is smoke will appear.*
And so hath it done; for I did lately hear
How flek and his make use their secret haunt-
    ing,   [ing.
By one bird, that *in mine ear was late chaunt-*
One swallow maketh not summer, (said I), men
    say.   [lay,
I have, (quoth she), *mo blocks in his way to*
For further increase of suspicion of ills :
Beside his jetting into the town to his gills,
With callets he consumeth himself and my
    goods;
Sometime in the fields, sometime in the woods,
Some hear and see him whom he heareth nor
    seeth not—   [wot;
But *fields have eyes and woods have ears,* ye
And also on my maids he is ever tooting.
Can ye judge a man, (quoth I), by his looking?
What, *a cat may look on a king,* ye know!
My cat's leering look, (quoth she), at first
    show,
Showeth me that my cat goeth a catterwawing;
And specially by his manner of drawing
To Madge, my fair maid; for may he come
    nigh her
He must needs bass her, as he cometh by her.
He loveth well sheep's flesh, that wets his
    bread in the wool—
If he leave it not, *we have a crow to pull.*
He loveth her better at the sole of the foot
Than ever he loved me at the heart root.
It is a foul bird that fileth his own nest;
I would have him live as God's law hath ex-
    pressed,
And leave lewd ticking : he that will none ill do
Must do nothing that belongeth thereto;

To tick and laugh with me he hath lawful leave.
To that I said nought, but laughed in my
    sleeve;
But when she seemed to be fixed in mind,
Rather to seek for that she was loth to find,
Than leave that seeking, by which she might
    find ease,
I fained this fancy, to feel how it would please.
Will ye do well? (quoth I), take pain to watch
    him;
And if ye chance in advoutry to catch him,
Then have ye him on the hip, or on the hurdle;
Then have ye his head fast under your girdle;
Where your words now do but *rub him on the*
    gall,   [wall.
That *deed without words* shall drive him to the
And *further than the wall he cannot go,*
But must submit himself; and if it hap so
That at end of your watch he guiltless appear,
Then all grudge, grown by jealousy, taketh
    end clear.   [she);
Of all folks I may worst watch him, (said
For of all folks himself most watcheth me;
I shall as soon try him, or take him this way,
As *drive a top over a tiled house:* no, nay!
I may keep corners or hollow trees with th' owl,
This seven years, day and night to watch a
    bowl,
Before I shall catch him with undoubted evil.
He must have a long spoon shall eat with the
And *the devil is no falser than is he.* [devil;
I have heard tell, *it had need to be*   [ear—
A wily mouse that should breed in the cat's
Shall I get within him then? nay, *ware that*
    gear!
It is hard halting before a cripple, ye wot;

A falser water drinker there liveth not.
When he hunteth a doe that he cannot avow,
All dogs bark not at him, I warrant yow.
Namely not I, I say, though as I said,
He sometime, though seldom, by some be be-
            wrayed.   [loweth;
Close hunting, (quoth I), *the good hunter al-*
But, be your husband never so still of mouth,
If ye can hunt, and will stand at receipt,
Your   maid   examined,   maketh   him   open
            straight.   [preef,
That were, (quoth she), as of my truth to make
To axe my fellow whether I be a thief.
They cleave together like burrs; that way I
            shall
Pike out no more than out of the stone wall.
Then like ye not to watch him for wife nor
            maid?   [I said;
No! (quoth she).   Nor I, (quoth I), whatever
And I mislike not only your watch in vain,
But also, if ye took him, what could ye gain?
From suspicion to knowledge of ill, forsooth!
Could make ye do but *as the flounder doeth—*
Leap out of the frying pan into the fire;
And *change from ill pain to worse is worth*
            small hire.   [doubt;
Let time try!   *Time trieth truth in every*
And *deem the best till time hath tried the truth*
            out.
And reason sayeth : *make not two sorrows of*
            one;
But ye make ten sorrows where reason maketh
            none.   [wink
For where reason, (as I said), willeth you to
(Although all were proved as ill as ye think),
Contrary to reason ye stamp and ye stare;

Ye fret and ye fume, *as mad as a March hare,*
Without proof to his reproof, present or past,
But by such report as most prove lies at last.
And *here goeth the hare away;* for ye judge all,
And judge the worst in all, ere proof in ought
  fall.   [saws;
But *blind men should judge no colours:* by old
And *folk ofttimes are most blind in their own*
  cause—
The blind eat many flies. Howbeit, the fancy
Of your blindness cometh not of ignorancy.
Ye could tell another herein the best way;
But *it is as folk do, and not as folk say;*
For they say, *saying and doing are two things*
To defend danger that double dealing brings:
As ye can seem wise in words, be wise in deed.
That is, (quoth she), *sooner said than done,* I
  drede;
But methinketh your counsel weigheth in the
  whole
To make me *put my finger in a hole;*
And so, by sufferance, to be so lither
In my house *to lay fire and tow together.*
But if they fire me, some of them shall win
More tow on their distaves than they can well
  spin;   [hands full—
And the best of them shall *have both their*
Bolster or pillow for me, be whose wull.
I will not bear the devil's sack, by Saint
  Audry !
For concealing suspicion of their baudry.
I fear false measures, or else I were a child;
For *they that think none ill, are soonest be-*
  guiled.
And thus, though *much water goeth by the mill*
That the miller knoweth not of, yet I will

Cast what may scape; and, as though I did
    find it,
With the clack of my mill to fine meal grind it.
And sure ere I take any rest in effect,
I must banish my maids such as I suspect :
Better it be done than wish it had been done.
As good undone, (quoth I), *as do it too soon.*
Well, (quoth she), till soon, fare ye well! and
    this
Keep ye as secret as ye think meet is.
Out at doors went she herewith; and hereupon
In at doors came he forthwith, as she was
    gone;
And, without any temperate protestation,
Thus he began, in way of exclamation.

Chapter VI.

Oh! what choice may compare to the devil's
    life
Like his that have chosen a devil to his wife?
Namely, such an old witch, such a macka-
    broine,
As evermore *like a hog hangeth the groyne*
On her husband, except he be her slave,
And follow all fancies that she would have.
'Tis said : *there is no good accord*
Where every man would be a lord.
Wherefore, my wife will be no lord, but lady,
To make me, that should be her lord, a baby.
Before I was wedded, and since, I made
    reckoning
To make my wife bow at every beckoning.
Bachelors boast how they will teach their
   wives good;

But *many a man speaketh of Robin Hood*
That never shot in his bow. When all is
    sought,   [*taught.*
Bachelors' wives, and maids' children be well
And this with this, I also begin to gather:
Every man can rule a shrew, save he that hath
    her.   [like wax;
At my will I weened she should have wrought
But I find and feel she hath found *such knacks*
In her bovget, and such toys in her head,
That to dance after her pipe I am nigh led.
It is said of old: *an old dog biteth sore;*
But, by God! th' old bitch biteth sorer and
    more;   [her tongue.
And not with teeth—(she hath none)—but with
If all tales be true, (quoth I), though she be
    stung,   [blame;
And thereby sting you, she is not much to
For, whatever you say, thus goeth the same.
When folk first saw your substance laid in
    your lap,   [good hap,
Without your pain, with your wife brought by
Oft in remembrance of haps happy device
They would say: *better to be happy than wise;*
Not minding thereby then to deprave your wit,
For they had good hope to see good proof of it.
But since their good opinion therein so cools,
That they say as oft: *God sendeth fortune to*
    fools;
In that, as fortune without your wit gave it,
So can your wit not keep it when ye have it.
Sayeth one: *this gear was gotten on a holy*
    day;
Sayeth another: *who may hold that will away.*
This game, from beginning, showeth what end
    is meant:

Soon gotten, soon spent; ill gotten, ill spent.
Ye are called not only too great a spender,
Too frank a giver, and as free a lender;
But also, ye spend, give, and lend, among such
Whose lightness minisheth your honesty as
    much
As your money; and much they disallow
That *ye brike all from her, that brought all to*
    yow;
And spend it out at doors, in spite of her,
Because ye would kill her to be quit of her.
For all kindness, of her part, that may rise,
Ye show all th' unkindness ye can devise.
And where reason and custom, (they say),
    affords
Alway to let the losers have their words,
Ye make her a cuckquean and consume her
    good;
And she must sit *like a bean in a monk's hood.*
Bearing no more rule than a goose turd in
    Thames;
But, at her own maids' becks, wings, or hems,
She must obey those lambs, or else a lambskin
Ye will provide for her, to lap her in.   [say;
This *biteth the mare by the thumb*, as they
For were ye, touching condition, (say they),
The castle of honesty in all things else,
Yet should this one thing, as their whole tale
    tells,
Defile and deface that castle to a cottage—
One crop of a turd marreth a pot of potage.
And some to this cry, Let him pass, for we
    think   [stink.
The more we stir a turd, the worse it will
With many conditions good, one that is ill
Defaceth the flower of all, and doth all spoil.

Now, (quoth I), if you think they truly clatter,
Let your amendment amend the matter:
Half warned, half armed. This warning for
    this I show,   [know.
He that hath an ill name is half hanged, ye

Chapter VII.

Well said! (said he). Marry, sir! here is a
    tale—
For honesty, *meet to set the devil on sale.*
But now am I forced *a bead roll to unfold,*
To tell somewhat more to the tale I erst told.
Grow this, as most part doth, I durst hold my
    life,
Of the jealousy of dame Julok, my wife,
Then shall ye wonder, when truth doth define,
How she can, and doth here both bite and
    whine.
Frenzy, heresy, and jealousy are three,
That men say hardly, or never, cured be.
And although jealousy need not or boot not,
What helpeth that counsel, if reason root not?
And in mad jealousy she is so far gone
She thinketh I run over all that I look on.
Take good heed of that, (quoth I), for at a
    word,   [sword
The proverb saith: *he that striketh with the*
Shall be stricken with the scabbard. Tush!
    (quoth he),
The devil with my scabbard will not strike me;
But, my dame taking suspicion for full prefe,
Reporteth it for a truth to the most mischief.
In words gold and whole, as men by wit could
    wish,

She will lie as fast as a dog will lick a dish.
She is, of truth, *as false as God is true;*
And, if she chance to see me, at a view,
Kiss any of my maids alone, but in sport,
That taketh she in earnest, *after Bedlam sort.*
The cow is wood; her tongue runneth on pat-
tens;
If it be morn, we have a pair of matins;
If it be even, evensong, not Latin nor Greek,
But English, and like that as in Easter week.
She beginneth, first with a cry a leison;
To which she ringeth a peal, a larum; such one
As folk ring bees with basins—the world run-
neth on wheels.
But except her maid *show a fair pair of heels,*
She haleth her by the boy rope, till her brains
    ache.   [make—
And bring I home a good dish, good cheer to
What is this? (saith she).   Good meat, (say I),
    for yow !   [sow !
God have mercy, horse! a pig of mine own
Thus when I see by kindness ease reneweth
    not,   [*reweth not;*
And then, *that the eye seeth not, the heart*
And that *he must needs go whom the devil doth*
    drive;
Her force forcing me, for mine ease to contrive
To let her fast and fret alone for me,
I go where merry chat and good cheer may be.
Much spend I abroad, which at home should
    be spent
If she would leave controlling and be content.
There leaped a whiting, (quoth she), and leaped
    in straight;   [ceit.
Take a hair from his beard, and mark this con-
He maketh you believe, by lies laid on by load,

My brawling at home maketh him banquet
    abroad.   [home.
Where his banquets abroad make me brawl at
For, as in a frost, a mud wall made of loam
Cracketh and crummeth in pieces asunder,
So melteth his money, to the world's wonder.
Thus may ye see, *to turn the cat in the pan,*
Or *set the cart before the horse,* well he can;
He is but little at home, the truth is so;
And, forth with him, he will not let me go;
And if I come to be merry where he is,
Then is he mad, as ye shall hear by this.
Where he, with gossips at a banquet late was,
At which, as use is, he paid all—but let pass!
I came to be merry; wherewith merrily :
Proface! *Have among you blind harpers,* (said
    I)—
The mo the merrier, we all day hear and see.
Yea, but *the fewer the better fare,* (said he).
Then here were, ere I came, (quoth I), too
    many;
Here is but little meat left, if there be any.
And *it is ill coming,* I have heard say,
To th' end of a shot and beginning of a fray.
Put up thy purse, (quoth he), thou shalt none
    pay;   [thy way.
And fray here should be none were thou gone
*Here is, since thou camest, too many feet
    a-bed;*   [errand sped.
Welcome! when thou goest: thus is thine
I come, (quoth I), to be one here, if I shall—
It is merry in hall when beards wag all.
What, bid me welcome, pig? I pray thee kiss
    me !
Nay, farewell, sow ! (quoth he), *our Lord bliss
    me*

From *bassing of beasts of Bearbinder Lane.*
I have, (quoth I), for fine sugar, fair rat's-bane.
Many years since, my mother said to me,
Her elders would say : *it is better to be*
An old man's darling than a young man's war-
     ling.
And God knoweth ! I knew none of this snarl-
     ing
In my old husband's days; for, as tenderly
He loved me as ye love me slenderly;
We drew both in one line.   Quoth he, *would*
     to our lord   [*cord.*
Ye had, in that drawing, *hanged both in one*
For I never meet thee at flesh, nor at fish,
But *I have* sure *a dead man's head in my dish;*
Whose best and my worst day, that wish might
     be,
Was when thou didst bury him and marry me.
If you, (quoth I), long for change in those
     cases,
Would to God he and you had changed places!
But best I change place, for here I may be
     spared,
And for my kind coming, this is my reward.
Claw a churl by th' arse, and he shitteth in my
     hand;   [band.
Knack me that nut, much good doyt you all this
Must she not, (quoth he), be welcome to us all,
Among us all, letting such a farewell fall?
Such carpenters, such chips, (quoth she); folk
     tell;   [*farewell.*
Such lips, such lettuce; such welcome, such
Thine own words, (quoth he), thine own wel-
     come marr'd.   [jarr'd.
Well, (said she), whensoever we twain have
My words be pried at narrowly, I espy.

Ye can see a mote in another man's eye,
But ye cannot see a balk in your own.
Yea, mark my words, but not that they be
    grown
By your revellous riding on every royle;
Well nigh every day a new mare or a moyle,
As much unhonest, as unprofitable,
Which shall bring us shortly to be *unable*
To give a dog a loaf, as I have oft said.
Howbeit, your pleasure may no time be denied,
But still you must have both the finest meat,
Apparel, and all thing that money may geat;
Like *one* of fond fancy so fine and so neat
That would have better bread than is made of
    wheat.
The best is best cheap, (quoth he), men say
    clear.
Well, (quoth she), *a man may buy gold too*
    dear;
Ye nother care, nor wellnigh cast what ye pay,
To buy the dearest for the best alway.
Then for your diet who useth feeding such,
Eat more than enough, and drink much more
    too much.   [school :
But temperance teacheth this, where he keepeth
He that knoweth when he hath enough is no
    fool.
Feed by measure, and defy the physician;
And, in the contrary, mark this condition :
A swine over fat is cause of his own bane;
Who seeth nought herein, his wit is in the
    wane.
But *pompous provision, cometh not all, alway*
Of gluttony, but of pride sometime, some say.
But this proverb preacheth to men haut or
    high :

HEY. II.   **G**

Hew not too high lest the chips fall in thine eye.
Measure is a merry mean, as this doth show:
Not too high for the pye, nor too low for the
    crow.
The difference between staring and stark blind
The wise man at all times to follow can find;
And i-wis an auditor of a mean wit,   [yit;
May soon accompt, though hereafter come not
Yet is he sure, *be the day never so long,*
Evermore at last they ring to evensong.
And where ye spend much though ye spent but
    lickle,
Yet *little and little the cat eateth the flickle;*
Little loss by length may grow importable;
A mouse in time may bite a-two a cable.
Thus, to end of all things, be we lief or loth,
Yet lo, *the pot so long to the water goeth,*
Till at the last it cometh home broken;
Few words to the wise suffice to be spoken.
If ye were wise, here were enough, (quoth she).
Here is enough, and too much, dame, (quoth
    he);
For, though this appear a proper pulpit piece,
Yet *when the fox preacheth then beware your*
    geese.
A good tale ill told, in the telling is marred.
So are, (quoth she), good tales well told, and
    ill heard.   [wit, wife:
Thy tales, (quoth he), show *long hair, and short*
But long be thy legs, and short be thy life.
Pray for yourself! I am not sick, (quoth she).
Well let's see, what thy last tale cometh to,
    (quoth he):   [wander;
Thou sayest I spend all; to this, thy words
But, *as deep drinketh the goose as the gander.*
Thou canst cough in the aumbry, if need be,

When I shall cough without bread or broth for
    thee.
Whereby, while thou sendest me abroad to
    spend,
Thou gossipest at home to meet me at land's
    end.   [mean—
Ah! then I beguile you, (quoth she), this ye
But sir! *my pot is whole, and my water clean.*
Well, thou wouldst have me, (quoth he), pinch
    like a snudge,
Every day to be thy drivel and drudge.
Not so, (quoth she), but I would have ye stir
Honestly; *to keep the wolf from the dur.*
I would drive the wolf out at door first, (quoth
    he);
And that can I not do, till I drive out thee.
A man were better be drowned in Venice gulf
Than have such a bearded bear, or such a wolf!
But had I not been witched, my wedding to
    flee,   [me.
The terms that long to wedding had warned
First, wooing for woeing; banna for banning;
The banns for my bane; and then this, thus
    scanning—
Marrying marring. And what married I than?
A woman! As who saith, woe to the man!
Thus wed I with woe, wed I Jill, wed I Jane—
I pray God, *the devil go with thee down the*
    lane!   [agreed),
I grant, (quoth she), this doth sound, (as ye
On your side in words, but on my side in deed.
Thou grant'st this grant, (quoth he), without
    any grace;
Ungraciously, to thy side, to turn this case.
Leave this, (quoth she), and learn liberality
To stint strife, grown by your prodigality.

Oft said the wise man, whom I erst did bury:
Better are meals many than one too merry.
Well, (quoth he), that is answered with this,
    wife: [*whole life.*
Better is one month's cheer than a churl's
I think it learning of a wiser lectour,
To learn to make myself mine own exectour,
Than spare for another that might wed thee,
As the fool, thy first husband, spared for me.
And as for ill places, thou seekest me in mo,
And in worse too, than I into any go.
Whereby this proverb showeth thee in by the
    week:
No man will another in the oven seek
Except that himself have been there before.
God give grace thou hast been good! I say no
    more;   [*couldst prove*
And would have thee say less except thou
Such process as thou slanderously dost move.
For slander, perchance, (quoth she), I not deny
It may be a slander, but it is no lie.
It is a lie, (quoth he), and thou a liar!
Will ye, (quoth she), drive me to touch ye
    nigher?   [*yit*
I rub the galled horse back till he winch; and
He would make it seem that I touch him no
    whit.   [*make:*
But I wot what I wot, though I few words
Many kiss the child for the nurse's sake.
Ye have many good children to look upon,
And ye bless them all, but ye bass but one.
This half showeth, what the whole meaneth,
    that I meve,
Ye fet circumquaques to *make me believe,*
Or think, *that the moon is made of a green*
    cheese.

And when ye have made me a lout in all these,
It seemeth ye would make me go to bed at
　　noon.
Nay, (quoth he), *the day of doom shall be done*
Ere thou go to bed at noon, or night, for me.
Thou art, to be plain, and not to flatter thee,
As wholesome a morsel for my comely corse
As a shoulder of mutton for a sick horse.
The devil with his dam hath more rest in hell
Than I have here with thee; but well, wife,
　　well!　　　　　　　　　　　　[buckets.
Well, well! (quoth she), *many wells, many*
Yea! (quoth he), and *many words, many*
　　buffets.　　　　　　　　　　　　[thus,
Had you some husband, and snapped at him
Iwys he would give you a recumbentibus.
A dog will bark ere he bite, and so thou
After thy barking wilt bite me, I trow now;
But *it is hard to make an old dog stoop,* lo!
Sir, (quoth she), *a man may handle his dog so*
That he may make him bite him, though he
　　would not.　　　　　　　　[wives scold not;
Husbands are in heaven, (quoth he), *whose*
Thou makest me claw where it itcheth not. I
　　would　　　　　　　　　　　　[cold;
Thy tongue were cooled to make thy tales more
That aspen leaf, such spiteful clapping have
　　bred,
That *my cap is better at ease than my head.*
God send that head, (said she), *a better nurse!*
For *when the head acheth all the body is the*
　　worse.
God grant, (quoth I), the head and body, both
　　two,
To nurse each other better than they do:
Or ever have done for the most times past.

I brought to nurse both, (quoth she), had it not
    been waste.   *[meal;*
Margery, good cow, (quoth he), gave a good
But then she cast it down again with her heel.
How can her purse for profit be delightful
Whose person and properties be thus spiteful?
A piece of a kid is worth two of a cat—
Who the devil will change a rabbit for a rat?
If I might change, I would rather choose to
    beg,
Or sit with a roasted apple or an egg
Where mine appetite serveth me to be,
Than every day *to fare like a duke* with thee !
Like a duke? like a duck! (quoth she), thou
    shalt fare,   *[yet spare.*
Except thou wilt spare, more than thou dost
Thou farest too well, (quoth he), but *thou art
    so wood,*   *[doth thee good.*
Thou knowest not who doth thee harm, who
Yes, yes ! (quoth she), for all those wise words
    uttered,
I know on which side my bread is buttered;
But *there will no butter cleave on my bread,*
And on my bread any butter to be spread;
Every promise that thou therein dost utter,
Is *as sure as it were sealed with butter,*
Or a mouse tied with a thread. Every good
    thing
Thou lettest even slip, like a waghalter slip-
But take up in time, or else I protest, [string.
All be not a-bed that shall have ill rest.
Now, go to thy darlings, and declare thy grief,
Where all thy pleasure is : *hop whore, pipe
    thief!*

CHAPTER VIII.

With this, thence hopped she; wherewith, O
    Lord! he cried,   [bide?
What wretch but I this wretchedness could
Howbeit, in all this woe, I have no wrong;
For it only is all on myself along.
Where I should have bridled her first with
    rough bit,
To have made her chew on the bridle one fit,
For lickorous lucre of a little winning,
I gave her the bridle at beginning;
And now *she taketh the bridle in the teeth,*
And runneth away with it; whereby each man
    seeth
It is, (as old men right well understand),
Ill putting a naked sword in a madman's hand.
She taketh such heart of grace that though I
    maim her,
Or kill her, yet shall I never reclaim her.
She hath, (they say), been stiff-necked ever-
    more;
And *it is ill healing of an old sore.*
This proverb prophesied many years agone:
It will not out of the flesh that is bred in the
    bone.   [sort
What chance have I, to have a wife of such
That will no fault amend, in earnest nor sport?
A small thing amiss lately I did espy,
Which to make her mend, by a jest merrily,
I said but this: *taunt tivet, wife, your nose*
    drops;
So it may fall, I will eat no browesse sops
This day.   But two days after this came in **ure**,
I had sorrow to my sops enough, be sure!

Well! (quoth I), *it is ill jesting on the sooth;*
Sooth bourd is no bourd, in ought that mirth
    doeth.
Such jests could not juggle her, were ought
    amiss,
Nor *turn melancholy to mirth;* for it is
No playing with a straw before an old cat.
Every trifling toy age cannot laugh at;
Ye may walk this way, but sure ye shall find
The further ye go, the further behind.
Ye should consider the woman is old :   [*cold!*
And what for? a hot word? *soon hot, soon*
Bear with them that bear with you, and she is
    scanned
Not only *the fairest flower in your garland,*
But also she is all the fair flowers thereof :
Will ye requite her then with a taunting scoff?
Or with any other kind of unkindness?   [*ness!*
Take heed is a fair thing: beware this blind-
Why will ye, (quoth he), I shall follow her will?
To make me John Drawlatch, or such a sneak-
    bill?
To bring her solace that bringeth me sorrow?
By'r lady ! then *we shall catch birds to-morrow:*
A good wife maketh a good husband, (they
    say).
That, (quoth I), ye may turn another way :
To make a good husband, make a good wife;
I can no more herein, but *God stint all strife!*
Amen ! (quoth he), and God have mercy,
    brother !
I will now mend this house and pair another.
And that he meant, of likelihood, by his own;
For, so apaired he that, ere three years were
    grown,
That little and little he decayed so long,

Till he at length *came to buckle and bare*
   thong.
To discharge charge, that necessarily grew,
There was *no more water than the ship drew.*
Such drifts drave he, *from ill to worse and*
Till he was *as bare as a bird's arse.*   [*worse,*
Money, and money worth, did so miss him
That *he had not now one penny to bliss him;*
Which, foreseen in this woman, wisely weigh-
   ing   [ing,
That meet was to stay somewhat for her stay-
To keep yet one mess for Alison in store,
She kept one bag that he had not seen before:
A poor cook that may not lick his own fingers.
But about her at home now still he lingers,
Not checker a-boord, all was not clear in the
   coast,
He looked like one that had beshit the roast.
But whether any secret tales were sprinkling,
Or that he by guess had got an inkling
Of her hoard; or that he thought to amend,
And *turn his ill beginning to a good end*
In showing himself a new man, as was fit,
That appeared shortly after, but not yet.

CHAPTER IX.

One day in their arbour—which stood so to
   mine,
That I might, and did, closely mine ear incline,
And likewise cast mine eye, to hear and see
What they said and did, where they could not
He unto her a goodly tale began,   [see me—
More like a wooer than a wedded man.
As ferre as matter thereof therein served

But the first part from words of wooing
    swerved,
And stood upon repentance, with submission
Of his former crooked unkind condition;
Praying her to *forgive and forget* all, free
And he *forgave* her *as he forgiven would be*;
Loving her now, as he full deeply swore,
As hotly as ever he loved her before.
Well, well! (quoth she), whatever ye now say,
It is too late to call again yesterday.
Wife! (quoth he), such may my diligence seem
That th'offence of yesterday I may redeem;
God taketh me as I am, and not as I was—
Take you me so too, and let all things past
    pass.   [think plain.
I pray thee, good wife! think I speak and
What! *he runneth far that never turneth again.*
Ye be young enough to mend, I agree it;
But I am, (quoth she), too old to see it;
And amend ye or not, I am too old a year
What is life where living is extinct clear?
Namely at old years of least help and most
    need;   [heed.
But no tale could tune you in time to take
If I tune myself now, (quoth he), it is fair;
And hope of true tune shall tune me from de-
    spair.   [(said she);
Believe well, and have well, men say; yea,
Do well, and have well, men say also, we see.
But what man can believe, that man can do
    well
Who of no man will counsel take, or hear tell?
Which to you, when any man any way tried,
Then *were ye deaf: ye could not hear on that*
    side.
Whoever with you any time therein wears,

He must *both tell you a tale, and find you ears.*
You had on your harvest ears, thick of hearing;
But this is a question of old inquiring :
Who is so deaf, or so blind, as is he
That wilfully will nother hear nor see?
When I saw your manner, my heart for woe
    molt ;   [*bolt :*
Then would ye *mend as the fletcher mends his*
Or *as sour ale mendeth in summer :* I know,
And *knew, which way the wind blew,* and will
    blow.
Though not to my profit, a prophet was I :
I prophesied this, too true a prophecy.
When I was right *ill believed, and worse hard,*
By flinging from your folks at home, which all
    marred,
When I said in semblance either cold or warm :
A man far from his good is nigh his harm.
Or willed ye to look, that ye lost no more,
On such as show that *hungry flies bite sore,*
Then would ye look over me, with stomach
Like as the devil looked over Lincoln. [swollen,
The devil is dead, wife, (quoth he), for ye see
I look like a lamb in all your words to me.
Look as ye list now, (quoth she), thus looked ye
    than ;
And for those looks I show this, to show each
    man,
Such proof of this proverb, as none is greater,
Which saith, that *some man may steal a horse*
    better
Than some other may stand and look upon.
Lewd huswives might have words, but I not
    one
That might be allowed.   But now if ye look,
In mistaking me, ye may see, *ye took*

*The wrong way to wood, and the wrong sow by
    th'ear;*
And thereby *in the wrong box* to thrive, ye
    were.
I have heard some, to some tell this tale not
    seeld:
When thrift is in the town, ye be in the field;
But contrary, you made that sense to sown,
When thrift was in the field, ye were in the
    town.   [any;
Field ware might *sink or swim* while ye had
Town ware was your ware *to turn the penny.*
But town or field, where most thrift did appear,
*What ye won in the hundred ye lost in the
    shire—*
In all your good husbandry thus rid the rock.
Ye stumbled at a straw, and leapt over a block.
So many kinds of increase you had in choice,
And nought increase nor keep, how can I re-
    joice?
Good riding at two anchors men have told,
For if the tone fail, the tother may hold.
But you leave all anchor hold, on seas or lands,
And so *set up shop upon Goodwin's sands.*
But as folk have a saying, both old and true,
In that they say: *black will take none other*
So may I say here, to my deep dolour, [*hue;*
It is a bad cloth that will take no colour.
This case is yours; for ye were never so wise
To take speck of colour of good advice.
Th'advice of all friends I say, one and other
Went in at the tone ear, and out at the tother.
And as those words went out, this proverb in
    came:
*He that will not be ruled by his own dame
Shall be ruled by his stepdame;* and so you,

Having lost your own good, and own friends
    now,
May seek your foreign friends, if you have any.
And sure one of my great griefs, among many,
Is that ye have been so very a hog   [*dog!*
To my friends.   What, man? *love me, love my*
But you, *to cast precious stones before hogs,*
Cast my good before a sort of cur dogs
And salt bitches; which by whom now **de-
    voured,**
And your honesty among them deflowered,
And that you may no more expense afford,
Now can they not afford you one good word,
And you them as few. And old folk under-
    stood :   [*good.*
When thieves fall out true men come to their
Which is not alway true; for, in all that bretch,
I can no farthing of my good the more fetch;
Nor, I trow, themselves neither, if they were
    sworn ;
Light come, light go ! And sure, since we were
    born,
Ruin of one ravine was there none greater ;
For, by your gifts, they be as little the better
As you be much the worse, and I cast away—
An ill wind that bloweth no man to good, men
    say.   [*the corn.*
Well, (quoth he), *every wind bloweth not down*
I hope, (I say), *good hap be not all outworn.*
I will now begin thrift, when thrift seemeth
    gone—   [*than one ;*
What, wife ! *there be mo ways to the wood*
And I will assay all the ways to the wood
Till I find one way to get again this good.
Ye will get it again, (quoth she), I fear,
As shortly as a horse will lick his ear.

The Dutchman sayeth, that *segging is good
    cope;*
Good words bring not ever of good deeds good
    hope;   [scorn—
And these words show your words spoken in
It pricketh betimes that will be a good thorn;
*Timely crooketh the tree, that will a good
    cammock be.*
And, *such beginning such end,* we all day see;
And you, by me at beginning being thriven,
And then to keep thrift could not be pricked nor
    driven—
How can ye now get thrift, the stock being
    gone?
Which is th'only thing to rise thrift upon.
Men say : *he may ill run that cannot go,*
And your gain, without your stock, runneth
    even so.
For, *what is a workman without his tools?—*
Tales of Robin Hood are good among fools.
He can ill pipe that lacketh his upper lip;
*Who lacketh a stock, his gain is not worth a
    chip.*
A tale of a tub, your tale no truth avoweth;
*Ye speak now as ye would creep into my
    mouth;*
In pure painted process—*as false as fair*—
How ye will amend when ye cannot appair?
But against gay glossers this rude text re-
    cites :
It is not all butter that the cow shites.
I heard once a wise man say to his daughter :
Better is the last smile than the first laughter.
We shall, I trust, (quoth he), laugh again at
    last,
Although I be once out of the saddle cast;

Yet, since I am bent to sit, this will I do:
Recover the horse or lese the saddle too. [hap,
Ye never could yet, (quoth she), recover any
To win or save ought, to stop any one gap.
For stopping of gaps, (quoth he), care not a
    rush,
I will learn *to stop two gaps with one bush.*
Ye will, (quoth she), as soon *stop gaps with
    rushes*
As with any husbandly handsome bushes.
Your tales have like taste, where temperance is
    taster,
To *break my head, and then give me a plaster.*
Now thrift is gone, now would ye thrive in all
    haste;   [*waste.*
And when ye had thrift, ye had *like haste to*
Ye liked then better an inch of your will
Than an ell of your thrift. Wife (quoth he),
    be still,
May I be holp forth an inch at a pinch,
I will yet thrive, (I say): *As good is an inch
As an ell.* Ye can, (quoth she), make it so
    well;
For when *I gave you an inch, ye took an ell,*
Till both ell and inch be gone, and we in debt.
Nay, (quoth he), *with a wet finger* ye can fet
As much as may easily all this matter ease;
And this debate also pleasantly appease. [now,
I could do as much with an hundred pound
As with a thousand afore, I assure you.
Yea, (quoth she), *who had that he hath not
    would*
Do that he doeth not, as old men have told.
Had I, as ye have, I would do more, (quoth
    he),   [see.
Than the priest spake of on Sunday, ye should

Ye do, as I have, (quoth she); for nought I have
And nought ye do. What, man! I trow ye rave :   [*cake?*
Would ye both *eat your cake and have your*
Ye have had of me all that I might make;
And, *be a man never so greedy to win,*
He can have no more of the fox but the skin.
Well! (quoth he), if ye list to bring it out,
Ye can give me your blessing in a clout.
That were for my child, (quoth she), had I ony ;
But husband! I have neither child, nor money.
Ye cast and conjecture this much, like in show,
As the blind man casts his staff, or shoots the
crow.   [none,
Howbeit, had I money right much, and ye
Yet to be plain, ye should have none for Joan.
Nay, he that first flattereth me, as ye have done,
And doth as ye did to me after, so soon,
He may be in my Pater noster indeed ;
But be sure, he shall never come in my Creed.
Ave Maria! (quoth he), how much motion
Here is to prayers, with how little devotion;
But some men say : *no penny no Pater noster!*
I say to such (said she) : *no longer foster,*
No longer lemman. But fare and well then,
Pray and shift each one for himself, as he can :
Every man for himself, and God for us all.
To those words he said nought; but, forthwith did fall   [speech.
From *harping on that string* to fair flattering
And, as I erst said, he did her so beseech,
That things *erst so far off* were *now so far on,*
That as she may wallow, away she is gone

Where all that was left lay with a trusty friend,
Dwelling a good walk from her at the town's
    end.
And back again straight a halting pace she
    hobbles,
Bringing a bag of royals and nobles;
All that she had, without restraint of one jot—
She brought bullock's noble, for noble or groat
Had she not one mo : which I after well knew.
And anon smiling, toward him as she drew,
Ah, sir ! *light burden far heavy* (quoth she);
This light burden in long walk well-nigh trieth
    me.
God give grace I play not the fool this day ;
For here *I send th'axe after the helve away.*
But if ye will stint and avoid all strife,
Love and cherish this as ye would my life.
I will, (quoth he), wife, by God Almighty !
This gear *cometh* even *in pudding time rightly.*
He snatched at the bag. *No haste but good,*
    (quoth she);
Short shooting leseth your game, ye may see.
Ye missed the cushion, for all your haste to it,
And *I may set you beside the cushion yit,*
And *make you wipe your nose upon your sleeve*
For ought ye shall win without ye axe me leave.
Have ye not heard tell, *all covet, all lose?*
Ah, sir ! I see *ye may see no green cheese*
But your teeth must water—a good cockney
    coke!
Though ye love not *to buy the pig in the poke,*
Yet snatch ye at the poke, that the pig is in,
Not for the poke, but the pig good cheap to
    win.
Like one half lost, till greedy grasping gat it,
Ye would be over the stile ere ye come at it.

But abide, friend ! *your mother bid till ye were*
     born :   [morn.
Snatching winneth it not, if ye snatch till to
Men say, (said he), *long standing and small*
     offering   [proffering
Maketh poor persons ; and, in such signs and
Many pretty tales and merry toys had they,
Before this bag came fully from her away.
Kindly he kissed her, with words not tart nor
     tough :   [*enough.*
But *the cat knoweth whose lips she licketh well*
Anon, the bag she delivered him, and said
He should bear it, for that it now heavy
     weighed.
With good will, wife ! for it is, (said he to her),
A proud horse that will not bear his own pro-
     vender.
And oft before seemed she never so wise,
Yet was she now, suddenly waxen *as nice*
As it had been a halporth of silver spoons.
Thus *cloudy mornings turn to clear afternoons* ;
But so nigh noon it was, that by and by,
They rose, and went to dinner lovingly.

CHAPTER X.

This dinner thought he long, and straight after
To his accustomed customers he gat ;   [that
With whom, in what time he spent one groat
     before,
In less time he spent now ten groats or more ;
And in small time he brought the world so
     about   [*out.*
That *he brought the bottom of the bag clean*
His gadding thus again made her ill content ;

But she not so much as dreamed that all was
    spent.
Howbeit, suddenly, she minded on a day
To pick the chest lock, wherein this bag lay;
Determining this : if it lay whole still,
So shall it lie—no mite she minish will ; [best
And, if the bag began to shrink, she thought
To take for her part some part of the rest.
But straight as she had forthwith opened the
    lock,
And looked in the bag *what it was a clock,*
Then was it proved true, as this proverb goeth :
He that cometh last to the pot is soonest wroth.
By her coming last, and too late to the pot,
Whereby she was *potted* thus *like a sot*
To see the pot both skimmed for running over,
And also all the liquor run at rover.
At her good husband's and her next meeting,
The devil's good grace might have given a
    greeting,
Either for honour or honesty, as good [wood ;
As she gave him : she was, (as they say), horn
In no place could she sit herself to settle,
It seemed to him *she had pissed on a nettle.*
She nettled him, and he rattled her so,
That at end of that fray asunder they go;
And never after came together again—
He turned her out at doors to graze on the
    plain,
And himself went after; for, within fortnight,
All that was left was launched out quite.
And *thus had he brought haddock to paddock,*
Till they both were *not worth a haddock.*
It hath been said : *need maketh the old wife*
    trot—
Other folk said it, but she did it, God wot !

First from friend to friend, and then from dur
    to dur,
A-begging of some that had begged of her.
But as men say : *misery may be mother*
Where one beggar is driven to beg of another.
And thus wore and wasted this most woeful
    wretch,   [fetch.
Till death from this life did her wretchedly
Her late husband, and now widower, here and
    there   [where;
Wandering about, *few know and fewer care*
Cast out as an abject, he leadeth his life
Till famine belike fet him after his wife.
    Now let us note here : First, of the first
    twain,
Where they both wedded, together to remain,
Hoping joyful presence should wear out all
    woe :
Yet *poverty brought that joy to joy*-fail, lo !
But, notably note these last twain : whereas he
Took her only for that he rich would be,
And she him only in hope of good hap
In her doting days to be danced on the lap.
In condition they differed so many ways,
That lightly *he laid her up for holy days ;*
Her good he laid up so, lest thieves might spy
    it,
That nother she could, nor he can, come by it.
Thus failed all four, of all things less and
    more,
Which they all, or any of all, married for.

Chapter XI.

Forsooth! said my friend, *this matter maketh
  boast*
Of diminution. For, *here is a mill post*
Thwitten to a pudding prick so nearly,
That I confess me discouraged clearly.
In both my weddings, in all things, except one,
This spark of hope have I, to proceed upon:
Though these and some other speed ill as ye
  tell,
Yet other have lived and loved full well.
If I should deny that, (quoth I), I should rave;
For, of both these sorts, I grant, that myself
  have
Seen of the tone sort, and heard of the tother,
That liked and lived right well, each with
  other.
But whether fortune will you that man declare,
That shall choose in this choice, your comfort
  or care,
Since, before ye have chosen, we cannot know,
I thought to lay the worst, as ye the best show,
That ye might, being yet at liberty,
With all your joy, join all your jeopardy.
And now, in this heard, in these cases on each
  part,
I say no more, but *lay your hand on your heart.*
I heartily thank you, (quoth he); *I am sped*
*Of mine errand: this hitteth the nail on the
  head.*
*Who that leaveth surety and leaneth unto
  chance,*
When fools pipe, by authority *he may dance.*
And sure am I, of those twain, if I none choose,

Although I nought win, yet shall I nought
    lose.
And to win a woman here, and lose a man,
In all this great winning what gain win I
    than?
But, mark how folly hath me away carried;
How, like a weathercock, I have here varied:
First, these two women to lose I was so loth,
That if I might, I would have wedded them
    both;   [them;
Then thought I since, to have wedded one of
And, now know I clear, I will wed none of
    them.
They both shall have this one answer by letter:
As good never a whit as never the better.
Now let me ask, (quoth I), and yourself
    answer
The short question that I asked while're.
A foul, old, rich widow, whether wed would ye,
Or a young, fair maid, being poor as ye be?
In neither barrel better herring, (quoth he).
I like thus richesse as ill as poverty;
Who that hath either of these pigs in ure,
He hath *a pig of the worse pannier* sure.
I was wedded unto my will; howbeit,
I will be devorst, and be wed to my wit;
Whereby, with these examples past, I may
    see
Fond wedding, for love, as good only to flee.
Only for love, or only for good,
Or only for both I wed not, by my hood!
Thus, no one thing only, though one thing
    chiefly
Shall woo me to wed now: for now I espy,
Although the chief one think in wedding be
    love,

Yet must mo things join, as all in one may
     move
Such kind of living, for such kind of life,
As lacking the same, *no lack to lack a wife.*
Here is enough, I am satisfied, (said he).
Since *enough is enough,* (said I), here may we,
With that one word take end good, as may be
     guessed
For folk say : *enough is as good as a feast.*

F<small>INIS</small>

The firste hundred of Epigrammes.

Inuented and
made
by
John Hey=
wood.

LONDINI
1562.

TO THE READER

Rhyme without reason, and reason without
    rhyme—
In this conversion deep difference doth fall
In first part whereof, where I am fallen this
    time.
The folly I grant; which granted, (readers all),
Your grant, to grant this request, require I
    shall.
Ere ye full reject these trifles following here,
Perceive, (I pray you), of the words th'intents
    clear.
In which, (may ye like to look), ye shall espy
Some words show one sense, another to dis-
    close;
Some words, themselves sundry senses signify;
Some words, somewhat from common sense, I
    dispose
To seem one sense in text, another in glose.
These words in this work, thus wrought your
    working tool   [fool.
May work me to seem, (at least), the less a
Then in rough rude terms of homely honesty—
For unhonest term, (I trust), there none here
    sounds
Wherein fine tender ears shall offended be—

Those follies, being searched in reason's
    bounds,
Reason may be surgeon salving those wounds;
Turning those sores to salves; for reason doth
    guess
Homely matters homely terms do best express.
But where all defence standeth in exemption,
To defend me herein out of folly's bands—
So that to redeem me there's no redemption,
Granting, and submitting folly, that so
    stands—
This last refuge I crave to have, at your hands,
Those follies standing clear from intent of ill;
In lieu or lack of good wit, except good will.

THE TABLE TO THIS BOOK.

Finis Tabulæ.

THE FIRST HUNDRED OF EPIGRAMS

1. "AN EPIGRAM ON THIS BOOK OF EPIGRAMS."

This book may seem, as it sorteth in suit,
A thin trim trencher to serve folk at fruit.
But carver or reader can no way win
To eat fruit thereon, or compt fruit therein.

2. "OF THREE SAGES."

Three manner sages nature doth devise—
The sage herb, the sage fool, and the sage
    wise.
And who for most wise himself doth accept,
May match any sage, the sage wise except.

3. "QUESTIONS ANSWERED."

Trust they any
That trust not many? } Yea.

Please they any
That serve many? } Nay.

Help they any
That help not many? } Yea.

Friend they any
That flatter many? } Nay.

Fear they any
That fear not many? } Yea.

Keep they any
That keep too many? } Nay.

4. "Of Water, Wine, and Ale."

Water under a boat, wine in a bottle,
The tone I can bear, th'other beareth me well;
And whereas nother boats nor bottles be,
Nother can I bear wine, nor water bear me.
But, above all liquor, well fare ale, (I say),
For I with ale, and ale with me, wag away.

5. "Too Much or Too Little."

If that I drink too much, then am I dry;
If I drink too little, more dry am I;
If I drink no whit then am I dryest.
Too much, too little, no whit—nought is the
    best.
Thus drink we no whit, or drink till we burst,
Yet poor dry souls we be ever a-thirst.

6. "Of the Senses."

Speak not too much, lest speech make thee
    speechless;
Go not too much, for fear thou go behind;
Hear not too much, lest hearing bring deaf-
    ness;   [blind;
Look not too much, lest looking make thee
Smell not too much, lest smelling lose his kind;
Taste not too much, lest taste mistaste thy
    chaps;
Touch not too much for fear of afterclaps.

7. "Of Talking."

Thy tail can talk, and knoweth no letter;
Thy tongue can talk, and talketh much sweeter;
But except wisdom be the greater
Of tongue and tail, thy tail talketh better.

8. "OF EARS AND WITS."

Thin ears and thick wits be dainty;
Thick ears and thick wits be plenty;
Thick ears and thick wits be scant;
Thin ears and thin wits none want.

9. "A DRUNKARD."

A goose is harnessed in her white feathers;
A drunkard in drink against all weathers;
A fool in his fool's hood, put all togethers.

10. "THE FOX AND THE MAID."

Although that foxes have been seen there
    seeld,
Yet was there lately, in Finsbury field,
A fox sat in sight of certain people,
Nodding, and blissing, staring on Paul's
    steeple.
A maid toward market, with hens in a band,
Came by, and with the fox she fell in hand.
"What thing is it, Reynard, in your brain
    plodding,   [ding?"
That bringeth this busy blissing and nod-
"I nother nod for sleep, sweetheart," the fox
    said,   [maid.
"Nor bliss for spirits, except the devil be a
My nodding and blissing breedeth of wonder,
Of the wit of Paul's weathercock yonder.
There is more wit in that cock's only head,
Than hath been in all men's heads that be dead.
As thus, by common report, this we find,
All that be dead did die for lack of wind.
But the weathercock's wit is not so weak
To lack wind; the wind is ever in his beak.
So that, while any wind bloweth in the sky,

I 2

For lack of wind that weathercock will not
      die.''
She cast down her hens, and now did she bliss,
'' Jesu ! '' (quoth she), '' *in nomine patris !*
Who hath ever heard, at any season,
Of a fox's forging so feat a reason? ''
And while she praised the fox's wit so,
He gat her hens in his neck, and to go.
'' Whither away with my hens, fox? '' (quoth
      she).
'' To Paul's pig as fast as I can,'' (quoth he).
'' Between these hens, and yonder weathercock,
I will assay to have chickens a flock.
Which, if I may get, this tale is made good,
In all Christendom not so wise a brood.
Maiden,'' (quoth he), '' these hens be forbodden
Your sight till the weathercock hath trodden.''
'' Woe, worth ! '' (quoth she), ''all crafty in-
      ventions,
And all inventors, that by false intentions,
Invent with intent to blind or blear blunt eyes,
In case as this fox to me doth devise.''

11. '' OF AN ILL GOVERNOR CALLED JUDE.''

A ruler there was, in country a-fer,
And of the people a great extortioner ;   [Jude.
Who, by name, (as I understand), was called
One gave him an ass ; which gift, when he had
He asked the giver for what intent   [viewed,
He brought him that ass.   '' For a present
I bring master Jude,'' (quoth he), '' this as[s]
      hither
To join master Jude and this as[s] together.
Which two, joined in one, this is brought to
      pass :
I may bid you ' Good even,' master Judas.''

"Macabe or Iscariot, thou knave?" (quoth
    he).   [be."
"Whom it please your mastership, him let it

12. "OF GIVING AN ALMS."

Into a beggar's hand, that alms did crave,
Instead of one penny, twopence one gave.
Which done, he said, "Beggar, happy thou
    art!
For to thee my hand is better than my heart."
"That is," (quoth the beggar), "as it chanceth
    now;
The better for me, and the worse for you."

13. "OF A SURFEIT."

A man, from a fever recovered new,
His greedy appetite could not eschew
From meat contagious, whereto he had a lust;
But one morsel, one evening, needs eat he
    must.
Which, forthwith, brought good approbation
Of his return into residivation.
"What cause causeth this?" (quoth the
    physician).
"I know," (quoth he), "no cause of suspicion;
Howbeit, my wonder is great as can be
By what means this fever attacheth me
More for eating a little this night last, [past.
Than for eating much more the night before
I did eat a capon nigh every whit
The last night; after which, I felt no fit.
And this night I ate but one bit of fresh beef,
And yet I am shaken with the whoreson thief."
"Now," (quoth the physician), "appeareth the
    cause why:
Capon is wholesome, and the beef contrary;

And a little ill meat giveth sickness more food
Than a little too much of meat that is good.''
" Sir, I thank you much,'' (quoth the patient);
" This lesson shall henceforth make me to con-
    sent
When I shall needs surfeit, by unruly will,
Rather to surfeit on that is good, than ill.''

14. '' REPUGNANCY IN APPEARANCE.''

Much contrariety may seem to stand
Where none is; as by example, my son:
In London is the best ale of all England;
And yet, as good ale in England as in London.

15. '' THE APE AND THE ASS.''

The ape and the ass stood where they beheld
A course with a greyhound at the hare in a
    field;   [ground wan,
They well perceiving the greyhound great
As long as the hare and he forthright ran;
And like advantage they saw in the hare
When she list lightly to turn here and there.
The ape, to know whether the ass's talking,
Were any quicker than his assish stalking,
Asked the ass, " If thou should'st choose one
    of both—
To ren as swiftly as the greyhound yonder
    go'th,
Or turn as light as the hare—which one of
    twain   [obtain? ''
Wouldst thou in thy choosing by choice
" I,'' (quoth the ass), " being at liberty [thee.
Will choose none of both feats, I may say to
What winneth the dog by his swift footman-
    ship   [a whip?
When the hare, at pinch, turneth from him at

And what win'th the hare in her turns so
    lightly,
The dog out-running her again, by and by?
Renning or turning so, run or turn who will,
I will go softly, or else stand even still."
" Howbeit, to assoil thy question," (quoth he),
" If I should choose one, like the hare would I
    be ;
For, where the dog renneth the hare for to kill,
She turneth for defence, offering the dog none
    ill.
And better is this part in this case, brother,
Myself to defend, than offend another."

16. "A Fool and a Wise Man."

A fool and a wise man riding, one espied.
He asked the horse that the wise man did ride :
" Whither goest thou, horse? " " Whither go
    I ? " (quoth he)—   [me ! "
" Ask him that guideth the bridle, ask not
" Whither ridest thou, fool ! " (quoth he),
    " with look so fell? "
" Ask my horse, knave ! " (said he), " what
    can I tell? "
" When fools ride," (quoth he), " that cannot
    rule the rein,
Their horses be their herbengers, I see plain.
And when wise men ride, I right well espy,
Themself, not their horse, appoint where they
    lie."

17. "Of Sight."

Who needs will look, and would not see,
The sight once seen thou lookest for,
Close up thine eyes. For, trust thou me,
Much looking so breedeth much eye sore.

18. "Feigned News."

From a field fought, one of the beaten side
Ran home, and victory on his part he cried;
Whose prince, by him thus informed of this,
Made bonfires and bankets, as the use is.
In short time, after all which joy and cost,
The king was ascertained the field was lost.
Wherewith he, (in as great haste as great
     grief),
Charged the first messenger to make preef
Where he had this lie: that the field was won.
"Myself, sir," (quoth he), "this lie first be-
     gun;
Which, for commodity unto your grace,
And all your subjects, I brought it in place.
Where the truth should have brought watching
     and weeping,
My lie brought two days of laughing and sleep-
     ing.
And if ye all this year took my lie for true
To keep you merry, what harm could ensue?
Better is," (quoth he), " be it new or stale,
A harmless lie than a harmful true tale."
How his lie was allowed, I know none that
     knoweth;
But it was at least winked at, I heard of
     trowth.

19. "Two, Arm in Arm."

One said to another, taking his arm,
" By licence, friend, and take this for none
     harm."
" No, sir," (quoth the other), " *I give you leave
To hang on my arm, but not on my sleeve."*

20. " OF HEARING AND SPEAKING."

Who heareth all
And speaketh nought,
Chance may so fall
He is well taught.
Who speaketh all
And heareth nought,
Fall what shall fall,
He is ill taught.
Who heareth all
And all babbleth,
Whatever fall
He oft fableth.
Who heareth nought
Nor nought can speak,
May soon be thought
A hoddypeak.
Say nought, hear all;
Say all, hear nought;
Both, none, these fall
Extremely wrought.
Who heareth oft
And speaketh seeld,
Be wit aloft
He winneth the field.

21. " OF WIT, WILL, AND WISDOM."

Where will is good, and wit is ill,
There wisdom can no manner skill.
Where wit is good, and will is ill,
There wisdom sitteth all silent still.
Where wit and will are both two ill,
There wisdom no way meddle will.
Where wit and will well ordered be,
There wisdom maketh a trinity.

22. "The Wren, and her Birds."

Of a nest of wrens late bred in a hedge,
Which the dam forsaking, when they were
        fledge,
One said: " Alas! mother, what is the why
That ye draw from us unnaturally? "
" Child," (quoth the dam), " I do now unto
        thee
As my dam, in my youth, did unto me.
Whereby I am blameless in that I do,
Since I do but as I have been done to."
" Mother," (quoth he), " to deal as ye be dealt
        with
Is not alway meet; but this is the pith:
As ye would your dam should have dealt with
        yow,   *[now."*
So should ye, our dam, deal with your birds
" Why, son," (quoth she), " thinkest thou me
        such a fool,
That my child shall set his mother to school?
Nay, adieu," (quoth she), and away she is
        flown;
This child, for this check, refusing for her own.
Which done, the wren calleth his brothers and
And unto them this lesson he whisters. [sisters,
" I see, and ye may see," (quoth he), " by this
        case,
The trial of taunts out of time and place.
Where fair words haply my mother might have
        won,
This taunt maketh her refuse me for her son.
Which may teach us all, wherever we become,
Rather by silence alway to be mum
Than in ought at liberty, or forbidden,
To taunt our betters, openly or hidden."

23. "THE MASTER AND THE MAN."

A man, and his man, chanced late to be
Nigh where a crow stood crying in a tree.
"James," (quoth the master), "the crow hath
    spied thee."   [(quoth he).
"Nay, by God! he looketh on you, master,"
"Taunts," (quoth the master), "rebound some-
    times I see;   [me."
Where I thought to taunt thee, thou dost taunt

24. "UPON PENANCE."

Two men of one man were confessed but late,
And both two had penance after one rate.
Which was: each of them a penny should give
To a penniless man, him to relieve.   [more;
Th'one of these twain had one penny, and no
Th'other, no penny nor farthing had in store.
They disclosing each to other in this case,
This penny father drew his purse apace,
Saying: "Since thou art penniless, I will
Give thee this penny, my penance to fulfil."
"God thank thee!" (quoth the tother), "and
    since thou
Art now penniless, as I was even now,
For penance I give this penny to thee,
As freely as ever thou gavest it to me."
"Well done!" (quoth the other), "here may
    we boast:
Penny dole dealt without one penny cost."

25. "JACK AND HIS FATHER."

"Jack," (quoth his father), "how shall I ease
    take?
If I stand, my legs ache; and if I kneel,
My knees ache; if I go, then my feet ache;

If I lie, my back acheth; if I sit I feel
My hips ache; and, lean I never so weel,
My elbows ache." "Sir," (quoth Jack),
    "pain to exile,
Since all these ease not, best ye hang awhile."

26. "Of a Daw."

With a crossbow, late, in hand ready bent,
To shoot at a daw in a tree, I went
Saying to one by: "I will assay to hit
Yonder I see a daw, if she will sit."
"She is, if she sit, a daw indeed," (quoth he);
"But if she sit not, what is she then, say ye?"
"A daw also," (said I).   Then said he, "I see,
Whether a daw sit, or whether a daw flee,
Whether a daw stand, or whether a daw lie,
Whether a daw creak, or whether a daw cry,
In what case soever a daw persever,
A daw is a daw, and a daw shall be ever."

27. "Of Showing the Way."

Twain met in a highway what time they did go,
Each one toward the place the tother came fro.
"What is my way," (said the fone), "I pray
        thee?"   [ings," (quoth he);
"Fool!" (quoth th'other).   "That is ill tid-
"I can tell thee better tidings than this:
Thy way, both fair and smooth as a die is.
My tidings," (quoth he), "is better than thine,
But I think thy tidings truer than mine."
"This is," (quoth the tother), "so well
        brought about,
That it brought, and shall bring me, in doubt
Which of these twain is most ill to view:
Good tales that be false, or ill tales that be
        true."

28. "A Quiet Neighbour."

Accompted our commodities,
Few more commodious reason sees
Than is this one commodity—
Quietly neighboured to be;
Which neighbourhood in thee appears.
For, we two, having ten whole years
Dwelt wall to wall, so joiningly,
That whispering soundeth through wellnigh,
I never heard thy servants brawl
More than thou hadst had none at all.
Nor I can no way make avaunt,
That ever I heard thee give them taunt.
Thou art to them, and they to thee,
More mild than mute; mum ye be.
I hear no noise mine ease to break;
Thy buttery door I hear not creak;
The kitchen cumbreth not by heat;
Thy cooks chop neither herbs nor meat.
I never heard thy fire once spark;
I never heard thy dog once bark;
I never heard once in thy house
So much as one peep of one mouse;
I never heard thy cat once mew—
These praises are not small nor few.
I bear all water of thy soil,
Whereof I feel no filthy foil,
Save water which doth wash thy hands,
Wherein there none annoyance stands.
Of all thy guests set at thy board,
I never heard one speak one word;
I never heard them cough nor hem;
I think, hence to Jerusalem,
For this neighbourly quietness,
Thou art the neighbour neighbourless.

For ere thou wouldest neighbours annoy,
These kinds of quiet to destroy,
Thou rather wouldest to help that matter,
At home alone fast bread and water.

29. "Of Dogs and Thieves."

To keep thieves by night out of my house,
I keep dogs to aid me in my yard,
Whose barking at stir of every mouse,
By lack of sleep killeth me in regard—
Thieves or dogs then, which may best be
    spared?
Murder is the most mischief here to guess;
Thieves can do no more, and dogs will do no
    less.

30. "A Keeper of the Commandments."

If it be, (as it is), much commendable
To keep God's precepts, given Moses in table:
In keeping the same, (as thou hast pretended),
Thou may'st well be marvellously commended.
First, for thy having any mo gods but one:
Thou keepest within that bound: for God thou
    hast none.
Having or worshipping of god, false or true,
Thou hast nor worshippest God, old nor new.
And, as for the committing of Idolatry,
By graving to thyself any Imagery:
This twenty years, day in, weather hot or cool,
Thou handledst no carving nor working tool.
The name of God in vain: thou consentest not
    till;   [good or ill,
Thou never swearest but for some purpose
And as for the holy day, thou dost break none:
For thou wilt rather make twenty than break
    one.

Father and mother not dishonoured by thee :
For thou never comest where any of them be.
And where thou shalt not kill; to clear thee of
     that,
Thou never durst abide to fight with a gnat.
Than all adultery or fornication :
Chastity dischargeth, by this approbation;
All women hardly can bear thee their favour
To abide thy sight; and in no wise thy savour.
For stealing or theft : whatever thou hast been,
Thy hands at this day are known to be clean.
How canst thou steal ought in house, field, or
     street ?—   [feet.
Thou sittest in Newgate fast bound, hands and
By false witness thou never hurtest man : for
     why?
Every word thou speakest, every man thinkest
     a lie.
Now, to covet in mind thy neighbour's ass,
Or his house : when bondage will not let thee
     pass
To ride to the tone, or go to the tother;
Or, in consented thought, one way or other.
For to covet thy neighbour's maid or his wife :
Thou knowing they cannot love thee for their
     life.
Or, of thy neighbour's things to covet any-
     thing :
When covetousness can no way bring winning;
But that lack of credit, liberty, or love,
Keepeth thee from that coveting can move.
Thou hast too shrewd a wit in desire to dwell,
To have things from which despair doth thee
     expel.   [appear,
Thus in God's precepts, except thou clear
I know not who the devil can say he is clear.

31. "OF A NOSE."

But for blemish of a face to look upon,
I doubt which were best, to have a nose or
        none.
Most of our savours are more sour than sweet :
A nose or no nose, which is now most meet?

32. "LETTING OF A FARM."

By word, without writing, one let out a farm,
The covenants wherein the lessee brake amain :
Whereby the lessor, lacking writing, had
        harm.   [plain,
He said and sware, he would make promise
Without writing, never to let thing again.
" Husband ! " cried this wife, " that oath again
        revart :
Else, without writing, ye cannot let a fart."

33. "AGE AND YOUTH."

Though age and youth together can seeld
        agree,
Yet once, two young and two old folk did I see
Agreed like lambs together, divers years :
The story whereof forthwith appears.
A woman old, and a man young were led,
She him for love, and he her for good, to wed.
A young woman, and old man, in like case,
Were wed for like cause at the same time and
        place.
Into one house these two couples wedded were,
And during their lives, together must live there.
And they once acquainted, and one month
        married,
All their lives after they never varied.
Company and condition these four folk hold,

As nature naturally willeth young and old :
Coupling themselves together thus every day ;
Th'old fools all day prate, the young fools all
    day play.

34. "A Rose and a Nettle."

What time herbs and weeds, and such things
    could talk,
A man in his garden one day did walk,
Spying a nettle green, (as Themeraude), spread
In a bed of roses like the ruby red.   [eye,
Between which two colours he thought, by his
The green nettle did the red rose beautify.
" Howbeit," he asked the nettle, " what thing
Made him so pert? so nigh the rose to
    spring? "   [nettle ;
" I grow here with these roses," said the
" Their mild properties in me to settle ;
And you, in laying unto me your nose,
Shall smell how a nettle may change to a
    rose."
He did so : which done, his nostrils so pritcht,
That rashly he rubbed where it no whit itched ;
To which smart mock, and wily beguiling,
He, the same smelling, said smoothly smiling—
" Roses convert nettles? Nay, they be too
    fell ;
Nettles will pervert roses rather, I smell."

35. "Of the Wife's and her Husband's Waste."

"Where am I least, husband? " Quoth he,
   " In the waist :   [strait-laced."
Which cometh of this; thou art vengeably

" Where am I biggest, wife? " " In the
    waste," (quoth she);
" For all is waste in you, as far as I see."

36. " An Old Wife's Boon."

In old world, when old wives bitterly prayed,
One devoutly, as by way of a boon,
Axt vengeance on her husband, and to him
    said :
" Thou wouldst wed a young wife ere this
    week were doon   [soon."
Were I dead, but thou shalt wed the devil as
" I cannot wed the devil," (quoth he).
    " Why? " (quoth she).   [he).
" For I have wedded his dam before," (quoth

37. " A Talk of Two Conies."

In time when dumb beasts, as well as birds
    spake,
Two conies their minds in this matter brake.
" Were all conies in such case," (said the one),
" That of two winters' weather we must choose
    one :   [snow ever?
Which were best choice—frost never, and
Or else to choose frost ever, and snow never? "
" Frost," (quoth the other), " maketh us lusty
    and fat ;   [(quoth he), " for that?
And snow lameth us for lean." " What,"
Forty fat conies be oft killed in one night,
When lean conies with life 'scape away quite."
" Yea," (quoth the tother), " but where snow
    too long lieth,
Conies by famine well-nigh every one dieth.
Better all be fat, though some die as lots fall,
Than linger in leanness, and thereby die all."

38. " A Prisoner."

In prison, a prisoner condemned to die,
And for execution waiting daily,
In his hands for worms looking on a day,
Smiling to himself these words did say:
" Since my four quarters, in four quarters
        shall stand,   [hand?
Why harm I these seely worms eating my
Nought else in this deed do I, but myself show
Enemy to the worm and friend to the crow."

39. " Two Blind Men."

One blind man to supper another bad;
Which twain, sitting at such meat as they had,
" Methinketh," (quoth the blind host), " this
        candle burneth dim."   [him.
" So thinketh me, sir," said the blind guest to
" Wife," (said the good man), " with sorrow
        mend this light."   [bright;
She put out the candle, which burned very
And chopped down empty candlesticks two or
        three.   [(quoth he).
" So lo! now eat and welcome, neighbour,"

40. " Debility of Senses."

" Wife, my hands for feeling are oft very ill;
And, as th'one hand mendeth, th'other ap-
        paireth still."   [feeleth, evermore,
" Ye say sooth," (said she), " th'one hand
Worse the day present than the day before.
Th'other hand feeleth, by ointments excellent,
Better the day before than the day present.
But how doth your eye-sight? " " Worse and
        worse," (said he);   [thee."
" For worse this day, than yesterday, I see

"Though you were blind," (quoth she), "that
    should no love break;   [speak."
I would your eyes were out, so you could not
"Take hearing too," (quoth he), "thou
    makest my ears such   [too much.
That thou hast made them hear enough, and
And going may go too. For wherever I am,
I go not an inch from the devil or his dam."
"In faith, if thou didst," (quoth she), "yet
    could I well
Find means to find out a fool by the smell.
And here may we hear and see, how this tale
    fits,   [wits."
With my good man's goodly limbs, and good

41. "A FOOLISH HUSBAND."

"Husband, *two wits are better than one,*
    clerks say,   [way:
To debate matters; which seemeth true this
When we two contend, what's my wit without
    thine
To convince thyself thy wit conducteth mine?"

42. "A WITTY WIFE."

"Jane," (quoth James), "to one short demand
    of mine   [thine,
Answer not with a lie from that mouth of
And take this noble." Which when she had
    ta'en: [Jane?"
"Is thy husband," (quoth he), "a cuckold,
She stood still, and to this would no word
    spake.   [break,
From which dumb dump when he could her not
He axt his noble again. "Why," (quoth she),
"Made I any lie to thee?" "Nay," (quoth
    he).

" Then walk, fool ! " (quoth she), " this wager
    I win clear,
And thou of my counsel never the near."
" Gog's soul ! " (sware he), and flung away
    amain :
" I will never talk with that woman again.
For, as she in speech can revile a man,
So can she in silence beguile a man."

43. " Handsome Handling."

Some wonder to see thy handling of things
But it is no wonder as the case stands.   [neat;
The toes of thy feet, in handling of things feat,
Are as handsome as the fingers of thy hands.

44. " A Saying of Patch, my Lord Cardinal's Fool."

Master Sexten, a person of known wit,
As he at my Lord Cardinal's board did sit,
Greedily wrought at a goblet of wine :
" Drink none," (said my lord), " for that sore
    leg of thine."   [provide
" I warrant your grace," (quoth Sexten), " I
For my leg : For I drink on the tother side."

45. " Certain Follies."

To cast fair white salt into wise
    men's meat,
To make them count salt sugar, } a folly.
    when they eat :

To bear a man in hand he itcheth
    in each part
When the man feeleth an universal } a folly.
    smart :

To speak always well, and do
    always ill,
And tell men those deeds are done } a folly.
    of good will :

Thy lusty-limbed horse to lead in
    thy hand,
When on thy lame limbs thou canst } a folly.
    scantly stand :

Of kicks for cage work, to build
    thy house high,
And cover it with lead to keep thy } a folly.
    house dry :

46. " OF TWO STUDENTS."

Two scholars young, in the university late
Kept in thin diet, after scholars' rate,
Th'one being an eater greedy and great,
Th'other a weak feeder, said at his meat :
" Oh this smart, small pittance and hungry
Maketh us to study aptly and quiet."   [diet
" Sure," (said the tother), " small meals are
    induction
To th'increase of study, for deeper instruction ;
This dinner shall drive me to study, anon,
Where I may get more meat when this is
    gone."

47. " A MERRY WOMAN."

There came, by chance, to a good company
A lady, a wanton and a merry.   [light,
And though every word of her own showed her
Yet no man's words else to her might that
    recite.

She had all the words; she babbled so fast
That they, being weary, one said at the last:
" Madame, ye make my heart light as a kyx,
To see you thus full of your *meretrix*."
This trick thus well tricked in the Latin phrase,
Brought to this tricker nother muse nor mase;
She nought perceiving, was no whit offended;
Nor her light behaviour no whit amended;
But still her tongue was clapping like a patten.
" Well," said the said man, " in language of
    Latin
I never told woman any fault before,
Nor never in Latin will tell them fault more."

48. " A Louse and a Flea."

A louse and a flea, set in a man's neck,
Began each other to taunt and to check;
Disputing at length all extremities
Of their pleasures, or discommodities:
Namely this I heard, and bare away well.
" If one," (quoth the louse), " scrat within
    an ell
Of thy tail, then forthwith art thou skipping;
Like Jack of Bedlam, in and out whipping.
Half an hour after thou dar'st nowhere sit,
To abide the biting of one good bit.
And when any man herein shall prove me,
His nails do, (as a writ doth), remove me;
Which nails, once removed from the man's
    head,
I am straight at feeding, within a hair bread
Where I fed before in my dainty diet.
" Ye be hardy," (quoth the flea), " I deny not;
But how many lice have abidden by it
When they would have done as fleas do, fly
    it? "

With this the man to his neck his hand
    wrought;
The flea skipped away, but the louse he caught.
" Now, now? " (quoth the flea). " Alas ! "
    (quoth the louse);
" My head is well served to serve for souse
That thus, like a souse head, forsaw not this
    grief,
Till feeling hath put painful practise in preef."

49. " OF HIM THAT FORGOT HIS PATER NOSTER IN LATIN."

An old, homely man at shrift commanded,
By his curate, his *Pater noster* to bid,
After long study, he said: " Master vicar !
By Jis ! cham ashamed my wit is no quicker.
Ich said it within little more than fortnight;
And now, like a beast, cha forgot it quite.
Fie on age ! In youth ich had ever such wit,
That whatsoever ich had to do, yet
At shrift chad my *Pater noster* evermore,
When ich said it not twice in the year before."

50. " OF HIM THAT COULD NOT LEARN HIS PATER NOSTER IN ENGLISH."

A man of the country, shriven in Lent late,
(According to th'injunction), his curate
Bade him the *Pater noster* in English say.
" Ich can it not, master," (quoth he), " by my
    fay ! "   [the rest miss."
" Say a piece of it," (quoth he), " though ye
" Ich cannot one word of it," (quoth he), " by
    Jis !
And yet, master vicar, by God's sacrament !
Cha jumbled about it ever since last Lent;
And some of it ich had in the cleansing week;

But now, when ich should say it, all is to
    seek.''   [far decayed,
'' Well,'' (quoth the priest), '' if your wit be so
Say the *Pater noster* ye have always said.''
'' Nay, by the Mass ! '' (sware he), '' if you will
    have all told,
Cha so grated on the new, cha forgot th'old.''

51. '' Of the Fist and the Heart.''

One cursed another's heart for a blow in a
    fume :
'' Curse not his heart,'' (quoth one by), '' curse
    his fist.''
'' His heart,'' (quoth he), '' to mine ear did
    not presume ;
But his heart to mine ear did his fist assist.''
Since each limb must frame in feat, as the
    heart list,
When the heart willeth any limb in any fault
    to fall,
No man blame any man, to blame the heart
    for all.

52. '' Of This Word, *Enough*.''

A merry man by his master at meat set :
'' Methinketh,   (quoth the master), '' thou
    canst no drink get.''   [he.
'' Here is enough, though there be none,'' said
'' Then art thou not dry? ''   '' Yes, so mote I
    thee,
And fain would drink.''   '' How be thy words
    true then? ''
'' Thus : This word *enough* two ways we may
    scan ;
Th'one much enough, th'other little enough ;
And here is little enough.''   His master lough,

Calling in his wife to discant upon this.
"How sayest thou, wife? our man in this case
    ·is
Dry, and would drink, and drink nothing nigh
    him;
And yet proveth he drink enough by him."
"Since he," (quoth she), "proveth drink
    enough in store,
More than enough, were waste: he getteth
    no more."

53. "OF TABLE-PLAY."

"Wife, I will no more play at tables with thee;
When we come to bearing, thou beguilest me
In bearing of thy men; while thou hast any,
Each other cast thou bearest a man too many."

54. "THE COCK AND THE HEN."

A cock and his hen perching in the night,
The cock at his hour crowed loud as he might;
The hen, heavy of sleep, prayed the cock that
    he
Would leave off his crowing; but it would not
    be.
The hen saw the cock stick to his tackling:
In her treble voice she fell so to cackling
That the cock prayed her, her cackling to
    cease,
And he of his crowing would hold his peace.
"Nay, churl," (quoth she), "be sure that will
    I not;
And for thy learning henceforth mark this
    knot:
Whenever thou wouldest seem to overcrow me,
Then will I surely overcackle thee."

55. "Cheapening of a Face of Fur."

Into a skinner's shop, while his wife there
    wrought,
In haste ran a gentleman, there to espy
A fair face of fur which he would have bought.
" What fur," (quoth he), " would your master-
    ship buy? "   [nigh? "
" Harlots' wombs," (quoth he), " know ye any
" Harlots' wombs," (forsooth !), " I have
    none," (quoth she);
But ye shall have knaves' shanks, meet as
    can be."

56. "Buying of Shoes."

When I at the shoemaker's shall shoes assay,
If they be too little, they will stretch, (saith
    he);   [way.
If they be too much, they will shrink straight-
Too long, too short, how narrow or wide they
    be,
All is one matter as he shapeth them to me.
For may he once get his shoes on my feet,
Without last or lingel his words make them
    meet.

57. "A Suspicion Cleared."

One to his friend, kindly
Gave monition friendly,
That ill was reported
By one that resorted
To him : whom, (as they thought),
Enticed him to nought.
He thanked him, and said,
" My friend, be not afraid.
The hearing of that fool

Setteth me no whit to school.
I hear him when he list;
And follow him when me list.''

58. '' OF SPITE.''

If there be any, as I hope there be none,
That would lese both his eyes to lese his foe
    one,
Then fear I there be many, as the world go'th,
That would lese one eye to lese their foes both.

59. '' OF THE LETTER 'H.' ''

'' H '' is worst among letters in the cross row;
For if thou find him other in thine elbow,
In thine arm, or leg—in any degree—
In thy head, or teeth, in thy toe or knee,
Into what place soever '' H '' may pike him,
Wherever thou find ache, thou shalt not like
    him.

60. '' ILL FLYING OF IDLENESS.''

If flight from idleness may be deemed
Main means to virtue being fled warely:
How mayest thou then thereby be esteemed?
Thou fleest that vice not meanly nor barely,
But mainly; scrupulously, and so charely,
That in thee, ere idleness shall be spied,
Thou wilt yet rather be ill occupied.

61. '' A TONGUE AND A CLOCK.''

'' Thy tongue should be a clock, wife, had I
    God's power,
For then would it strike but once in one hour.''
'' Yet it might run,'' (quoth she), '' and strike
    ere the time;

And should that clock have, (as my tongue
    hath), a chime,
I, being sexton, might set the clock forth soon
To strike and chime twelve two hours before
    noon."

62. " A Hearer of a Sermon."

" What bringeth thou from the sermon, Jack?
    declare that ! "
" Forsooth, master ! " (quoth he), " your cloak
    and your hat."
" I can thee good thank, Jack, for thou art
    yet sped
Of somewhat in thy hand, though nought in
    thy head."

63. " A Man without Wit, Strength, and Cunning."

Thou art a wight to wonder at :
Thy head for wit showeth thee a wat ;
Thy body for strength showeth thee a gnat ;
Thy voice for tune showeth thee a cat—
Do, say, or sing, in any what,
Thou art a minion marmsat.

64. " How to Wish."

" How may I have thee, Gill, when I wish for
    thee ? "
" Wish not for me, Jack, but when thou
    mayest have me."
This is a lesson Gill, proper and pleasant ;
For, by these words, this winning Jack may
    avaunt.   [before,
Though Jack be no nearer Gill than Jack was
Yet Jack is nearer his wit, by Jis ! by ten
    score.

65. "A Doubtful Demand of Choice."

" If thou must choose, Hodge, touching
 cuckoldry,   [commonly
Which wouldst thou choose? to know thyself
To be taken for one, and take thyself none;
Or, to be taken for none, and take thyself
 one? "
" The best or worst of these twain, (Hugh), tell
 me which :
Claw where it doth smart, or tickle where it
 doth itch? "   [brother."
" I know small difference herein, Hodge
" And I, (Hugh), know as little in the tother."

66. "An Old Widower and a Young Maid."

A widower rich, with riveled face old,
Wooing a fair young woman, his mind he told
Boasting what he had, as wooers do, that can.
Wherein he boasted of a goodly young man,
A son of his own, whom God had him sent,
Of conditions and qualities excellent.
In this hot wooing this old man's behaviour,
So far forth, had won this young woman's
 favour   [done,
That, in short tale, when his long tale was
She prayed him to go home and send her his
 son.

67. "Gaping Oysters."

" On whom gape thine oysters so wide, oyster-
 wife? "   [life ! "
" Mine oysters gape on you, sir, God save your
" Wherefore gape they? " " Sir, they gape
 for promotion;   [tion."
They hope, (to promote them), you have devo-

" Nay," (quoth he), " the peril were pernicious
To promote oysters that be ambitious."

68. " THE JUDGE AND THE JUGGLER."

To a justice, a juggler did complain
Of one that dispraised his liger de maine.
" What's thy name? " (said the justice).
    " Dawson," said he.   [pardie ! "
" Is thy father alive? " " Nay, dead sir,
" Then thou shalt no more be Daw's son, a
    clear case,   [place."
Thou art Daw thyself now, in thy father's

69. " OF LOOKING."

To save mine head when I upward cast mine
    eye,
And look not to my feet, to the ground fall I.
When I look downward to my feet, to take
    heed,   [bleed.
A tile, fallen from a house maketh my head
And look I right forth, between my feet and
    head,
Broken head, breakneck falls, of both I am
    sped.
I think it as good, by ought I can devise,
To be stark staring blind, as thus to have eyes.

70. " OF CONSTANCY."

Some say thou art inconstant, but I say nay—
What though thy wit be wavering every way?
Whose wit, like the wind, hath been wavering
    ever,
And in unsteady wavering doth persever.
A constant man I affirm him constantly,
For he is constant in inconstancy.

71. "Of a Face and a Wit."

In thy youth and age these properties are
    sprung :   [young.
In youth thy face was old : in age thy wit is

72. "Of Blowing."

What wind can there blow that doth not some
    man please?
A fart in the blowing doth the blower ease.

73. "To the Flatterer."

Thy flattering of me, this followeth thereupon :
Other thou art a fool, or else I am one.
Where flattery appeareth, at least by wise
    men's school,
The flatterer, or the flattered, is a fool.

74. "Of Contentation."

Is not the poor man rich that is contented?
Yes : rich by his contentation consented.
Is not the rich man poor that is not content?
Yes : poor by lack of contentation here meant.
Then riches and poverty in men's minds lie?
Yea : but we may far sooner learn, (think I),
To think ourselves rich having no riches nigh,
Than make ourselves rich having much riches
    by.

75. "Of Waiting."

I would see a man wait to his master's mind
As the weathercock waiteth on the wind ;
Blow it here or there, blow it low or high,
The weathercock's beak is still in the wind's
    eye.

76. "OF FOREKNOWLEDGE."

Foreknowledge of things that must fall
To man, I think it were not best.
The foreknown ill to man would call
Forefelt grief of foreknown unrest.
By foreknown good, to man were ceast
Sweet sudden joy, which evermore
Cometh when joys come unknown before.

THE SAME IMPUGNED WITHOUT CHANGE OF WORDS, EXCEPT FOUR OR FIVE.

Foreknowledge of things that must fall
To man, I think it were the best.
The foreknown ill to man would call
Digestion of foreknown unrest.
By foreknown good, to man were ceast
Distemperate joy, which evermore
Cometh when joys come unknown before.

77. "MISTAKING AN ERRAND."

Feasting a friend, the feaster, (whose man did
    wait),   [conceit.
Bade him at the last course fetch the clouted
"What bringest thou here, knave?" (quoth
    he), "what hast you doon?"
"I have," (quoth his man), "brought here
    your clouted shoon."
"Clouted shoon, carterly knave! what dost
    thou dream?
Eat thou the clouted shoon, fetch us the
    clouted cream."

78. "OF HOLDING AN INN."

Being holden in Newgate, thou canst not be
An innholder, for thine inn holdeth thee.

79. "A Wife's Defence of her Beetle Brow."

"Were I to wed again, wife, I make a vow
I would not wed a wife with a beetle brow."
"And I," (quoth she), "rather would a husband wed
With a beetle brow, than with a beetle head."

80. "The Shrewd Wife's Tongue."

"A dog, dame, ruleth in degree
Above a devil with thee;
At least sour wind a dog letteth flee,
Thy nose will stopped be;
But no devil's word may make decree
To stop thy tongue I see."
"Since thou appearest to be," (quoth she),
"A dogged devil to me,
To tame thy devilish property
My tongue shall still be free."

81. "A Fool's Tongue."

Upon a fool's provocation
A wise man will not talk;
But every light instigation
May make a fool's tongue walk.

82. "Of Glass and Lattice."

Where glaziers and lattice-makers work in
    sight,
This one difference in their two feats we find:
Glass keepeth out the wind and letteth in the
    light;   [wind.
Lattice keepeth out the light and letteth in the
Of both sorts I wish when I shall wish any,
Lattice-makers few, and glaziers many.

83. "Two Wishers for Two Manner of
Mouths."

" I wish thou hadst a little narrow mouth,
wife !
Little and little to drop out words in strife."
"And I wish you, sir, a wide mouth for the
nonce,
To speak all that ever you shall speak at once."

84. "Of Dispraise."

All men must be blind and deaf ere thou praise
win ;
For no man seeth or heareth ought to praise
thee in.

85. "A Discharge from Hypocrisy."

Thou art no bird of hypocrisy brood,
For thou fleest all things that might show thee
good.

87. "Of the Fool and the Gentleman's
Nose."

One gentleman having another at meat,
That guest having a nose deformed, foul and
great,   [by,
The fool of that house, at this time standing
Fell thus in hand with that nose suddenly.
" Nose *autem*, a great nose as ever I saw ! "
His master was wroth, and cried, " Hence with
that daw !"   [fool,
One said : " Talk no more of great noses, ye
Lest ye be talked withal in the whipping
school."   [speak,
The fool, warned of great noses no more to

L 2

To mend that fault this way these words did
    break.
" Said I, this is a foul, great spittle nose?
By'r lady! I lied, it is a fair little nose."
" Will not that fool be had hence? " (quoth
    the master).
" Thou wilt, fool! " (quoth one), be walked
    with a waster,
If thou speak of any nose, great or small."
The fool at third warning, minding to mend
    all,
Stepped to the board again, crying as he goes:
" Before God and man! that man hath no
    nose."
The fool was feaked for this; but what of that?
The great fault, here to note, he amended nat;
Which is this: not the wise, but the fool, ye
    see,
In cloaking of one fault maketh two or three.

87. " A Fool Taken for Wise."

Wisdom and folly in thee, (as men scan),
Is as it were a thing by itself sool:
Among fools thou art taken a wise man;
And, among wise men, thou art known a fool.

88. " Things to Forbear."

Displeasures that fume and fret,
Good to forgive and forget.
All oaths, what, when, and where,
Better forbear than forswear.
Other men's livings all,
As good forsteal as forstall.
Not at bottom, but at brink,
Better foresee than forthink.

89. " MEDDLERS."

To feed of any fruit at any feast,
Of all kinds of meddlers, meddle with the least.
Meddle not with great meddlers; for, no ques-
    tion,   [gestion.
Meddling with great meddlers maketh ill di-

90. " OF DWELLING."

Between Ludgate and Newgate thou canst dwell
    never;
For in Ludgate or Newgate thou must dwell
    ever.

91. " OF THE MILNER AND THE SEXTON."

The milner tolleth corn, the sexton tolleth the
    bell;
In which tolling, tollers thrive not alike well.
Th'one tolleth with the clapper, th'other in the
    hopper;   [copper.
Th'one savour'th of silver, th'other soundeth of

92. " OF BOOKS AND CHEESE."

No two things in all things can seem only one;
Because two things so must be one thing
    alone.   [cheese,
Howbeit, reading of books and eating of
No two things, for some things, more like one
    than these.
The talent of one cheese in mouths of ten men
Hath ten different tastes in judgment—most
    times when
He saith " 'tis too salt "; he saith " 'tis too
    fresh ";   [nesh."
He saith " 'tis too hard "; he saith " 'tis too
" It is too strong of the rennet," saith he;

" It is," saith he, " not strong enough for
    me."
" It is," saith another, " well as can be."
No two of any ten in one can agree; [books.
And, as they judge of cheese, so judge they of
Onlookers on which, who that narrowly looks,
May look for this : Saith he, " that book is too
    long."   [" ye say wrong,
" Tis too short," saith he. " Nay," saith he,
'Tis of meet length; and, so fine phrase, or
    fair style,
The like that book was not made a good while;
And, in touching the truth, invincibly
    wrought."   [nought."
" Tis all lies," saith another, " the book is
No book, no cheese, be it good, be it bad,
But praise and dispraise it hath, and hath had.

93. "OF HEADS."

Some heads have taken : two heads better than
    one;
But ten heads, without wit, I ween as good
    none.

94. "THE WOODCOCK AND THE DAW."

A woodcock and a daw sat upon a plain,
Both showed comparison each other to disdain.
" Back ! " (quoth the woodcock). " Straw for
    thee ! " (quoth the daw);   [awe? "
" Shall woodcocks keep daws now in dreadful
" None awe," (quoth the woodcock), " but in
    behaviour;   [favour ! "
Ye ought to reverence woodcocks, by your
" For what cause? " (quoth the daw), " for
    your long bills? "

"Nay," (quoth the woodcock), "but lords
    will, by their wills,
Rather have one woodcock than a thousand
    daws;
Woodcocks are meat, daws are carron—weigh
    this clause."   [agree;
"Indeed, sir," (said the daw), "I must needs
Lords love to eat you, and not to eat me—
Cause of daws' courtesies!—so, if woodcocks
    thus gather,
Ye shall have courtesy; for this, I would rather
Be a daw, and to woodcock courtesy make,
Than be a woodcock, and of daws courtesy
    take.
I were double a daw, had I not liever
Birders should, (in their birding endeavour),
Take up gins and let me go when they geat me,
Than set gins to get me, for lords to eat me."

95. "Of Few Words."

Few words show men wise, wise men do de-
    vise;
Which is ofttime true, and oft otherwise.
In some case silence may as stiffly stand
With folly, as with wisdom, wisely scanned.

96. "Wotting and Weening."

Wotting and weening—were those two things
    one,   [none!
Who could wot himself wise like thee? I ween

"Otherwise."

"I would give the best fardle in my pack
To be as wise as thou weenest thou art, Jack."
"And to be as wise as I wot thou art—
What would I give, trowest thou? what? not a
    fart!"

97. "A Much Like Matter."

"Tom, thou thinkest thyself wise."   "Yea,
     what of that, Hugh?
Thou thinkest thyself wiser than I?"   "Yea,
     Tom, true."
"It seemeth," (said a third man), "by this
     device,
No mastery for fools to ween themselves wise."

98. "Wisdom and Folly."

Thy wisdom and folly both, nay no one
Can be contained in volumes great nor small.
Thy wisdom being none, occupieth place none;
Thy folly being all, occupieth place all.

99. "Of Lack."

One lack of late in thee saw we,
Which lacketh not now; for this we see:
Thou hast lacked lack of honesty;
But now that lack lacketh not in thee.

100. "The Weathercock, the Reed, and the Wind."

The weathercock and the reed, comparing late
Their service done to the wind, fell at debate.
"The wind," (quoth the weathercock),
     "windeth nowhere;   [there."
But straight, bolt upright, I stand waiting
"Forsooth!" (said the reed), "and where the
     wind is found,
At every blast I bow down to the ground."
"Surely," (said the wind), "the waiting of
     the tone,
And curtsey of the tother I take both one?

And none of both good; but rather ill to me:
For, when I oft in corners secret would be,
Other the crooked curtsey of the reed,
Or weathercock's waiting, bewrayeth me with
    speed.
As lief is to me, in such serving pretence,
Single negligence as double diligence."
The weathercock and the reed, being both
    blank,   [thank."
Each told himself: "much service have small

FINIS.

❧ Three hundred Epi=
grammes, vpon
three hundred
prouerbes,

Inuented and made by
John Heywood

LONDINI.

1562.

THE TABLE OF THIS BOOK.

FINIS.

EPIGRAMS UPON PROVERBS

1. "OF AMENDMENT."

If every man mend one, all shall be mended:
This mean to amendment is now intended.
For though no man look to mend himself,
    brother;   [other.
Yet each man looketh to control and mend

2. "WAGGING OF BEARDS."

It is merry in hall when beards wag all:
" Husband, for this, these words to mind I
    call :
This is meant by men, in their merry eating;
Not to wag their beards in brawling and
    threating."   [pins
" Wife, the meaning hereof differeth not two
Between wagging of men's beards and
    women's chins."

3. "OF HASTE."

The hasty man wanteth never woe:
In hasty women not ever so.
With suffering husbands hasty wives
Have oft, we see, full merry lives.

4. "BREAKING OF SQUARE."

An inch breaketh no square: which, since thou
    hast heard tell,
Thou dost assay how to break square by an ell.

" OTHERWISE."

An inch breaketh no square: thou breakest
    none, though it do;
Thou rather bringest square than breakest
    square between two.

5. " LOOKING AND LEAPING."

Look ere thou leap: nay, thou canst in no wise
    brook   [look.
To look ere thou leap, for thou leapest ere thou

6. " WEDDING AND HANGING."

" Wedding and hanging are destiny, I see;
Wedding or hanging, which is best, sir? "
    (quoth she).
" Forsooth ! good wife, hanging I think best,"
    (quoth he).   [me."
" So help me God, good husband ! so thinketh
Oh, how like lambs, man and wife here agree.

7. " OF DELAY."

He that will not when he may,
When he would he shall have nay:
But to that nay, nay I say :
If of my wife I delay
To take shrewd words, yet that stay
Stayeth them not from me next day.

8. " OF WITS."

So many heads, so many wits: nay, nay !
We see many heads and no wits, some day.

9. " NO LACK IN LOVE."

In love is no lack: true, I dare be borrow ;
In love is never lack of joy or sorrow.

" OTHERWISE."

In love is no lack: no, in no wooing day;
But after wedding day, let's hear what ye say.

10. " OF HOMELY HOME."

Home is homely: yea, and too homely sometime
Where wives' footstools to their husbands'
heads climb.

11. " GIVING AND TAKING."

Better give than take: all say, but so think
none.   [one.
All think better take twenty pounds than give

12. " JACK AND GILL."

All shall be well, *Jack shall have Gill:*
Nay, nay! Gill is wedded to Will.

13. " OF THE END OF A WIT."

Thou art *at thy wits' end:* which I wonder in
To see a wit at end before it begin.

14. " OF BOUGHT WIT."

Wit is never good till it be bought:
Thy wit is dear bought, and yet stark nought.

" OTHERWISE."

" *Wit is never good till it be bought,* Will."
" Jack, to buy or sell that ware fools can no
skill."

15. " OF HASTE AND WASTE."

Haste maketh waste: which, perceived by
sloth,   [truth !
Sloth will make no haste, he sweareth by his

16. "Making of Malt."

Soft fire maketh sweet malt: as malt-makers
tell.
Then, to make sweet malt fire is too rash in
hell;
Whereby, since in hell no good ale is to sell,
Dry drunken souls cannot like in hell to dwell.

17. "Of an Aching Eye."

Better eye out, than alway ache:
In rage of ache, true as I spake:
But in mean ache, meanly to moan,
Better an aching eye than none.

18. "What Thing Beggars Choose."

Beggars should be no choosers: but yet they
will;
Who can bring a beggar from choice to beg
still?

19. "Of Robbing."

Rob Peter and pay Paul: thou sayest I do;
But thou robbest and poulst Peter and Paul too.

20. "Of Need and Law."

Need hath no law: in some case, in very deed,
Need hath no law; and yet of law we have
need.

21. "Of Beginning and Ending."

Of a hard beginning cometh a good ending:
Truth, on this term, is not alway depending;
Some hardly begin by the feet to sit fast,
That end with hard hanging by the necks at
last.

22. "Of Grace."

In space cometh grace: I grant grace may
      come in space;
But in rule, by thy rule, never look for grace.

23. "Of Fore Provision."

Whoso that knew what would be dear,
Should need be merchant but one year:
But thou hast known years, two or three,
That good conditions would, in thee,
Both dear and daintily be grown;
And yet for all this, thus foreknown
To warn thee of great fore provision,
Thou hast not now one good condition.

24. "Of Saying and Doing."

Saying and doing, are two things, we say:
But thy sayings and doings every way
Join, jump in one; thy words and deeds pro-
      ceed,
But thou art good, nother in word nor deed.

25. "Of Treading on a Worm."

Tread a worm on the tail, and it turneth again:
But thou treadest on the worm's head that to
      restrain.

26. "Of Ease in an Inn."

Thou takest thine ease in thine Inn, so nigh
      thee
That no man in his Inn can take ease by thee.

"Otherwise."

Thou takest thine ease in thine Inn: but I see
Thine Inn taketh nother ease nor profit by
      thee.

27. "How to Prove a Friend."

Prove thy friend ere thou need: that canst thou
    no way;
For without need of thy friend thou art no day.

28. "Unwise Wedding."

*Who weddeth ere he be wise shall die ere he
    thrive:*
Then shalt not thou be wedded and rich alive.

29. "Something and Nothing."

Something is better than nothing:
In something I grant this othing;
In some I deny; for I see
As good have nothing as have thee.

30. "The Sleeping Dog."

It is ill waking of a sleeping dog:
So think many, namely, the wroting hog.

31. "Of Hap."

*It happeth in an hour that happeth not in
    seven year.*
"That happeth this hour, wife, for thou
    makest me good cheer."

32. "Of Sight and Mind."

Out of sight out of mind: this may run right;
For all be not in mind that be in sight.

33. "Of Mirth with Wisdom."

'Tis good to be merry and wise:
How shall fools follow that advice?

34. "OF HOLDING OF A NOSE."

Thou canst *hold my nose to the grindstone*:
So cannot I thine for thou hast none.

35. "AN EYE-SORE."

It is but *an eye-sore*: but an eye-sore, fie!
That eye-sore is as ill as any sore eye.

36. "OF RECKONING."

Reckoning without thine host thou must reckon
    twice:
May not my hosts disappoint that device?

37. "SETTING UP A CANDLE."

To set up a candle before the devil:
Dim-sighted devils, I deem, deem it not evil.

38. "OF CLOUDS AND WEATHER."

After clouds black, we shall have weather
    clear: [black;
And after weather clear we shall have clouds
Now hot, now cold, now fair, now foul appear;
As weather cleareth, or cloudeth, so must men
    take.

39. "OF MAKING AND MARRING."

Make or mar I will, so sayest thou ever;
But thou dost ever mar, thou makest never.

40. "OF BIRDS AND BIRDERS."

Better one bird in hand, than ten in the wood:
Better for birders, but for birds not so good.

41. "OF SORROWS."

Make not two sorrows of one, if thou can;
Lest making of two sorrows mar one man.

42. "OF FEEDING AND TEACHING."

Thou art better fed than taught, I undertake:
And yet art thou skin and bone, lean as a rake.

43. "OF SUFFERANCE."

Of sufferance cometh ease: " How shall I know
     that, wife? "
" I have suffered thee, without ease, all my
     life."

44. "OF HIM THAT SET HIS HAND ON HIS
MONEY."

" *Thy hand is on thy halfpenny:* and must
     John;   [on."
For thou hast no more coin to set thy hand

45. "OF A HORSE CURRYING."

A short horse is soon curried: that is, to wit,
When short horse and short curriers do meet.

46. "OF SHAME."

Shame take him that shame thinketh: for thou
     dost think none;   [on.
Thou art too far past shame, shame to think

47. "A LORD'S HEART AND A BEGGAR'S
PURSE."

*There is nothing in this world that agreeth
     worse*
Than doth a lord's heart and a beggar's purse:
And yet, as ill as those two do agree,
Thou canst not bring them asunder to be.

48. "OF FORGETTING."

*The parish priest forgetteth he was parish
     clerk:*
And the parson forgetteth he was parish priest;

But priest, clerk, and no clerk, all who will
    mark,
To forget what we were shall see us enticed.

49. "OF THE HEART AND THE HEEL."

Shall *I set at my heart that thou settest at*
    thy heel?   [weel.
Nay, a heart in a heel'd hose can never do

"OTHERWISE."

Shall *I set at my heart that thou settest at thy*
    heel?   [not weel.
Nay, however kibed heels do, kibed hearts do

50. "PRAISE OF A MAN ABOVE A HORSE."

A man may well lead a horse to the water
But he cannot make him drink, without he list.
I praise thee above the horse, in this matter;
For I, leading thee to drink, thou hast not
    missed
Alway to be ready, without resistance,
Both to drink, and be drunk, ere thou were
    led thence.

51. "OF WEEPING."

Better children weep than old men, say wise
    men :   [and then.
But old men weep when children laugh, now

52. "OF TWO FALSE KNAVES."

Two false knaves need no broker: but it is need
That brokers break false knaves' fellowship
    with speed.

53. "A HEART IN A HOSE."

Thy heart is in thy hose: which jail is not
    strong :
Thy hose are too full of holes to keep it long.

54. "Of Creeping and Going."

Children must learn to creep ere they can go:
In the spittle old knaves learn to do so.

55. "Of Floating and Fleeting."

Thou art afloat, thou weenest, being in the
fleet :
But floating and fleeting agree not there meet.

56. "A Man at an Ebb."

Thou art at an ebb in Newgate : thou hast
wrong ;
But thou shalt be afloat at Tyburn ere long.

57. "Sight in a Millstone."

Thou *seest far in a millstone :* thank God, therefore !
Thou seest in a millstone ; in nothing more.

58. "Of Throwing."

Throw no gift again at the giver's head :
Namely, no gift of thy wife given in check ;
If thou do, the rebound may be so red
That the red blood may run down in thy neck.

59. "Of Store."

Store is no sore : yes, store may be a sore ;
I think it a sore of sores to have store.

60. "Of One in Prison."

" Thou art *in by the week.*" " Nay, sir, I
am here,
Not in by the week, I am in by the year."

61. "Saints and Devils."

Young saint, old devil: there's mo of womankind   [find.
Than young devils, old saints in mankind, as I

62. "Of Botching."

God is no botcher: but, when God wrought you
two,
God wrought as like a botcher as God might
do.

63. "Of a Year's Fair."

The fair lasteth all the year: "but wife, I tell
thee,
In this year's fair, for fair, I cannot sell thee."
" I have worse luck," (quoth she), and began
to scowl :
" I cannot sell thee there for fair nor for foul."

64. "Of a Cap and a Head."

Thy cap is better at ease than thy head :
Between which twain, might I at wish be sped
To choose one of the twain, which I would first
crave—
Thy whole cap before thy sick head I would
have.

" Otherwise."

My cap is better at ease than my head :
Thy cap is better than thy head, 'tis said.

65. "A Thief that hath no Fellow."

Ask my fellow whether I be a thief :
No way, can that way of thy theft make preef ;
Thou hast no fellow in theft to catch thee ;
For there is no thief, (in theft), can match thee.

HEY. II.   N

66. " False Measures."

Thou fearest false measures : which are things
    to fear sore ;
But I fear false measures as much and more.

67. " Of Clean Sweeping."

New broom sweepeth clean, which is thus
    understand—
New broom sweepeth clean in the clean
    sweeper's hand.

68. " Turning of Tippets."

He hath turned his tippet—that turn showeth
    plain
Our tippets have been turned, and turned again.

" Otherwise."

He hath turned his tippet, dyed it, and dressed
    it   [it.
Upon the right side and fair, and plain pressed

" Otherwise."

He hath turned his tippet, and pressed it so
    close,
That for a turned tippet it hath a fair gloss.

" Otherwise."

He hath turned his tippet : Lord ! how he pro-
    vides   [both sides.
Tippets turned, dyed, shorn, and worn bare on

" Otherwise."

He hath turned his tippet twice in my sight :
First on the wrong side, and last on the right.

"OTHERWISE."

He hath turned his tippet: an honest turning
To turn his tippet, and turn round for burning.

"OTHERWISE."

He hath turned his tippet, shorn against the
   wool full,
And more against his will than against the
wool.

"OTHERWISE."

He hath turned his tippet: that have we turned
   all;   [as a ball.
Some half turn, some whole turn, turned round

"OTHERWISE."

He hath turned his tippet; yea, for a while:
But might he turn again, Lord! how he would
   smile.

"OTHERWISE."

He hath turned his tippet; yet mo turns ye
   mock:
But who doth wear his tippet a weathercock?

"OTHERWISE."

He hath turned his tippet: now for a novelty;
And, for a novelty, would turn straight again
   he.

"OTHERWISE."

He turneth his tippet, or *his tippet turneth*
   him,   [Saint Sim!
But which turneth which, I see not, by sweet

"OTHERWISE."
He hath turned his tippet,
For simony a sippet.

"OTHERWISE."
He turneth his tippet: if that turning turn him
Into the pulpit, that turning is turned trim.

69. "OF THEFT AND RECEIPT."
Where are *no receivers,* there are *no thieves:*
Where nought is to receive, thieves bring no
grieves.

70. "OF WORK AND PLAY."
*As good to play for nought, as to work for
    nought:*   [for ought.
But thou wilt play for nought, and not work

71. "OF A PAINTED SHEATH."
*Thou makest much of thy painted sheath: and
    wilt do,*
It having not one good knife longing thereto.

72. "THE HARE AND THE HOUND."
Hold with the hare and run with the hound:
    run there
As wight as the hound, and as wise as the hare.

73. "OF BEGGARS SINGING."
Beggars sing before thieves: but what of that?
When beggars sing so, thieves see nought to
    laugh at.

74. "OF TWO FACES."
Thou bearest *two faces in one hood:*
Thou hast one ill face, both be not good.

75. "OF BEGGING."

Thou beggest at wrong door, and so hast
  begged long :   [wrong.
Thy getting, by begging, showeth every door

76. "OF NOTHING."

Nothing hath no savour: which savourless
  show   [we know.
Showeth nothing better than something that

"OTHERWISE."

Nothing hath no savour: as ill is this othing—
Ill savoured something as unsavoured nothing.

77. "OF VENTURING."

Nought venture, nought have: and venturing
  of much
May have a little, venturing is now such.

78. "OF SHALL BE AND SHALL NOT BE."

That shall be, shall be: but all that should be
Shall not be, nor hath been, as far as I see.

79. "THE BLACK OX."

The black ox never trod on thy foot:
But the dun ass hath trod on both thy feet.
Which ass, and thou, may seem sprung of one
  root ;
For the ass's pace, and thy pace, are meet.

80. "OF BRIDLING."

" I will bridle thee with rough bit, wife."
  Quoth she :
" If thou wilt bridle me, I will snaffle thee."

81. "MENDING AND 'PAIRING."

I will mend this house, and 'pair another:
Yea, but when wilt thou mend thyself, brother?

82. "OF RUNNING WITHOUT TURNING."

He runneth far that never turneth again: nay,
    nay!   [far way.
Though the snail never turn he runneth no

83. "BUYING A PIG."

I will never *buy the pig in the poke:*
There's many a foul pig in a fair cloak.

84. "HUNGRY FLIES."

Hungry flies bite sore: which shall bite us
    ever;
For without hungry flies we shall be never.

85. "OF LOVING A DOG."

Love me, love my dog: by love to agree
I love thy dog as well as I love thee.

86. "OF PRECIOUS STONES."

"Folly to cast precious stones before hogs,
    Hugh,"
"Hodge, except they be precious hogs, thou
    sayest true."

"OTHERWISE."

Cast precious stones before hogs: cast stones
    to hogs? nay!
But precious stones have been given to hogs,
    some say.

87. "Of Ill and Good Wind."

It is an ill wind that bloweth no man to good:
And like good wind that bloweth no man ill.
But, fearing ill winds, old men most times
    stood
Out of all extreme winds under the hill.

88. "Of Sooth Boord."

Sooth boord is no boord: sooth boord soundeth
    ill
In false fair flattering boord, boord as ye will.

89. "Of Tales Told in the Ear."

In at the tone ear and out at the tother:
If tales told thee go in and out so, brother,
Then the travel of those tales show much
    wonder:
Thy two ears be two hundred mile asunder.

90. "Of Going."

The further we go the further behind:
Meet footmen to go with crabs, in my mind.

"Otherwise."

The further I go the further behind:
Stand still, fool! till thou better footing find.

91. "Of Need."

Need maketh th'old wife trot: is she a trotter
    now?   [you?
Gallop, young wives! shall th'old trot out-trot

92. "Taking Heart of Grass."

"*Thou takest heart of grass,* wife, not heart
    of grace."   [in one place."
"Come grass, come grace, sir, we graze both

93. "Of Nothing and All Thing."

Where nothing is, a little thing doth ease:
Where all thing is, nothing can fully please.

94. "Coveting and Leesing."

All covet, all lose: this cometh oft in ure.
But nought have, nought lose: this is ever
　　　sure.

95. "Of the March Hare."

As mad as a March hare: where madness com-
　　　pares, 　　　　　　　　　　　　　　　　[hares?
Are not Midsummer hares as mad as March

96. "How God will Not Do for Us."

Every man for himself, and God for us all:
God will not seal that writing, write it who
　　　shall?

97. "Of Harping on a String."

Harp no more on that string, for it standeth
　　　too high;
And soundeth as basely as a halter, well nigh.

98. "A Loss by the Devil's Death."

The devil is dead: then hast thou lost a friend;
In all thy doings the devil was at tone end.

"Otherwise."

The devil is dead: one devil is dead, but we see
Mo devils left alive, as ill or worse than he.

"Otherwise."

The devil is dead: who shall inherit his land?
Enough: the devil hath left children a thousand.

" OTHERWISE. "

The devil is dead: who shall his land rightly
   win?
Thou ! for thou, by condition, art next of kin.

" OTHERWISE. "

The devil is dead: nay, the devil is in a sown ;
But the devil reviveth again, chil lay my gown.

" OTHERWISE. "

The devil is dead: what helpeth the death of
   the devil?
The devil hath heirs as ill as he, and more evil.

99. " OF A SHEEP'S EYE. "

He cast a sheep's eye at her: a strange eye
   spread
To see a sheep's eye look out of a calf's head.

100. " OF RULE. "

Better rule than be ruled: wife ! thy endeavour
Hath showed thee to be ruled by that rule ever.

101. " OF BLIND BAYARD. "

Who so bold as blind Bayard? no beast, of
   truth ;   [showeth
Whereof my bold, blind Bayard, perfect proof
Both of his boldness, and for his bold blind-
   ness.
By late occasion, in a cause of kindness,
A company of us rode in certain ground ;
Where we wellnigh an impassable slough
   found.

Their horses, ere they entered, began to stay;
Every one horse giving another the way—
Of good manner, as it were—and more and
      more
Each horse gave back to set his better before,
Save this rude rusty, bold, blind Bayard of
      mine,   [fine,
As rashly, as rudely, chopped forth; and in
Without any curtsey, ere any man bids,
Blindly and boldly, he leapt into the mids.
And look how boldly, the mids he leapt in till;
Even, with like boldness, in the mids he lay
      still;   [there,
And trow you the jade, at the best men's words
Would stir one joint? nay, not the breadth of
      one hair.   [ance
But stared on them, with as bold a counten-
As that whole had been his by inheritance;
He having no more to do there than had I.
But straight there cometh a cartwear of good
      horse by;
By force whereof, and help of all that rout,
Blind Bayard and I were drawn together out.
Which blind boldness, by this admonition,
Except he amend in some meet condition,
Rather than ride so, I will afoot take pain
Blind bold Bayard shall not thus bear me again.

102. "OF THE SPINSTER'S THRIFT."

Thus rideth the rock: if the rock be riding,
The spinster's thrift is set a-foot sliding.

103. "OF DEAFNESS."

Who is so deaf as he that will not hear?
Not the devil till will draw his hearing near.

104. "OF A GOOD HORSE."

It is a good horse that never stumbleth:
Then have I a good horse, for my horse
    tumbleth,   [never.
And falleth down right; my horse stumbleth
So well am I horsed, and have been horsed
    ever,
And so loth to lend him, to field or town's end,
That, as soon shall my foe ride him as my
    friend.

105. "OF WAYS TO THE WOOD."

There be mo ways to the wood than one:
Of all good ways to wood, thou goest none.

106. "OF ONE THAT MAY SOON AMEND."

He may soon amend, for he cannot appair:
A good evidence to prove him the devil's heir.

107. "AN ILL HEARER."

I cannot hear on that side: no, truth to tell,
Of any side thou couldst never yet hear well.

108. "OF A GOOD FACE."

" I did set a good face on the matter, Joan."
" Thou didst borrow it then, Bess, for thou
    hast none."

109. "A SHARP THORN."

It pricketh betimes that shall be a sharp thorn:
" I ween thou prickest, wife! ere time thou
    were born."

110. "COMING AND GOING."

As fast as one goeth another cometh in ure:
Two buckets in a well come and go so, sure;
But go or come who shall, while all come and
go,
Seldom cometh the better : practise preveth so.

111. "THE BETTER COMETH SELDOM."

Seldom cometh the better, come or go who
will :
One nail driveth out another, we see still.

112. "ONE DRIVETH OUT ANOTHER."

One nail driveth out another : with strokes so
stout
That the hammer-head which driveth them
weareth quite out.

113. "OF BURDEN."

Light burden, far heavy : that dost thou try ;
A feather borne far will tire thee well nigh.

"OTHERWISE."

Light burden, far heavy, borne for other men ;
For ourselves, heavy burdens light enough
then.

"OTHERWISE."

Light burden, far heavy : thy brain lacketh
strength
To bear a pint of wine a pair of butts' length.

"OTHERWISE."

Light burden, far heavy : thou dost find that
lack
In all light good burdens that lie on thy back.

" OTHERWISE."

Light burden, far heavy: how can lame folk prove,   [remove?
Who in all their lives, their lengths do not

114. " RUNNING AND GOING."

He may ill run that cannot go:
He that sitteth by the feet find so.

115. " A LACK OF TOOLS."

What is a workman without his tools?
How may baubles be missed among fools?

116. " TASTE OF A MAN'S TALES."

A tale of a tub, *thy tales taste all of ale:*
Not of pescod ale, sir; my tales are not stale.

117. " OF A CAT'S LOOK."

A cat may look on a king: and what of that?
When a cat so looketh, a cat is but a cat.

118. " ONE PUT OUT OF A CREED."

Thou mayest *be in my pater noster,* indeed;
But surely thou shalt never come in my creed.
I care not, though I do not; what can I win
To come in a creed, which creed God is not in?

119. " ALL THAT MAY BE WON OF THE FOX."

We can have no more of the fox but the skin:
And the fox thinketh that too much for us to win.

120. " THE SURETY OF SOME SEAL."

As sure as it were sealed with butter: forsooth !
Some butter seal lasteth as long as some wax doth.

121. "The Hares Going Away."

There goeth the hare away: is she gone, say
you? [enou'.
Let her go! we have hares and hare-heads

122. "Judgment of Colours."

Blind men should judge no colours: should they
nat?
Blind men will judge all colours, for all that.

123. "Hap and Wit."

Better be happy than wise: here art thou hit;
Thy hap hath ever been better than thy wit.

"Otherwise."

Better be happy than wise: not so, some say;
He that can be wise shall be happy, say they.

124. "Of Fortune to Fools."

God sendeth fortune to fools: not to everyone;
Thou art a fool, and, yet, fortune thou hast
none.

"Otherwise."

God sendeth fortune to fools: and to wise men
still [ill.
God sendeth good fortune, or the devil sendeth

125. "Of Loosers' Words."

Let the loosers have their words, all at once:
Shall the loosers talk? there will be chat for the
nonce.

126. "Getting and Spending."

Ill gotten, ill spent: be that tale true to tell,
Thou art never like to spend penny well.

127. "Matters Not Laid a-Water."

My matter is laid a-water: that's a false tale;
Thy matters lie, not in water, they lie in ale.

128 "Measure."

Measure is a merry mean
Which, filled with noppy drink,
When merry drinkers drink off clean
Then merrily they wink.

"Otherwise."

Measure is a merry mean,
But I mean measures great;
Where lips to little pitchers lean,
Those lips they scantly wet.

"Otherwise."

Measure is a merry mean:
But inch, foot, yard, or ell,
Those measures are not worth a bean;
They measure no drink well.

"Otherwise."

Measure is a merry mean:
Be drink dear or good cheap,
From measure no wight may thee wean;
Thou measurest drink by heap.

"Otherwise."

Measure is a merry mean:
Good liquor may not shrink;
Thou takest no triacle of Gean
So wholesome as good drink.

" OTHERWISE."

Measure is a merry mean
Showing indifference;
Would th'ale-wife play the polling quean?
Yet measure will not lie.

" OTHERWISE."

Measure is a merry mean
That doth diligently;
Attend the taps of stand and stean
To moist thy lips full dry.

" OTHERWISE."

Measure is a merry mean:
And measure is thy mate
To be a deacon, or a dean:
Thou wouldst not change the state.

" OTHERWISE."

Measure is a merry mean:
Who that shall enterprise
This measure from thee, for to glean,
Right early must he rise.

" OTHERWISE."

Measure is a merry mean:
In volumes full or flat;
There is no chapter, nor no scene
That thou appliest like that.

129. " GOING BEYOND THE WALL."

Furder than the wall we cannot go:
Thine visage showeth otherwise, then so;
Thou goest, when thou must start out of sight,
To the wall, and over the wall quite.

130. "Of Harm."

A man far from his good is nigh his harm:
Nigh thy good, next thy harm, as chance may
  charm.

"Otherwise."

A man far from his good is nigh his harm:
For thee to fear that it were worse than wood-
  ness;
Movables, unmovables, land or farm,
Thou hast not one groat's worth of good or
  goodness.

"Otherwise."

A man far from his good is nigh his harm:
This showeth thee nigh harm; for, hadst thou
  an arm   [stantine,
That could and would reach hence to Con-
That arm could not reach to any good of thine.

131. "Wit Kept by Warmth."

Thou art wise enough if thou keep thee warm:
But the least cold that cometh killeth thy wit
  by harm.

132. "Light Coming and Going."

Light come, light go, that cometh in ure by
  light feet;   [street.
But light heads make light feet lie lame in the

"Otherwise."

Light come, light go: for that thou art well
  wrought;
For thou art as light as a thing of nought.

HEY. II.   O

" OTHERWISE."

Light come, light go: pass, come and go
     lightly;
In a juggler that lightness is sightly.

" OTHERWISE."

Light come, light go: thy light going doth
     excel;
But thy light coming I like not half so well.

233. " OF KISSING."

Unknown, unkissed: and being known, I ween
Thou art never kissed where thou mayest be
     seen.

" OTHERWISE."

" *Unknown, unkissed:* from that desire, wife,
     bless thee;   [thee."
For no man that seeth thee desireth to kiss
" From kissing in sight, husband, such as
     flee me,   [me."
Let them come kiss me where they do not see

134. " OF LEAVE."

Leave is light: light enough as thou wilt make
     it;
If thy master give no leave thou wilt take it.

" OTHERWISE."

Leave is light: yea, and leave is axed lightly;
And may be granted lightly, axed rightly.

135. " GOD IN THE ALMONRY."

There is God in th'almery: a well-played part;
Shut God in thine almonry out of thy heart.

136. " THE DEVIL IN TH'OROLOGE."

The devil is in th'orologe, the hours to try;
Search hours by the sun; the devil's dial will
lie.

" OTHERWISE."

The devil is in th'orologe: now cheer in
bowls;
Let the devil keep our clocks while God keep
our souls.

137. " THE BEST."

The best is behind: the worst is before;
Between both, beware drift to the worst shore.

" OTHERWISE."

The best is behind: we go before too fast;
Bide for the best, else it will be lost at last.

" OTHERWISE."

The best is behind: start thou back and fet it,
Abide, abide! a wiser man must get it.

" OTHERWISE."

The best is behind: even so I thought it would;
The best lacketh feet, foot pace with us to hold.

" OTHERWISE."

The best is behind: behind, nor yet before,
Would I have the best but with us evermore.

138. " THE WORST."

The worst is behind:
There art thou assigned.

" OTHERWISE."

The worst is behind : but the way is not rough ;
The worst will get before again, time enough.

" OTHERWISE."

The worst is behind : yet behind worse evil
We see our fare ; at next course cometh the
    devil.

" OTHERWISE."

The worst is behind : God keep it behind us ;
Or us before it, as it never find us.

139. " LASTING OF WONDER."

A wonder lasteth but nine days :
Yes, thou didst nine years gone
But one good deed, for which some says,
Thou art yet wondered on.

140. " OF A GALLED HORSE."

*Rub a galled horse on the back and he will
    kick :*   [prick.
But the galled ass will stand still, rub, spur, or

141. " GOOD BEGINNING AND END."

Of a good beginning there cometh a good end :
Nay, Lucifer began well, and now a fiend ;
But of good beginning and ending, truth to
    tell,
The best way to end well is to begin well.

142. " THE STILL SOW."

The still sow eateth all the draff : my sow eateth
    none ;   [gone.
The devil stealeth not my sow till her grain be

143. " Of Stumbling."

Stumble at a straw and leap over a block:
Such stumblers are blockheads, or else they
    do mock.

" Otherwise."

Stumble at a straw and leap over a block:
The ass and the ape seem here joined in one
    stock.

144. " Of the Shoe and the Sole."

The shoe will hold with the sole: no man
    knoweth it
But he that knoweth how the shoemaker
    seweth it.

" Otherwise."

The shoe will hold with the sole: what should
    the shoe do
But hold with the sole? the sole will hold with
    the shoe.

145. " Might and Right."

Might overcometh right: God keep us from
    that might;   [right.
God give us that might that striveth not with

146. " Birth and Teaching."

Better unborn than untaught: but, of truth,
    thou   [now.
Were as well taught afore thou were born as

147. " Of Hanging."

I have hanged up my hatchet: and 'scaped thy-
    self?
Thou shouldest rather be hanged than thy
    hatchet, else !

148. "An Old Knave."

An old knave is no babe: no, but we know
Of an old knave's babe an old knave may
grow.

149. "A Man's Ear and his Hood."

Thy ear groweth through thy hood: is thy hood
torn?
Or doth thy ear pierce through thy hood, like
a horn.

150. "Gains and Losses."

Light gains make heavy purses:
Light losses make heavy curses.

"Otherwise."

Light gains make heavy purses: and light
purses
Make heavy hearts, and heavy-hearted curses.

"Otherwise."

Light gains make heavy purses: so brag merchants bare
When they take three halfpence for twopenny-
worth ware.

151. "Thieves Falling Out."

*When thieves fall out true men come to their
good:*
Come betimes, or else it is gone, by rood!

152. "Of a Shorn Face."

Thy face is shorn against the wool, very deep:
Have I wool in my face? yea, thou art a sheep.

153. "A Bench Whistler."

" Thou art a *bench whistler:* a shrill, whistling
wench;   [Bench? "
But how long hast thou whistled in the King's
" I have whistled in the King's Bench,
(Geoffrey),   [sea."
As long as thou hast marched in the Marshal-

154. "What God Said to One."

Thou art *one of them to whom God bade Ho!*
God took thee for a cart-horse, when God bade
so.

"Otherwise."

Thou art *one of them to whom God bade Ho!*
I ween thou went'st too far when God bade so.

155. "Bowing and Breaking."

Better bow than break when straining shall
stretch;
Nay, as good break as bow beyond our reach.

"Otherwise."

Better bow than break: I praise this that ye
spake;   [break.
But some bend, or be bent and bowed, till they

"Otherwise."

Better bow than break: it is truly spoken:
Bowed wands serve for somewhat, so do not
broken.

156. "Of Wrestling."

The weaker hath the worse in wrestling alway:
Best for the weak to leave wrestling then, I
say.

157. "God and the Church."

The nearer to the church, the farther from God:
Both one to thee, a ream thence, or a rod.

158. "Of One Tale in All Men Told."

It must needs be true that every man saith:
Till all men say one thing, the judgment
    stayeth.

"Otherwise."

It must needs be true that every man saith:
Must it so? then art thou a fool, in faith!

159. "Of Malkin."

There be mo maids than Malkin: "thou sayest
    truth, Joan;
But how may we be sure that Malkin one?"

160. "Rash Venturing."

I will *set all* even *at six and at seven:*
Yea, and repent all between ten and eleven.

161. "A Scabbed Horse."

*A scabbed horse is good enough for a scalded
    squire:*   [hire.
Your mastership need not care what horse ye

162. "Of Sitting."

*Between two stools my tail goeth to the
    ground:*
Better stand than sit till sure seat be found.

163. "Ale and Wit."

When ale is in wit is out:
When ale is out wit is in;

The first thou showest, out of doubt,
The last in thee hath not been.

164. "OF RESTITUTION."

Steal a goose and stick down a feather:
In a feather, and such conscience,
If I should stick them down together
I can devise no great difference.

165. "EATING OF FLIES."

" *The blind eateth many a fly:* not thou, wife !
For, though blindness have banished thine eyes'
    defence,
Yet when flies in flying to thy mouth be rife,
Thy tongue is a fly-flap, to flap flies from
    thence."

166. "OF THE FOX'S PREACHING."

When the fox preacheth then beware our géese:
You that fear your geese learn wit here a-piece;
Keep foxes from pulpits your geese to teach,
Or keep geese from sermons when foxes do
    preach.

167. "OF POOR MEN'S SOULS."

Poor men have no souls: no, but poor men had
    souls   [ale-bowls.
Till the drunken souls drowned their souls in

"OTHERWISE."

Poor men have no souls: yes, but we see
Poor men's souls as poor as their purses be.

"Otherwise."

Poor men have no souls: no, have rich men
   any?
I fear but few; for they have lost souls many.

"Otherwise."

Poor men have no souls: No, no! the devil
   made them;
The sots could not keep their souls while they
   had them.

168. "Promise of Licence."

I will say no more till the day be longer:
No, no! say no more till thy wit be stronger.

169. "Of Little Saying."

Little said, soon amended:
Little good, soon spended;
Little charge, soon attended;
Little wit, soon ended.

170. "Of the Tide."

The tide tarrieth no man: but here to scan—
Thou art tied so that thou tarriest every man.

171. "Praise of Good End."

" *All is well that endeth well:* a good saying,
   (wife);
But I would see it proved by th'end of thy life."

172. "Of Hearing and Judging."

Hear all parts ere ye judge any:
God send such hearers many!

173. "A Lesson for Looking."

Some man may better steal a horse
Than some may stand and look upon:
Where such suspicion standeth in force,
Flee sight of stolen horse—look on none!

174. "Of a Woman's Lives."

"Wife, *a woman hath nine lives like a cat.*"
"Sir, you have but one life, and yet enough of
   that."

175. "The Crow Called White."

I will *say the crow is white:* art thou so light?
What is thy credence when the crow cometh in
   sight?

"Otherwise."

Ye must *say the crow is white:* in any case
Not now; but we were made say so a long
   space.

"Otherwise."

I will *say the crow is white:* wilt thou so
When every man seeth her black? go, fool,
   go!

176. "Of the Old Fool."

There is no fool to the old fool:
Go, young fools, to th'old fools to school!

"Otherwise."

There is no fool to th'old fool: speak not that
   loud;   [proud;
That praise will make old fools vengeably

Which praise of old fools, young fools perceiv-
    ing plain :   [dain.
Young fools and old fools each will other dis-

177. " OF A BEAN."

A bean in a monk's hood : very good !
Here is the bean, but where is the hood?

178. " THE GIFT OF A PIG."

" Sir, *ye give me a pig of mine own sow.*"
" Wife, I give a sow pig to a sow now."

179. " CHANGE AND ROBBERY."

Change is no robbery : that is a tale not
    strange ;   [change.
Change is no robbery, but robbery maketh
Many sweet blessings change to bitter curses
When true men's money changeth into thieves'
    purses.

180. " OF FAIR WORDS."

Fair words make fools fain : that was by old
    schools ;   [fools.
But now we see fair words make wise men

" OTHERWISE."

Fair words make fools fain : yet fair words
    are cheerful ;
But foul words make all folk ireful or fearful.

181. " OF LAUGHING."

I *laughed in my sleeve,* faint laughings there
    to win ;
Sleeves be too narrow to laugh lustily in.

182. "OF SEEKING."

"I seek for a thing, wife, that I would not
    find."   [mind."*
"Good husband! ye are the more fool, in my

"OTHERWISE."

Thou seekest for a thing that thou wouldst not
    find:
And I find all things that I do not seek;
In my hap, and thy wit, what difference as-
    signed?
I ween not the value of a good green leek.

183. "OF A HEAD UNDER A GIRDLE."

He hath thy head under his girdle: take heed
He hang not thy head in his girdle, indeed.

184. "OF WIDE SHOOTING."

He shooteth wide: the cause why I see, even
    sith   [with.
He hath not one straight shaft to shoot straight

"OTHERWISE."

He shooteth wide:
On which side?

"OTHERWISE."

He shooteth wide: but he cannot amend that;
For he seeth not the mark that he shooteth at.

185. "THE FOOL'S BOLT."

A fool's bolt is soon shot, and fleeth ofttimes
    far;
But the fool's bolt and the mark come few
    times near.

186. " Of a Merchant."

He is a merchant without money or ware :
Bid that merchant be covered ; he is bare.

" Otherwise."

He is a merchant without money or ware :
He hath, in some respect, the less cause of
care.

187. " Of Tongue."

*" Tongue breaketh bone, and bone it hath
none :*
I wish, (wife), thy tongue may have a bone."
" And I wish," (quoth she), " a bone in your
hood."   [good."
" Wish that bone away," (said he), " 'tis not
" Then wish you the tother," (quoth she),
" away."   [may
They did so ; which done, now said she : " We
Witness both that you have your wish in fine,
But both cannot witness that I have mine."

" Otherwise."

Tongue breaketh bone itself having none :
Such tongues should have bones, or bodkins
the tone.

" Otherwise."

*Tongue breaketh bone and bone itself hath
none :*   [(Joan)."
" Yes, thy tongue is full of good ale-bones,

188. " Of Speech."

Spare to speak, spare to speed : If speech bring
speed,

Then wilt thou speed, for thou speakest more
than need.

189. "A Busy-body."

He will have an oar in every man's barge:
Even in Cock Lorel's barge he beareth that
charge.

"Otherwise."

He will have an oar in every man's barge:
Then with some of those oars he roweth at
large.

190. "Of Time."

Time is tickle: we may match time in this;
For we be even as tickle as time is.

"Otherwise."

Time is tickle:
Chance is fickle;
Man is brickle;
Frailties pickle
Powdereth mickle,
Seasoning lickle.

191. "Of Far Casting."

He casteth beyond the moon: great diversity
Between far casting and wise casting, maybe.

"Otherwise."

He casteth beyond the moon: what need that
be done?
We have casting enough a this side the moon.

192. "Of Hunger."

Hunger droppeth out of his nose:
That is the worst kind of the pose.

193. "Of Feeding."

He hath fed till he is as full as a tun:
I mean an empty tun—what food hath he
    won?

194. "Of Mortimer's Sow."

Backare, quoth Mortimer to his sow:
Went that sow back at that bidding, trow you?

"Otherwise."

Backare, quoth Mortimer to his sow: see
Mortimer's sow speaketh as good Latin as he.

"Otherwise."

Backare, quoth Mortimer to his sow:
"The boar shall back first," (quoth she), "I
    make a vow!

195. "Of Flea-biting."

'Tis but a flea-biting: friend, if fleas bite so,
They will bite men to the bare bones where
    they go.

196. "The Breechless Master."

The master weareth no breech: then I protest!
The master is a girl, a boy, or a beast.

197. "Of Meat and Sauce."

Sweet meat will have sour sauce: to this reason
    feat
Join this conversion: sour sauce will have
    sweet meat.
Thus, sourness and sweetness, the one and
    th'other,
In fear of the tone, we hope of the tother.

" OTHERWISE. "

Sweet meat will have sour sauce: where that
    is seen,   [ween.
As good lack that meat as have that sauce, I

198. " OF PROFFERED SERVICE. "

Proffered service stinketh: thou art deceived
    else;
Thy proffered service stinketh not; thou
    stinkest thyself.

" OTHERWISE. "

Proffered service stinketh: more fool thou to
    proffer it!
Thou shouldest season thy service ere thou
    offer it.

199. " OF COMMON MEDDLERS. "

He that meddleth with all thing may shoe the
    gosling:
If all such meddlers were set to goose-shoeing,
No goose need go barefoot between this and
    Greece;
For so: we should have as many goose-shoeers
    as geese.

200. " OF ENOUGH AND A FEAST. "

As good enough as a feast: yea God save it!
Enough were even as good if we might have it.

" OTHERWISE. "

As good enough as a feast:
This for a truth say most and least.
But what enough is justly meant,
And with enough to be content,

HEY. II.   P

Those are two points that few or none
Can learn to know, and stand upon.

201. "OF PLAIN FASHION."

The plain fashion is best: what! plain without
    pleats?   [bleats.
That fashion commendeth the calf when it

"OTHERWISE."

The plain fashion is best: and accepted best
In things that please ears, but not in the rest.

"OTHERWISE."

The plain fashion is best: that's truly expressed
Where fashioners of plain fashions are honest.

202. "OF HIM THAT COMETH LAST."

He that cometh last make all fast: to this, say
    some,
All is made fast ere the last comer come.

"OTHERWISE."

He that cometh last make all fast:
Who shall make him fast that cometh last?

203. "OF STRIVING."

He striveth against the stream: by custom's
    school
That striver is either a fish or a fool.

204. "OF SITTING."

Better sit still than rise and fall:
If all fall ye may hang when ye shall.

205. "OF WRITING TO FRIENDS."

*Ye may write to your friends that ye are in
    health:*   [wealth?
Who may write to his friends that he is in

206. "Of Great Clerks."

The greatest clerks be not the wisest men:
Be small learned, or unlearned fools, wisest
   then?

207. "Of Killing."

He will kill a man for a mess of mustard:
He will kill ten men then for a custard.

208. "Of Falsehood."

There is falsehood in fellowship: there is so;
The fellowship is small else as the world doth
   go.

"Otherwise."

There is falsehood in fellowship: no wonder;
Falsehood and fellowship are seldom asunder.

209. "Of Bleeding."

Here lieth all and bleedeth: all? that's false
   and foolish;   [fish.
Thou never sawest blood bleed out of a stock-

210. "Of Seeing."

Seest me and seest me not: both one thing,
   forsooth!   [doeth.
As good unseen as seen whose sight no good

211. "Of Ills."

Of two ills choose the least: of ills many
The least is too great to choose any.

"Otherwise."

Of two ills choose the least: may we choose ills
   now?   [yow.
Choose on, choosers! the like choice never had

P 2

212. "Of Pepper."

Thou takest pepper in the nose: and yet thy nose   [rose.
Looketh not black like pepper, but red like the

"Otherwise."

Thou takest pepper in the nose; which needeth not—
Thy nose without pepper is fiery red-hot.

"Otherwise."

Thou takest pepper in the nose, which so seasoned,
Showeth thy nose better seasoned than thy head reasoned.

213. "Of an Ill Stake."

An ill stake that cannot stand one year in a hedge:
If the stake self fail, the stake is as ye allege;
But, if stake stobbers will not let stakes stand,
Blame not the stake; blame the stake stobber's hand.

214. "Of Sufferance."

Sufferance is no quittance: but, suffering too long   [wrong.
Showeth much like a quittance in suffering of

215. "Of Misreckoning."

Misreckoning is no payment: yes! as doth fall
In some reckoners, misreckoning is payment all.

"Otherwise."

Misreckoning is no payment: to avoid that,
Some debtors with their creditors reckon nat.

216. " OF EVEN RECKONING."

Even reckoning maketh long friends:
Odd reckoning maketh many friends.

217. " OF TAKING."

I will take as falleth in the sheaf: wherever it
    fall   [all.
In the sheaf, or out of the sheaf, thou takest

218. " OF MUM."

Mum is counsel in every man we see;
But mum except, nothing is counsel in thee.

219. " OF STOPPING A MOUTH."

" He shall not stop my mouth." " No, Nan, I
    think that;
I believe all the devils in hell stoppeth it nat."

220. " OF CASTING."

He is cast in his own turn: that is likely;
And yet in all turns he turneth wondrous
    quickly.

221. " OF JACK."

He is Jack out of office: curtsey, withdraw!
Jack once out of office, all hail Jack daw!

222. " OF THE WINKING CAT."

Let the cat wink and let the mouse run: run,
    mice!
Or else the cat's claws will catch you at a trice.

" OTHERWISE."

Let the cat wink and let the mouse run: run,
    rats!   [cats.
Small holes keep small mice from wily winking

"Otherwise."

Let the cat wink and let the mouse run: creep,
    mouse, creep!   [sleep.
Run not before cats that wink more than they

223. "Of Saying Nay."

Say nay, and take it: yea, say nay and take it;
But say nay or say ye never forsake it.

"Otherwise."

Say nay and take it: hear me say this othing:
Say nother yea nor nay; tak't and say nothing.

224. "Of the Pie and Crow."

Not too high for the pie nor to low for the
    crow:
High pies made low crows; we have enough,
    I trow.

225. "Of Saying Nought but Mum."

I will *say nought but mum:*
Thou showest the more wit some.

"Otherwise."

I will *say nought but mum:* that I beseech;
Mum hath a grace in thee far more than
    speech.

226. "Of Tongue and Wit."

Thy tongue runneth before thy wit: that's no
    rash race;
For, so may it run running but a snail pace.

227. "Of Own."

Own is own
Where's own known.

" OTHERWISE."

Own is own: these words I speak with eyes
  weeping,
For all mine own is in other men's keeping.
But good is that riches where it is heapt
That from th'owner by no means can be kept.

228. " OF SPINNING."

She hath spun a fair thread: which showeth,
  indeed,
That a foul spinner may spin a fair thread.

229. " OF LAUGHING."

They laugh that win: falsely to win and keep,
Winners may laugh when they have cause to
  weep.

" OTHERWISE."

They laugh that win: by theft to win and keep,
Thieves at stealing laugh, thieves at hanging
  weep.

230. " OF PLAYING."

He playeth best that wins: that deny I will;
Many players win much that play very ill.

" OTHERWISE."

He playeth best that wins: there is a lie running;   [ning.
Many win much, much more by hap, than cun-

231. " OF THE WIND BLOWING."

Let this wind overblow: when over blow,
This wind will over blow us first, I trow.

232. "OF FAR AND NIGH."

I have seen as far come as nigh: come no near;
The ferder thou art hence, the better is it here.

233. "OF TH'INSTEP."

He is high in th'instep: his steps may be high,
But to step in good steps he steppeth nothing
  nigh.

234. "OF SMALL AND GREAT."

Many small make a great: and some great
  made small;
Thou hadst great good manners and thou hast
  none at all.

235. "OF THE KEYS."

The keys hang not all by one man's girdle:
  no!   [so?
Every key hath a clog: who would be clogged

236. "OF PROVENDER."

His provender pricketh him: prick him? gods
  forbod!
What is his provender? pins, by likelihood!

"OTHERWISE."

His provender pricketh him: where grew that
  corn?
Pricking provender as ill as boats borne.

"OTHERWISE."

His provender pricketh him: that horse must
  need stir;   [spur.
Pricked within with provender, without with

237. "OF SOME HERE AND THERE."

Here some and there some: yea, here and there
  some;   [come.
But most when, and most where no some doth

238. "OF THE PARSON'S LEMAN."

She is as tender as a parson's leman:
Parson's lemans are tough enough now and
 than.

239. "OF ILL WEED."

Ill weed groweth fast: it groweth fast indeed;
The corn can scantily grow for the weed.

"OTHERWISE."

Ill weed groweth fast: that is showing
In the show of thy fast growing.

240. "OF SINKING."

He shall sink in his own sin: yea, when he
 sinketh;
But he fleeth in his own sin yet, methinketh.

241. "OF GOOD SILVER."

She thinketh her farthing good silver: but, trust
 me!
She is quicksilver what ever her farthing be.

242. "OF THE PROUD COCK."

Every cock is proud on his own dunghill:
The hen is proud enough there, mark who will.

243. "OF FAT IN THE FIRE."

The fat is in the fire: that is a shrewd turn;
Cast the lean after; fat and lean, let all burn!

244. " Of Bow Bent."

I have the bent of his bow: that I know;
What bolts shootest thou from that bow? fools'
    bolts, I trow !

245. " Of God's Being."

God is where he was: yea, but so art not thou;
Thou were abroad late, and art in Newgate
    now.

246. " Of Kinsfolk."

Many kinsfolk, few friends:
Few friends and many fiends.

247. " Of Friendship."

A friend is never known till a man have need:
Nor then, nother, for any I know, indeed.

248. " Of Nothing."

*Where nothing is, the king must lose his
    right:*
Where all thing is, there right is lost by might.

249. " Of Poverty."

Poverty parteth fellowship: that's not true
    ever;
Poverty in beggars parteth fellowship never.

250. " Of Ears Glowing."

Thine ears may glow: "let's see whether they
    glow, John.   [none."
I lie: thine ears cannot glow, for thou hást

251. " Of Post and Pillar."

Tossed from post to pillar: thou art a pillar
    strong;   [long.
And thou hast been a pillar, some say, too

252. " Of May Be."

Be as be may is no banning:
But be as be shall hath much scanning.

253. " Of Use."

Use maketh mastery: this is a true tale to tell;
In that use hath made thee prick a purse so
    well.

254. " Of Spurning."

Folly to spurn or kick against the hard wall:
Being shod with cakebread that spurner
    marreth all.

" Otherwise."

Folly to spurn or kick against the hard wall:
But against soft walls spurners spurn and kick
    all.

255. " Of Tying the Bell."

Who shall tie the bell about the cat's neck
    now?   [I know."
" Not I," (quoth the mouse), " for a thing that

256. " Of Had I Wist."

" *Beware of Had I wist, wife.*" " Oh man !
    'tis too late   [mate."
To beware thereof since thou were my wedded

257. " Of Dancing."

He danceth attendance: are attendants danc-
    ing?   [ing.
Then have we much dancing with small avanc-

258. "OF THE CAT EATING FISH."

The cat would eat fish but she will not wet her
*   feet:*
She thinketh flesh with dry feet more sweet
    than fish with weet.

259. "OF THE BLIND."

The blind eat many a fly: that we find
Chiefly where carvers to the blind are blind.

260. "OF THE WORST AND BEST."

Provide for the worst: the best will save itself;
For that saving side thou art a subtle elf.
Of all kinds of things thou hast provision
    pressed,   [best.
For thy neighbours the worst, for thyself the

261. "OF FIVE EGGS."

He cometh in with his five eggs: what eggs to
    call?   [daws' eggs all.
Hen eggs, goose eggs, or duck eggs? nay,

262. "OF CLIMBING."

He that never climbed never fell: some men
    climb   [time.
For doves' nests and find daws' nests, some-

263. "OF THE WAY."

It is out of my way: so it lightly may;
To all good things thy way is out of the way.

264. "OF WAITING."

He waiteth for moonshine in the water:
Such waiting, such winning; that's a meet
    matter.

265. "Of Rhyme."

It may rhyme but it accordeth not: "'cordeth
    not, Will?
Beware of 'cording rhymes; those rhymes
    agree ill."

266. "Of Fishing."

It is ill fishing before the net:
Worse fishing behind, as nets are set.

267. "Of Good."

He knoweth none end of his good: mark his
    winning;   [ning.
He knoweth of his good none end, nor begin-

268. "Of the Hot Iron."

When the iron is hot, strike: strike hot iron and
    steel;
But gold or silver to strike we have no deal.

269. "Of the Purse."

Thy purse is threadbare, we see, on the out-
    side;
And more bare on the inside when both sides
    are tried.

270. "Of Many Hands."

Many hands make light work: many hands?
    yea, mark!
Ye must say thus: many light hands make
    light wark.

"Otherwise."

Many hands make light work: no work is
    'signed thee;

Thou canst not work; thy hands be bound
   behind thee.

271. "OF THE LOATH STAKE."

The loath stake standeth long: we have many
   loath stakes;   [makes.
Each stake well-nigh to other itself, loath

"OTHERWISE."

The loath stake standeth long; in some place,
   but some hand
Plucketh up all stakes, suffering no stake
   long to stand.

272. "OF HAVING."

Better to have than wish: nay, ye may so
   crave   [have.
That better to wish ten times than once to

"OTHERWISE."

Better to have than wish: not alway, cousin!
What if ye rashly wished stripes now, a dozen?

"OTHERWISE."

Better to have than wish: better have as we
   have   [crave.
Than to have at wish all that wishers would

273. "OF COUNSEL."

Three may keep counsel if twain be away:
But one fool doth oft his own counsel bewray.

"OTHERWISE."

Three may keep counsel if twain be away:
Some women, I hear say, that saying denay.

274. "Of· Rome."

Rome was not built on one day: that is well
    known;
Nor in one day Rome will not be overthrown.
For where Rome seemed pulled down in one
    day, brother,
There is Rome set up again in another.

275. "Of Speech."

Spare to speak, spare to speed:
Dumb men win nought indeed;
And speech, as speech may fall,
May win nought and lese all.

276. "Of One Had in the Wind."

I have him in the wind: well, sir, it is your
    mind   [wind.
To have him in the wind, or hang him in the

277. "Of One Ill Shod."

*Who is worse shod than is the shoemaker's
    wife?*
The devil's wife; she was never shod in her life.

278. "Of All and Nought."

He would all have and nought forego: no!
He may all forego and nought have, so!

279. "Of Warning."

I gave him *Scarborough warning:* Scar-
    borough?   [borough.
That warning came short to bring good har-

280. "Of Birds Flown."

The birds are flown: that bird's nest was ill
    watched;

Birds' wings once full summ'd birds will hardly
    be catched.

" Otherwise."

The birds are flown. Flown? that flight no
    wonder brings;   [wings.
Birds may soon flee where birders clip no birds'

281. " Of Leaving."

Leave it or it leave you: leave what? folly?
He can never leave it nor it him, wholly.

282. " Of Setting in Foot."

He hath set in foot: things by wit to be sped,
His foot shall do service as good as his head.

" Otherwise."

I will set in foot: friend, thou mayest set in fit
Foot, hand, and head, but thou canst set in
    no wit.

283. " Of Fast Binding."

Fast bind, fast find: nay, thou were 'prentice
    fast bound,
And yet rannest thou away where thou couldst
    not be found.

284. " Of Hap."

Happy man, happy dole: so say sick and
    whole;
But good hap is dainty: most men have seldom
    good dole.

" Otherwise."

Happy man, happy dole: hap is full of holes;
Hap catcheth and holdeth very few good doles.

285. "Of Time."

Take time when time cometh: we are ofttimes
    told of it;
But when time cometh yet can we take no hold
    of it.

"Otherwise."

Take time when time cometh: assay to be bold
    of it;
But slippery as an eel's tail is the hold of it.

"Otherwise."

Take time when time cometh: are we set time
    to take?   [break.
Beware time, in meantime, take not us in

"Otherwise."

Take time when time cometh: when time
    cometh—thou sayest well!   [tell.
But when cometh good time to take, I cannot

286. "Of the Fat Hog."

Every man basteth the fat hog: nay, friend,
    nay!
Mast faileth sore this year, fat hogs pine away.

"Otherwise."

Every man basteth the fat hog, 'tis agreed
That those hogs shall have most help that have
    least need.

287. "The Bale and Boot."

When bale is hekst, boot is next: though boot
    be nigh,   [high?
What helpeth boot where bale is ever most

288. "Of Sows."

" As meet as a sow to bear a saddle, John."
" A sow to bear a saddle? we have seen none;
But though sows bear no saddles, yet may we say
We see saddles bear sows, well-nigh every day.

289. "Of Making a Cross."

I will make a cross upon this gate: yea, cross on;
Thy crosses be on gates all, in thy purse none.

290. "Of a Pad."

It will breed a pad in the straw: very well!
Beware it breed not a padlock on thy heel.

291. "Of Long Standing."

Long standing and small offering maketh poor parsons :   [garsons.
Long waiting and small wages maketh poor

292. "Of the Weaker."

The weaker goeth to the pot: yea, and God wot!
Some the weaker for oft going to the pot.

293. "Of Catching."

Catch that catch may: after catching and snatching,
Pilling and polling, we fall now to patching.

294. "Of Holding."

Hold fast when ye have it : if it be not thine,
Hold fast and run fast when thou hast it, friend mine!

295. "Of Knowledge."

*I know him as well as the beggar knoweth his
     bag:*
Thou knowest him; but when wilt thou know
     thyself, wag?

296. "Of Smellings."

*I smelt him out further than he might smell
     thee.*
The smeller of smellers then, thou art even he!

297. "Of Nought Laid Down."

Nought lay down, nought take up: well said!
Nought lie down, nought rise up: well weighed!

298. "Of Sight and Fare."

Ye see your fare: a very strange fare to see;
A blind man may see our fare as well as we.

299. "Of the Pot Not Broken."

Neither pot broken nor water spilt: water
Thou spillest none; but thou spillest all other
     matter.

300. "Of Late and Never."

Better late than never: yea, mate!
But as good never as too late.

"Otherwise."

Better late than never:
That is not true ever;
Some things, to rule in rate,
Better never than late.

Finis.

The fifth hundred of Epygrams.

Inuented and
made by
John
Heywood.

LONDINI.
Anno Christi
1562.
*

To the Reader

Were it as perilous to deal cards at play,
As it is quarrelous to deal books this day,
One and forty men, among one and fifty,
Would flee one and thirty, to flee one un-
      thrifty.   [ing,
And yet cards so dealt should have, in reveal-
Foredeal of books in this hard time of dealing.
Cards be tooted on but on the tone side:
Books on both sides; in all places pored and
      pried.
Not to content, but to contend, upon spial
Of least tittle, that can come in trial.
If the best writer to write be much afraid,
More may I, (the worst), by fearful fear be
      stayed.   [me so,
And were not this one thing, fear should stay
That book or ballet, I never durst write mo.
In all my simple writing never meant I
To touch any private person displeasantly.
Nor none do I touch here by name, but only
      one,
Which is myself; whom I may be bold upon.
This meant in my making, since proof doth
      declare,
I pray you readers to scan this, by this square.
As I, for mirth, merrily did make it,
So you, in mirth, merrily will take it.

FINIS.

THE TABLE

Finis.

THE FIFTH HUNDRED OF EPIGRAMMES

1. "Of Weening and Wotting."

Wise men in old time would ween themselves
    fools;   [wise.
Fools now in new time will ween themselves
Ween wise and wot wise differ in wise schools:
To ween themselves wise, when fools so devise,
As foolish as fruitless is th'enterprise.
This case is thus adjudged, in wisdom's school:
Who weeneth himself wise, wisdom wotteth
    him a fool.   [one,
Made by John Heywood to these fools every-
And made of John Heywood when he weeneth
    himself none.

2. "Of a Man of Law and his Clients."

Twenty clients to one man of law
For counsel, in twenty matters, did draw.
Each one praying at one instant to speed,
As all at once would have speed to proceed.
"Friends all," (quoth the learned man), "I'll
    speak with none
Till one barber have shaven all, one by one."
To a barber they went all together:
And being shaven, they returned again thither.

" Ye have," (quoth the lawyer), " tarried long
    hence."   [shaven since
" Sir," (quoth one), " twenty could not be
Of one barber; for, ye well understand,
One barber can have but one shaving hand."
" Nor one lawyer," (quoth he), " but one talk-
    ing tongue."
Learn clients this lesson of this lawyer sprung:
Like as the barber, one after one must shave,
So clients, of counsellors, counsel must have.

3. "An Advice against Mocking."

Use to thy true friend no derision;
If thy friend spy it, he taketh it poison.
Though thy friend dissemble th'espial clearly,
Yet spied in a friend it toucheth him nearly.
Telling thy friend his fault, mocking him not,
If he thank thee not, then is he a sot.

4. "Of Itching and Smarting."

Itching and smarting, both touch us at quick.
When we itch, we scratch: when we smart,
    we kick.
But, in our kicking at our present smart,
Let us consider our former desart.

5. "Of a Sharp Tongue."

" Wife, I perceive thy tongue was made at
    Edgware."   [by there."
" Yea, sir, and yours made at Rayleigh, hard

6. "Of a Horse."

A tilt horse, *alias* a beer horse to be—
Which wouldst thou be? a beer horse, I say
    to thee.   [beer,
When the horse is seen cheerily to draw the
He is so praised that he may be proud to hear.

At tilt, when the horse runneth as fast as he
    can,   [the man.
All cry : " Well run ! " not to the horse, to
And if the horse fall, with the man overlaid,
Then cry they all : " A vengeance on that lame
    jade ! "

7. " OF A BUTLER AND A HORSE."

The butler and the beer horse both be like one :
They draw beer both ; that is truth to bide one.
" Both draw beer, indeed, but yet they differ,
    Joan ;
The butler draweth and drinketh beer, the
    horse drinketh none."

8. " OF BRASS."

I perceive well now that brass is waxen proud,
Because brass so much with silver is allowed ;
And being both joined, since they most by
    brass stand,   [hand.
That maketh brass bold to stand on the upper

9. " OF A LOUSE'S DWELLING-PLACE."

" Were thou a louse and shouldst choose one
    dwelling-place,   [this case :
Whither wouldst thou dwell, having choice in
In men's big breeches, or in women's thick
    ruffs ? "
" I would be, both for the places and stuffs,
In summer with women, in winter with men.
In summer the woman's neck pleasant then.
In winter the man's breech is close and warm :
Large walks for life to walk warm without
    harm ;   [halls—
Galleries, gable ends, cambers, parlours,
Cold frost to defend, a dozen double walls.

Some sealed, some hanged, some dyed, some
　　painted, some stained ;　　　　　[tained.
Rents of all size, great and small rents re-
And when, by louse biting, the leg is itching,
The bars of men's breeches have such strong
　　stitching,　　　　　　　　[and stamp !—
Such bolstering, such 'broidering—let men stare
The louse is as safe there as he were in a camp.
In winter, I say, these breeches are alone ;
But then in summer let the louse thence be
　　gone
For fear of a plague ; if he then thither get,
A thousand to one he shall die of the sweat."

10. "Of a Strange Glass."

Good God ! what a glass to view is this?
See what an unsightly sight here is :
Great promise, small performance ;
Great countenance, small continuance ;
Great winning, small saving ;
Great hoping, small having ;
Great hives, small honey ;
Great purses, small money ;
Great gaps, small bushes ;
Great spears, small pushes ;
Great wine, small water ;
Great words, small matter ;
Great bottom, small brink ;
Great brewing, small drink ;
Great rent, small place ;
Great space, small grace ;
Great drift, small shift ;
Great gift, small thrift ;
Great watching, small catching ;
Great patching, small matching ;

Great blood, small brute;
Great flowers, small fruit;
Great woods, small oaks;
Great staves, small strokes;
Great hens, small eggs;
Great hose, small legs;
Great study, small art;
Great desire, small desert;
Great giving, small taking;
Great marring, small making;
Great ships, small sailing;
Great loss, small availing;
Great marking, small minding;
Great seeking, small finding;
Great lawing, small loving;
Great stirring, small moving;
Great sowing, small growing;
Great trowing, small knowing—
I trow so great ill, and so small good
In one glass, together, never stood.

11. "Of Drinking and Drawing."

" If thou must be forced forth to take journey
      quick,   [forth, Dick? "
Whither wouldst thou be driven forth, or drawn
" I would be driven forth, Jack; for, as doth
      appear,
Drawing and hanging draw vengeable near.
I think it less ill, Jack, having choice in scope,
To be driven with the whip than drawn to the
      rope."

12. "Of Long Suits."

Suits hang half a year in Westminster Hall;
At Tyburn, half an hour's hanging endeth all.

HEY. II.   R

13. "Of Lightness."

"Nothing is lighter than a feather, Kit."
"Yes, Clim." "What light thing is that?"
　　"Thy light wit."

14. "Of a Disagreement."

Each one man wellnigh falleth out with
　　another;
And likewise each thing disagreeth with other:
Namely, malt and water; these two things are
So far fallen asunder, by scornful square,
That no brewer, be he lusty or lither,
Dare couch malt and water in house together.
But, chiefly sour water now beareth such sway
That, sweet malt from brewhouse, water
　　driveth away.

15. "Of Cheapening of Conies."

"Jane, thou sellest sweet conies in this poultry-
　　shop;
But none so sweet as thyself, sweet cony mop!
What is the price of thee?" "Forsooth!"
　　she told:
"At what price soever myself shall be sold,
Strange is the hearing, for ware or for money,
To hear a woodcock cheapen a cony."

16. "Of a Wife having Child."

"My wife hath a child now at four score and
　　ten!"
"At four score and ten years? nay, friend,
　　nay! what then?"   [meant."
"At four score and ten quarters of a year I

" Meant ye so? and I meant years; by which
  extent   [smell
Your wife might seem your mother; but now I
You may seem your wife's father wonderfool
  well."

17. " OF A BACHELOR AND A MAID."

" Is that bachelor a wooer to that maid? "
" The commons common so; 'tis commonly
  said."
" Where dwelleth that bachelor? " " Wide a
  bow of Bridewell."
" Where dwelleth that maid? " " At Broken
  Wharf very well."

18. " OF SHORT PAYMENT."

Thy debtor will pay thee shortly: shortly?
He will make that short lie, a long lie, dread I.

19. " WHENCE CERTAIN THINGS CAME FIRST."

Whence come great breeches? from Little
  Wittam.
Whence come great ruffs? from Small Brain-
  forth they came.   [Square Thrift.
Whence come these round fardingales? from
Whence come deep coped hats? from Shallow
  Shift.   [of Evil.
Whence come 'broidered gards? from the Town
Whence come uncombed staring heads? from
  the devil!   [Folly, John.
Whence come these women's scarves? from
Whence come their glittering spangs? from
  Much Wanton.   [osity.
Whence come perfumed gloves? from Curi-
Whence come fine trapped moils? from Super-
  fluity.   [shapen shoon.
Whence come corned crooked toes? from Short

Whence come wild high lookers? from Mid-
    summer moon.   [Painters' tools.
Whence come fair painted faces? from
Whence come all these? from the vicar of Saint
    Fools.

20. "Of Furred and Lined Gowns."

Thick furred gowns worn in summer show
    bare worn threads;   [Saint Needs.
Thin lined gowns worn in winter come from

21. "Of a Wine-drawer."

Drawer, thy wine is even with thee now I see:
Thou piercest the wine, and the wine pierceth
    thee.

22. "Short Checks Between a Man and His Wife."

" I am careful to see thee careless, Jill : "
" I am woeful to see thee witless, Will."
" I am anguished to see thee an ape, Jill : "
" I am angry to see thee an ass, Will."
" I am fretting to see thee flee from me, Jill : "
" I am sorry to see thee seek to me, Will."
" I am mad to see thee mate thy husband,
    Jill : "
" I am sad to see thee slander thy wife, Will."
" I am dumpish to see thee play the drab,
    Jill : "   [Will."
" I am knappish to see thee play the knave,

23. "Of a Woman decked in Two Colours."

My bonny Bess, black and white doth set thee
    out nett.
Thy ear white as pearl, thy teeth black as jet.

24. "Of Unsweet Breath."

Thine unsavoury breath lacketh salt, beale
    Belsabub: [tub.
It hath ta'en too much wind in the powdering-
Thy breath, Hodge, with salt is so savoury to
    smell,
That no seasoning liquor can season it well.

25. "Of Clipping and Cleansing."

Not clipping your beards, why clip you your
    nails?   [tails?
Not combing your heads, why wipe you your
These being superfluous things every one,
Comb, clip, or cleanse all: or clip or cleanse
    none.

26. "Of a Man and His Wife's Departing."

"Wife, I will go abroad—will ye take the
    pain?"   [again?"
"Be't; but when the devil will ye come in
"Makest thou me a devil? nay, then be out of
    doubt;   [goeth out."
The devil will come in when the devil's dame

27. "An Account of a Man's Children."

"Wife, of ten babes between us by increase
    grown,   [own:
Thou sayest I have but nine." "No mo of your
Of all things increasing, as my conscience li'th,
The parson must needs have the tenth for the
    tithe."

28. "Of a Woman of Huntington."

"Where dwel'st thou, Sis?" "I dwell at
    Huntington now."   [sow."
"Like so, for thou look'st like a now hunted

" Where dwel'st thou, Sim? "   " At Hammer-
    smith dwell I."   [hard by."
" A meet soil for thee! for hammer-head is

29. " OF A LAUNDRESS."

A like laundress to thee, never saw I.
Thy clothes washed but once a week commonly,
Thyself washed once in an hour usually;
And yet each week's end doth this thus try,
Thy clothes ever wet, thyself ever dry.

30. " OF A CUTTER OF PURSLANE."

This herb purslane thou cutt'st prettily I see:
But to cut a purse in a lane none like thee.

31. " OF ONE STANDING IN HIS OWN
CONCEIT."

He standeth well in his own conceit each man
    tells :   [else.
So had he need, for he standeth in no man's

32. "OF ONE THAT HEARD WITHOUT EARS."

I see men hear though they ears have none :
Thou dost hear me speak, thine ears being
    gone.

33. " OF AN ARCHER'S ROVING."

What a shaft shoots he with a roving arrow !
Still he hits the mark, be it wide or narrow.
" Where shooteth this sharp-shooting archer
    most, Will? "
" He shooteth most at rovers on Shooter's
    Hill."

34. "OF PERIL TO ONE BY THE NUMBER OF THREE."

In thy hand I see thy fortune shall be such
That the number of three shall danger thee
    much—   [thee;
Three bedfellows in thy bed shall displease
Three lice in thy bum breech shall oft disease
    thee;
Three cups full at once shall oft disguise thee;
Three bearers of the hum shall oft despise thee;
Three drinks—wine, ale, and beer—shall over-
    flow thee;   [thee;
Three wrestlers in one sign shall overthrow
Three wives in three years shall wonderfully
    wear thee;   [tear thee—
Three she-bears those three years shall all to
But in things numbered by three, above all
    these,   [three trees.
Bliss thee three thousand times from frame of

35. "OF GLORIA PATRI."

" Dick, I marvel much why, in every plate,
Gloria patri standeth before *Sicut erat*."
" Tom, *Gloria patri* is a gentleman :   [can.
In pleasant speech, speak so sweetly no tongue
Sicut erat is a churl, so rude and plain,
That to hear him speak all degrees do disdain."

36. "OF A DYER."

" Is thy husband a dyer, woman ? " " Alack ! "
" Had he no colour to dye thee on but black?
Dyeth he oft ? "   " Yea, too oft when cus-
    tomers call;
But I would have him one day die once for all.
Were he gone, dyer would I never mo wed,
Dyers be ever dyeing, but never dead."

37. "OF A JUG."

" Pot him Jack ! " " Pot him Jack ? " " Nay,
    pot him Jug !
To pot the drunkard, the jug is the dug."

38. "OF THE THREE CUPS."

" Where's thine inn, John? " " At Three
    Cups in Breadstreet, Joan." [bread alone;
" At Three Cups in Breadstreet? well, let
At those Three Cups whenever thou dines or
    sups,
Ere thou go to bed, thou hast in all thy cups ! "

39. "OF BRASS AND IRON."

Brass and old iron—who brought those two
    together ?   [hither.
Brass thinketh scorn to see them brought so
Old iron is rousty and rotten to view,   [new.
Brass with silver fair blanched and polished

"OTHERWISE."

Brass said to old iron with brass perking late :
" Back, ye cankered carl, ye be not my
    mate ! "   [most tallow;
" Back, brass," (quoth iron), " plainness is
I show as I am : and so dost not thou ! "

40. "OF JACK AND JOHN."

Jack and John in degree differ far, brother :
Jack daw is one, master John Daws is another.

41. "OF WRESTLING."

Where we wrestled by couples, we wrestle
    alone,   [gone.
And shall, till time our shackled breeches be

In stepping and striding it is a wonder
How we wrestle to get our legs asunder.

42. " OF PRIDE."

If thou will needs be proud, mark this, friend
    mine :
Of good deeds be not proud; they are not thine.
But when thou playest the knave, in ill deeds
    grown,
Be proud of those ill deeds : they are thine own.

43. " OF ONE HANGED."

" What fault had he done that was hanged
    yesterday?
Of any fault done by him I can nought say."
" Two or three two-penny trifles were laid to
    him,   [him."
But his fair gay hanged house, man, did undo
" Here is tit for tat, measure met very trim :
First he hanged his house, now his house hath
    hanged him."

44. " OF A DEBTOR."

" Doth your mastership remember your debt
    to me? "   [thee :
" Remember my debt? yea, friend, I warrant
I remember it so, that though I say it,
I'll never forget it, nor never pay it."

45. "OF LOVING OF A GOOSE."

" A goose, green or gray—which lovest thou
    better? "
" A green goose : for it is far the sweeter."
" Love both as thyself, for as proof showeth
    rife,
Thou art, and hast been, a goose all thy life."

" Otherwise."

Thou lovest a goose too much : 'ware surfeit,
    elf ;
I never saw goose yet, like thee, love himself.

46. " Of Harp-strings."

" Which string in all the harp wouldst thou
    still harp on ? "
" Not the bass : I will be none underling, John ;
Nor the standing tenor : for stiff standing ;
Nor the treble : for fear of too high hanging ;
Nor the counter tenor : for countering too
    long."   [harp thy song ? "
" Upon what harp-string then wouldst thou
" Above all strings, when we shall fall to harp-
    ing,   [string."
The harp-string to harp on, is the mean harp-

47. " Of Fortune."

Take thy fortune as it falleth, some adviseth :
But I would fain take fortune as it riseth.

48. " Of Choice."

Choice is good in most things, folk say; in
    which choice,   [rejoice :
For choice of one of two things, thou mayest
For man alive, like thee, frank choice can have
To play the knavish fool or the foolish knave.

49. " Of a False Brag."

" I was never but an honest man."
" Put out that *but*, and thou sayest truth
    than."

50. "Of Lying and True Saying."

"Wife, the people are disposed all to lie,
For thou art commended universally."
"Nay, sir! the people, to tell truth, are all
    bold,
For you are discommended of young and old."

51. "Of a Daw Pate."

"Thou art a very daw pate, as ever I saw."
"Sir! indeed the pate is chief part of a daw:
For when daws shall appear in any coast,
For all those daws' parts, their daw pates be
    most."

52. "Of Water and Wine."

Thou makest curtsy to wash hands with water
    of mine,   [wine.
Making no curtsy to wash thy mouth with my
But I pray thee make this change in this
    matter—
More curtsy at my wine, and less at my water.

53. "Between Dogs and a Deer."

"Set malice aside," said a buck to a grey-
    hound.
"Beware of pride," said that dog to that deer.
"Be patient in trouble," a hound said round.
Loving advice to this deer this did appear;
In which, counsel given, to kill him they run
    near: [seeth:
Which counsel amounteth to this, every man
Comfort him with their tongues, kill him with
    their teeth.

54. "OF TWELVE AND ONE."

" It is twelve o'clock."   " Sir ! 'tis more,
    wellnigh one."   [alone."
" Is one more than twelve? that's a reason
" Sir ! when the day to afternoon doth amount,
One is more than twelve, by our sexton's
    account."

55. "OF FARDINGALES."

Alas ! poor fardingales must lie in the street :
To house them, no door in the city made meet.
Since at our narrow doors they in cannot win,
Send them to Oxford, at Broadgates to get in.

56. "PRECEPTS OF A MAN TO HIS WIFE."

" Stand still, wife ! "   " I will : "
" Be still, wife ! "   " I nill."
" Now bark, wife ! "   " I will : "
" To wark, wife ! "   " I nill."
" Prove me, wife ! "   " I will : "
" Love me, wife ! "   " I nill."
" Now chat, wife ! "   " I will : "
" Leave that, wife ! "   " I nill."
" Keep chair, wife ! "   " I will : "
" Speak fair, wife ! "   " I nill."

57. "OF AN EXPERT MAN."

" Is he such an expert man? "   " An expert
    man?   [than."
Put out that *ex*, and no man more expert

58. "OF DELIVERANCE FROM ILL."

" Wife ! from all evil, when shalt thou de-
    livered be? "   [from thee."
" Sir ! when I," (said she), " shall be delivered

59. "Of Cutting of the Herb Thyme."

All times of the day, to-night from the prime,
Thou gardener wilt not leave cutting of thyme.
Thou wilt never leave cutting of thyme, I see,
Till such time, as time, shall in time cut off
thee.

60. "Of One Fearing the Sweat."

Sweating sickness so fearest thou beyond the
mark,   [wark.
That winter or summer thou never sweatest at

61. "Of One Thinking on Another."

"When doth your mastership think on me?"
    "Ever."   ["Never."
"When do you think upon my matter?"
"Me ye remember, my matter ye forget:
Remembrance and forgetfulness is wrong set;
For I would wish you rather, if it might be,
To remember my matter and forget me."

62. "Of One Being at a Point."

"Is he at a point with his creditors?" "Yea!
For he is not worth a point they all see."

63. "Of Testons."

Testons be gone to Oxford, God be their
speed!
To study in Brazennose, there to proceed!

64. "Of Red Testons."

These testons look red: how like you the same?
'Tis a token of grace: they blush for shame.

65. " OF STAMPING."

We stamp crabs; we stamp testons : which
    stamping doon
We stare upon testons now beyond the moon.
Which stamping of testons brought it not some
    skill,
Our staring on testons could judge them but ill.
But as the hot sun melteth snow away,
So shall hot fire melt cold testons, as folk say.
We, for testons leaving scolding and squaring,
And on testons leaving stamping and staring.

66. " OF JOHN LONG THE CARRIER."

" Of what length is John Long the carrier,
    Prat ? "   [thou that ? "
" A quarter of a year long."   " How provest
" Thirteen weeks past he should have brought
    me a wat ;   [cometh nat.
But yet 'long, John, John Long with that wat
Whereby I, John Short, am as short to com-
    pare,
As John Long by this length is long to declare.
For as John Long lurketh too long this wat to
    fet,
So I John Short leap too short this wat to get.

67. " OF TURNING."

" Wilt thou use turner's craft still ? "   " Yea,
    by my troth !   [grow'th.
Much thrift and most surety in turner's craft
Half turn, or whole turn, where turners be
    turning,   [ing."
Turning keeps turners from hanging and burn-

68. " Of Master Carter."

" Is that gentleman's name Master Carter? "
    " Yea ! "   [see !
" How his name and conditions differ now,
So cunning, so comely, so courteous, so kind,
So gentle a gentleman in each man's mind
That all men are stricken in pitiful wonder
To see Master Carter and the cart asunder."

69. " Of Going Far."

As he goeth far that never doth turn him back,
So goest thou far wide : thou never turnest
    again.
Where thou goest, or what thou doest, come
    luck, come lack,
Thyself or thy matters forth they go amain.
To turn again no counsel can thee strain ;
Except thy will shall show thy wit in the
    wane,   [lane.
Find means to take a house in Turn-again

70. " How Money is Made Lame."

" Money, with covetousness, thou dost rest so
That lack of use doth lame thee : thou canst
    not go ;
With prodigality thou trudgest so fast
That excess of too much exercise doth lame
    thee at last.
These two being lame lets of extremities,
Where wouldst thou be 'lotted to be from both
    these ? "
" With liberality would I be the mean."
" With liberality? nay, he is gone clean."

71. "Of an Old Wooer."

"Lady, I love you, in way you to wed:
But mine age with your youth disagreeth so
That, if I speak, I think not to be sped."
"Your age in your suit is no whit your foe;
To your years many, had ye many mo,
We would wed the sooner by years; showing
    plain
That I should the sooner be unwed again."

72. "Of a Young Wooer."

"I brought thee late an old, rich widow to
    woo;   [wouldst thou then do;
Whom thou mightest have had, but nought
Nor nought canst thou do now; thrift and
    thou art odd;
For now lieth she speechless at mercy of God."
"For the mercy of God bring me now to her;
I never saw meet time,'till now, to woo her."

73. "Of Weakness and Strength."

Weakness and strength, here showest thou
    both in preef:
Thou art a weak man and yet a strong thief.

74. "Warning of Pride."

Beware of pride, sayest thou to me?
Let pride, say I, beware of thee.
In every place thou dost so watch him,
That if pride stir, thou wilt sure catch him.

75. "Of Patience."

Be patient in trouble—how can that be
Since out of trouble nothing pleaseth thee?

76. "OF PLEASING."

"Be glad to please?" "Yea, be glad to
    please, brother!"
"But whom?" "Please thyself, see thou
    please none other."

77. "OF A HAND-GUN AND A HAND."

Thou hast a good hand-gun, but what's thy
    hand   [stand?
When thou shootest of['t], out of danger to
No standing more sure, in any place or plat,
Than to stand close to the mark thou shootest
    at.

78. "OF BRASS AND SILVER."

Brass hath been aloft, with silver set up.
Come down, brass, and drink on an ashen cup!

79. "OF DIFFERENCE BETWEEN WISE MEN AND FOOLS."

Between wise men and fools, among things
    many   [any
This one differeth, when both sorts get things
Which to their pleasures are pleasantly
    allowed—   [be proud.
Of those things won, wise men are glad, fools

80. "OF A PITHY WIT."

Good God! what a pithy wit hast thou, Dick!
The pith of thy words so deep and so trick,
Thy words so pithily pierce to the quick,
Pith of no words against thy words may kick,
No more than the pith of a gunstone may
    prick
Against the pithy pith of an elder stick.

HEY. II.   S

81. "Of Choice to be a Wise Man or a Fool."

"A wise man or a fool: if thou must be one,
Which wouldst thou be in winter, John?"
        "A fool, Joan.   [cold,
Where best men in winter sit next fire from
There stands the fool warm while all his tales
    be told."
"Which wouldst thou be in summer, when
        winter is gone?"   [showeth hereupon:
"A fool!" "A fool, why?" "That *why*
In summer when states sit from fire in the cool,
At that board's end in cool air there stands the
    fool."   [work,
"Winter and summer what time men must to
Which wouldst thou be?" "A fool, to look
    on and lurk:
All times of the year, for one thing or other,
Better be a fool than a wise man, brother!"

82. "Of a Knight's Carterly Collar."

I bade this carter bring my collar of gold:
And he bringeth me my horse-collar—"Hold,
    knave, hold!"   [ing,
"Sir, if I may speak my thought without fear-
This collar of both showeth best for your
    wearing."

83. "Of Males and Male Horses."

Of all horses, a male horse would I not be;
Where he erst bare one male, now beareth he
    three;
Those are: one behind, and one on each side.
The man, who on the male horse doth ride,

Weareth on each leg one male; for his slops
 are,
Each one slop one male (kindly to declare)—
Long, round, wide, weighty as a male each
 one.
But all horses are now male horses every one;
For every one horse beareth two males at
 least—   [feast.
Of male horses and male men, friends here's a

84. "A Man Discommended."

Not once a year ought seen in thee to allow :
Not once a year thy knee to God dost thou
 bow ;
Not once a year openest thou thy lips to pray;
Not once a year showest thou goodness any
 way;
Not once a year givest thou alms to the poor;
Not once a year dost thou repent thee there-
 fore;   [stood
But all times a year thou wouldst all under-
Thou never dost repent, but when thou dost
 good.

85. "Of Running."

" In post haste run, whoreson, run ! Art thou
 here yet? "   [of thy wit."
" Shall I run out of breath? " " Nay, run out

86. "Of Polling."

Our heads grow too long, God give our barbers
 curses;   [purses.
Our barbers poll no heads, our barbers poll

87. "Of Plate Lent Forth."

" Where is thy plate? " " Lent out to a
 marriage."

S 2

" Whither ? "   " To   Saint   Needs. "   " To
    whom ? "   " To Master Gage. "

88. " OF A MAN OF LAW AND HIS WIFE. "

You, being a pleader at law excellent,
Yet hath your wife brought you to an exigent.
Pray her to let fall th'action at law now,
Or else, so God help me ! she will overlaw yow.

89. " OF PENS AND PENCE. "

Pens and pence differ far in proportion—
The penny flat and round, the pen straight and
And yet for aids, in case of extortion,   [long.
Pens and pence are like in working of wrong.

90. " OF A WOMAN'S THIN TONGUE. "

" I never saw wife like thine for this thing,
    Dick—   [wondrous thick. "
Her tongue wondrous thin, and her speech
" Tom, I have spent much in vain, since she
    was young,   [tongue. "
To have her thick speech as thin as her
" It is the tongue of tongues, Dick, for running
    round ;
I take the tip for silver, by the shrill sound. "
" It hath, Tom, a shaking sharp sound in the
But it is no silver, would God it were ! " [ear,

91. " OF DRINKING TO A MAN. "

" I drink to thee, John. " " Nay, thou drinkest
    from me, Joan ;   [leavest none. "
When thou drinkest to me, drink for me thou

92. " OF RUNNING AT TILT. "

We apply the spigot till tub stand a-tilt.

Yea, run at the spigot tilt, leave the spear tilt
thou wilt.

93. "Of Expense."

" What may he spend? " " Ten pound a year
he might spend." [penny lend
" Is't mortgaged? " " Nay; no man will one
Upon it." " Is't sold? " " Nay; no man
will buy it."
" Then he holdeth it? " " Nay; he cannot
come nigh it."
" Why, fool! how may he spend ten pound
by year than? " [man;
" I said not, he *may*, but he *might* spend it,
Meaning, he might spend it if he had it."
" O, if he had it—a sir, the devil made it! "

94. "Of Fraying of Babes."

When do mothers fray their babes most from
dugs? [bear bugs.
When they put on black scarves, and go like

95. "Of Reeds and Oaks."

" Will you reeds at the wind's will still make
low becks? [your necks?
Will you oaks stand stiff still while wind break
Will you reeds, like apes, still tuck and bow
each joint? [one point?
Will you oaks, like asses, still stand stiff at
Will you reeds be still bending bowing bodies?
Will you oaks be still stout. stiff-necked
noddies? [avails?
Will you reeds be staggering still for vain
Will you oaks be stern still till your tops kiss
your tails? [towardly?
Will you reeds shrink still to all winds

Will you oaks swell still at all winds fro-
    wardly?   [footstools?
Will you reeds crouch still to be the wind's
Will you oaks crake still to be the wind's head
    fools?"   [reeds.
" Oaks will do as we have done; so will we
Wherein, for our purpose, mark what end
    proceeds: [blown;
In each one storm a thousand oaks down are
In a thousand storms not one reed over-
    thrown."

96. " Of Buying a Mortar."

" That spice mortar to sell it be you willing? "
" Yea, mistress? " " What's the price? "
    " Ten shilling."
" Ten shilling? Friend! I am hither enticed
To buy a spice mortar, not a mortar spiced."

97. " Of a Stepmother."

Thy father's second wife, thy stepmother—
For a stepmother there's not such another.
At three steps I saw her step, since she was
    wed,   [head.
From a stair foot, straight up to thy father's

98. " Of a Liar."

" Where doth Francis Fabler now lie, Jane? "
" At sign of the Whetstone, in Double-Tongue
    Lane,
He lieth by night; and, by day, daily he
Lieth down right in what place soever he be.
That he lieth still day and night, this thing
    doth try—
He never speaketh word but it is a lie.

99. "Of Tongues and Pinsons."

One difference this is on which our tongues
    may carp,   [sharp;
Between pinching pinsons and taunting tongues
Where these two nippers nip anywhere or
    when,
Those pinsons nip dead things, those tongues
    nip quick men.

100. "Of Heywood."

"Art thou Heywood with the mad merry
    wit?"   [hit."
"Yea, forsooth, master! that same is even
"Art thou Heywood that applieth mirth more
    than thrift?"
"Yea, sir! I take merry mirth a golden gift."
"Art thou Heywood that hath made many mad
    plays?"   [days."
"Yea, many plays; few good works in all my
"Art thou Heywood that hath made men merry
    long?"
"Yea, and will, if I be made merry among."
"Art thou Heywood that would be made merry
    now?"
"Yea, sir! help me to it now I beseech yow."

FINIS.

A sixt hundred of
Epi=
grammes.

Newly inuented and made
by
John Heywood.

❦

LONDINI.

Anno Christi

1 5 6 2.

To the reader.

Readers, read this thus: for Preface, Proface.
Much good do it you: the poor repast here,
A six hundred dishes I bring in place
To make good welfare, nay to make good
    cheer.   [dear,
Fare is food: cheer is mirth: since meat is
Not of meat but of mirth, come young come
    old,
Come who come will, here is open household.

FINIS.

THE TABLE

FINIS.

THE SIXTH HUNDRED OF EPIGRAMS

1. " OF REBELLION."

Against God I daily offend by frailty;
But against my prince, or native country,
With as much as bodkin, when I rebel,
The next day after hang me up fair and well.
The next day after? nay, the next day before
Wish thou thyself hanged, in that case, ever-
more.
Before, thou hangest honestly unworthily;
After, thou hangest worthily unhonestly.
But ho! at our first dish in our merry feast
Why talk we of hanging our mirth to molest?
Be our cheese no better than our pottage is,
Better fast than feast at such feasts as is this.
But being true to God, queen, country, and
crown,   [down.
We shall at all feasts, not hang up, but sit

" OTHERWISE."

Wilt thou be taken for a true Englishman?
Yea? be true to God, thy queen, and country
than.   [it;
Stand fast by thy country whoever would win
Better stand fast by it than hang fast in it.

2. "OF TONGUE, MOUTH, TEETH, AND WISDOM."

The tongue is assigned of words to be sorter;
The mouth is assigned to be the tongue's
        dorter;   [porter;
The teeth are assigned to be the tongue's
But wisdom is 'signed to tie the tongue shorter.

3. "OF SILVER TO BE BORROWED."

"Hast thou any bowed silver to lend me,
        Joan?"   [me?" "None."
"Nay." "Hast thou any broken silver for
"Hast thou any clipped silver?" "I had,
        but 'tis gone."
"Hast thou any cracked groat?" "Cracked
        groat? nay, not one."   [nor cut—
"No silver—bowed, broken, clipped, cracked,
Here's a friend for friendship, not worth a
        cracked nut."

4. "OF AN UNKINDLY MARCH."

This like March? as like as I am a March hare.
March is not so like March, friend; I would it
        were.   [thee,
Though shape of the March hare show not in
Yet hast thou the March hare's mad property.

5. "OF GOING TO HEAVEN AND HELL."

Of heaven or of hell, which go folk fastest to?
To hell, fool! to hell go far more fast they do.
The highway to both lieth thus as clerks tell,
Uphill to heavenward, downhill to hell.

6. "Of the Highway and a Maid's Face."

The more the highway is washed the fouler it
   is :   this !
Maid, the highway and thy face are like in

7. "Of One that Would be Praised."

"Wouldst   thou   be   praised?"   "Yea."
   "Why?"   "Praise pleaseth me well."
"Yea, but how doth desert of praise please
   thee, tell ! "

8. "Of Looking."

"Look upward to heaven, my friend; what !
   where lookest thou? "
"Sir, I was looking downward to hell for you."

9. "Of a Hare Afoot."

I hear by the hounds the hare is afoot;
Then must she to horseback, none other boot.
Nothing doth more a hare's hope of life quail
Than doth a hound's nose nigh a hare's tail.

10. "Of Hob and John."

Horse and harness up, on all hands ! Hob and
   John.
Hob and John? Nay, Lob and John would
   now be gone;   [start,
But, till your prince stir you to harness to
Harness you your horse, and get ye to the
   cart.

11. "Of Seeking a Daw."

"I have sought far to find a daw."   "Why,
   thou elf !   [thyself."
When thou wouldst quickly find a daw, seek

" What is Domine Daw in English to say? "
" No mo daws; thou Daw art daws enough for
    this day."

12. " Of Saying Grace."

To say grace fair, and to say grace oft, John,
From Gracechurch to Grantham thy like there's
    none.
At breakfast, at dinner, at supper, at all,
At sitting, at rising, have grace we shall.
There's no man alive, in house, street, or field,
That saith grace so oft, and showeth grace so
    seeld.

13. " Of Debt."

What difference in true debt, and blue debt, to
    rate?
Difference as in distance Ludgate and Newgate.

14. " Of Stepping."

In stepping one foot back, stepping forward
    twain,
My steps so stepped are not stepped in vain.
If one backstep be as much as foresteps three,
By your stout stepping your winning let us see.
Where wide-striding stepping gets no gain
    ought worth,   [forth.
As good to stand stone-still, as step one step

15. " Of Writing a Gentleman."

Thou writest thyself gentleman in one word,
    brother !
But gentle is one word, and man is another.

16. "Of a Wife's Affection to Her Husband."

I ween there's no wife like the wife of thine—
Thy body being hers, yet doth she incline,
Fairest, or foulest, whom fancy doth prefer,
To take whom thou list, so thou touch not her.

17. "Of a Man's Thrift."

Lord! what thrift ariseth in thy behalf?
Thy sow great with pig; thy cow great with
    calf;   [whelp;
Thy ewe great with lamb; thy bitch great with
Thy cat great with kit (and more increase to
    help);   [thrift, fool!
Thy wife great with child; and to show thy
Thy mare great with foal; and thyself great
    with fool.

18. "Of Learning the Law."

Thou wilt learn the law wherever thou be—
Lincoln's Inn, or Lincoln town, both one to
    thee.

19. "Of Good Will and Good Deeds."

Is good will the best part of a friend? nay,
    nay!   [may.
Beggars with lords so, for friendship compare
Good deeds by good will had, differ there,
    brother!
A pudding prick is one, a millpost is another.

20. "Of Newgate Windows."

All Newgate windows bay-windows they be;
All lookers out there stand at bay we see.

21. "Of Treading a Shoe Awry."

My wife doth ever tread her shoe awry.
Inward, or outward? nay, all outwardly :
She treadeth so outward, that if she outwin,
She will by her will never tread foot within.

22. "Of a Fair Sow."

I never saw a fairer sow in my life.
Ah sir, thy sow is even as fair as thy wife!

23. "Of Prayer."

Some pray *familorum familarum* :
Some say, that is folorum, solarum.

24. "Of Cheese."

I never saw Banbury cheese thick enough;
But I have oft seen Essex cheese quick enough.

25. "Of a Lease."

Thy lease of Freshwharf bindeth thee there to
        dwell;   [tell.
Which thou hast forfeited, as thy neighbours
These four years at Freshwharf, as folk con-
        sither,   [together.
Thou hast not been fresh full four hours

26. "Of Stocks."

Thy upper stocks, be they stuffed with silk or
        flocks,
Never become thee like a nether pair of stocks.

27. "A Taunt of a Wife to Her Husband."

" Wife, I ween thou art drunk or lunatic ! "
" Nay, husband ! women are never moonsick;

Come that conjunction in time, late, or soon,
We say, not the woman, the man in the moon.''

28. "Of Pride."

Fie on pride when men go naked : naked or
    clothed,
Pride is in all men a thing to be loathed ;
But yet may we see, though it do ill accord,
Some naked beggar as proud as some clothed
    lord.

29. "To Walk, Talk, Drink, or Sleep."

Walk groundly ;
Talk profoundly ;
Drink roundly ;
Sleep soundly.

30. "Of a Lanthorn and Light."

A lanthorn and a light maid—mannerly said :
But which to be light ? the lanthorn, or the
    maid.

31. "Of a Cry."

Thou lost'st a mark in issues, criers cry—
Cry not so for me, crier ! and mark this, why ?
I would rather give thee a gown of tissue
Than be in dread to lese my mark in issue.

32. "Of a Waterman's Rowing."

Thy fares over the water thou shouldst row
    them,
But under the water thou dost bestow them.

33. "Of Tongue and Wit."

Thou hast a swift-running tongue ; howbeit,

Thy tongue is nothing so quick as thy wit.
Thou art, when wit and tongue in running con-
tend,
At thy wits' end ere thou be at the tale's end.

34. "Of a Painter."

Thou art the painter of painters, mark who
shall,
In making and setting colours above all,
No painter painting within England's bounds,
Can set so fair colours upon so foul grounds.

35. "Of Peter and Paul."

I dwell from the city in suburbs at rowles;
I pray to Saint Peter to bring me near Powles.
Alas, thou pray'st all in vain, poor silly fool—
Peter will set no hand to bring thee to Poule.

36. "Of Loss of Health and Wealth."

How lost you your health?
That gluttony tell'th.
How lost you your wealth?
That lost I by stealth.
Who was your wealth's wringer?
My thumb and my finger.

37. "Of Looking Out."

Stand in and look out; hang out and look
not out—
Newgate and Tyburn do bring both these
about.

38. "Of Chafing Dishes."

Wife, all thy dishes be chafing dishes placed;
For thou chafest at sight of every dish thou
hast.

39. "Of Hanging and Standing."

Whether wilt thou hang up with ropes of
inions?
Or stiffly stand up with roperipe minions?
Forsooth! both for number and stuff, truly
cast,   [last.
As good hang with the first as stand with the

40. "Of a Man's Head and the Pillory."

Upon the pillory, your worshipful head
Unto the pillory doth worship far spread,
Which worship the pillory requiteth ill now;
For, as you worship it, so it shameth yow.

41. "A Praise of One."

See how some above some other praises win—
I praise thee for one thing above all thy kin.
They, without teaching could never practise
ought;   [taught.
Thou canst play the knave, and never was

42. "Of Divers Bands."

"All kinds of bands to be bound in being
scanned,   [or husband—
Headband, smockband, flailband, houseband,
Which shall bind thee?" "Not the last on sea
nor land;   [stand."
Before husband's bands, in devil's bands I will

43. "Of Covenants, &c."

Many poses without apposition;
Many covenants without good condition;
Many promises without good payment;
Many arbitraments without good dayment.

44. "Of Promise and Payment."

"May I trust that he promised?"
"Yea: scantly to be performed."
"Promiseth he thrice or he once pay?"
"Sometimes he doth; but not alway.
Some things he promiseth to pay ever;
Which things so promised he payeth never."

45. "Of One that Dare Not Steal."

"Thou borrowest, and thou beggest, but when
    wilt thou steal?"
"Never; for to be hanged, sir, I have no zeal."
"Thou wouldst steal if thou durst?" "Yea,
    but I dare not."   [care not.
"Well then, for thy hanging, in this world
And in the world to come, as well thou shalt
    speed   [indeed."
For good will to steal as thou hadst stolen

46. "Of the Creation of the Devil's Dam."

When was the devil's dam created, th'old
    withered jade?   [made,
The next leap-year after wedding was first
In an ill time; when the devil will that devil
    die,
At that year's end, that endeth wedding finally.

47. "Of Reward to a Serving Man."

"Wait well; thy master will do for thee I wis:
Canst thou spy nothing to ask of him?"
    "Yis;
But when I ask I cannot have that I crave."
"No? ask him blessing, and that shalt thou
    surely have."

48. "Two Properties of a Servant."

Whoso that hath a good servant, keep him
    well—
Well must I keep thee then, by this that I tell.
Singular in many things; in this above all—
To take thy wages great, and make thy service
    small.

49. "Of Toughness and Tenderness."

For toughness and tenderness both in one man
    seen,   [been.
One like your mastership few or none hath
Axe ought of ye : then are ye so tart and tough
That your taunts would touch a horse's heart
    most rough.   [you;
Give ought to ye : thus tender and meek are
Tears, like tears from your eyes, your knees to
    ground bow.

50. "A Question to a Child."

"Who is thy father, child?" axt his mother's
    husband.   [stand."
"Axe my mother," (quoth he), "that to under-
"The boy dallieth with you, sir; for, verily !
He knoweth who is his father as well as I."
The man, of this child's wit was wrapped in
    such joy   [boy.
That he knew not what he might make of the

51. "Seeking for a Dwelling-place."

Still thou seekest for a quiet dwelling-place :
What place for quietness hast thou now in
    chase?   [water.
London Bridge? That's ill for thee, for the

Queenhithe? That's more ill for another
matter.
Smart's Key? That's most ill for fear of
smarting smart.
Carter Lane? Nay, nay! that soundeth all on
the cart.   [the chain.
Powles Chain? Nay, in no wise dwell not near
Wood Street? Why wilt thou be wood yet
once again?
Bread Street? That's too dry; by drought
thou shalt be dead.
Philpot Lane? That breedeth moist humours
in thy head.   [fie!
Silver Street? Coppersmiths in Silver Street;
Newgate Street? 'Ware that, man! New-
gate is hard by.
Faster Lane? Thou wilt as soon be tied fast,
as fast.
Crooked Lane? Nay, crook no more, be
straight at last.   [against brother.
Creed Lane? They fall out there, brother
Ave Mary Lane? That's as ill as the t'other.
Paternoster Row? Paternoster Row?
Agreed! that's the quietest place that I know.

52. "OF THREE SOULS."

Thou hast three souls in charge: thy body
soul one;   [alone.
Thy feet soles twain; but let thy feet soles
Discharge thy body soul, and feet soles, poor
elves,   [themselves.
They shall pay their own fees and discharge

53. "OF ONE SAYING OF A HAT."

"Said he that hat on his head?" "Nay!
chance so led

That by that time the hat came, he had no
    head.''

54. '' Of Buying a Coat.''

'' I must buy a new coat for shame.''
'' To get shame? '' '' Nay, t'avoid the same.''
'' T'avoid shame? Thou mayest desire it,
But ten new coats will not hire it.''

55. '' Of Paring Nails.''

'' Pare my nails, wife ! '' '' Nay, man ! if
    your nails fail,   [scab'd tail? ''
Where can ye find friends to scratch your
'' Pare thine own nails then; for, as they be
    led,   [head.''
They prove fiendly friends in scratching my
'' That may be; but, as those words are soon
    spoken,
So even as soon is a scal'd man's head broken.''

56. '' Of a Man's Head.''

Thy head is great, and yet seemeth that head
    but thin;
Without hair without, and without wit within.

57. ''Of Money in One's Purse.''

He hath in his purse forty or fifty pound.
Put *n* to *or*, and mark then how that doth
    sound.

58. '' Of Friends and Foes.''

The devil shall have friends; and, as good
    reason goes   [have foes.
That the devil shall have friends as God shall

59. "Of Difference in Sundry Things."

Small difference between receiving and tak-
    ing:
Great difference between marrying and making.
Small difference between sighing and sobbing:
Great difference between bassing and bobbing.
Small difference between fair looks and fair
    words: [swords.
Great difference between blunt words and sharp
Small difference between talking and telling:
Great difference between smarting and smell-
    ing.   [ing:
Small difference between true love and trust-
Great difference between rubbing and rusting.
Small difference between lowering and snower-
    ing: [ing.
Great difference between laughing and lower-
Small difference between waste-ware and
    weeds: [deeds.
Great difference between good words and good
Small difference between closeness and conceal-
    ing:
Great difference between giving and stealing.

60. "Of Calling One Flibergibet."

"Thou flibergibet!" "Flibergibet, thou
    wretch!   [doth stretch?
Wott'st thou whereto last part of that word
Leave that word or I'll baste ye with a libet;
Of all words I hate words that end with gibet."

61. "Of Crows Breeding."

I would wish some good provision, to provide
That crows should never breed by the high-
    way's side.

They so mistrust every man to steal their birds,
That no man can 'scape their opprobrious
    words.
No man passeth by, whatsoever he be,
But those crows beknave him to the ninth
    degree.   [and raves,
Should the crow's word stand when he rages
We should have in England forty thousand
    knaves.

62. "Of Powles."

Thanks to God and good people Powles goeth
    up well :
Powles goeth up? but when goeth polling
    down : that tell !

63. "Of a Crow-keeper."

There be many called crow-keepers; but, in-
    deed,   seed ;
There's no crow-keeper but thou in time of
Where others keep crows out, like starvelings
    forlorn,
To keep crows in plight, thou keepest crows
    in the corn.

64. "Of Rape-seed."

" Hast thou any rape-seed? " " Yea; if you
    to rape fruit fall,   [mixed withal."
Here is rape-seed; but there's hemp-seed

65. "Of Red Roses."

" What think ye worth one bushel of red
    roses? "   [noses."
" More worth than are two bushels of red

66. "OF PENNYROYAL."

"I seek pennyroyal: have ye any?"
"Seek further; I have neither royal nor
      penny."

67. "OF MARJORUM."

"Hast any marjorum, gentle?"   "Yea, in-
      deed;
But it is somewhat mingled with nettle-seed."

68. "OF POPPY."

"Let's see poppy-seed."   "My poppy-seed is
      gone;   [alone!"
But, for your ground, I have puppy-seed

69. "OF THYME-SEED."

"Have ye any thyme-seed?"   "Thyme-seed?
      yea, by rood!   [good."
But it is so mistimed that it bringeth no thyme

70. "OF RUE."

"I would have a groatworth of your seed of
      rue."   [new."
"Ye shall have rue-seed enough, both old and

71. "LIVERWORT."

"What lack you, sir?"   "Liverwort-seed I
      come to crave."   [have."
"Liverwort I have none; but lipwort-seed I

72. "OF PINEAPPLE."

"Hast thou any graffs of the pineapple-tree?"
"Yea; pining graffs, great growers as can
      be."

73. " Of Heartsease."

" Have you any heartsease-seed? " " Yea,
    for God, I !   [buy? "
But what other ware with heartsease will ye
" None."   " Then have I no heartsease for
    you, brother.   [another;
We seed-sellers must sell seeds one with
To buy heartsease-seed of me, that no man
    shall,   [withal."
Except he buy some seeds of arse-smart

74. " Of Parsnip-seed."

Here is parsnip-seed that will nip you, as near
As ye were nipped with any parsnip this year.

75. " Of Aniseed."

This aniseed is brown; but, to occupy,
Brown Anne's as sweet, as white Anne's, like
    I.

76. " Of Lettuce-seed."

" I would buy lettuce-seed for my garden,
    Joan."   [none.
" Lettuce-seeds? forsooth, good master ! I have
But put out *u c e*, and these seeds, I'll avow,
Best seeds in England for your garden and
    you."

77. " Of Good News to a Man."

" What news? " " Good news for thee as wit
    can scan ;
We have news that thou art an honest man.
This news coming even now thus fresh and
    new,

All men take for good; no man taketh for
    true."

78. "Of Least and Most Mastery."

"What is the least mastery thou canst
    devise?"   [wise."
"Least mastery is a fool to ween himself
"What is the most mastery that thy wit
    spies?"
"The most mastery is, to make a fool wise."

79. "Of a Man and a Clock."

Men take man of earthly things most excellent,
But in one thing thou seemest under that ex-
    tent :
A clock after noon above thee I avow—
A clock can go alone then; so canst not thou.

80. "Of a Spare Horse."

"Hast thou any spare horse, to lend me one?"
"A spare horse? There's one; take him and
    begone."
Saddled and bridled he was, and with that,
As the man leapt up, the horse fell down flat.
He fell without help; but then up to get,
Five men were too few him on foot to set.
"A spare horse," (quoth he), "the devil may
    spare him;
He that shall occupy him must bear him."
"Since this spare horse will not serve thee,
    brother !
Yet of my spare horses here's another."
Up leapt the man, hence ran the horse amain;
In ten miles galloping he turned not again.

For judgment in spare horse, let this be com-
    pared :   [spared?
Run ever, run never—which may best be

81. " Of a Husband Hanged."

" Is thy husband hanged? "   " He was; but
    he is nat;
In spite of his foes I found friends to ease that.
For or my dear heart had hanged fully hours
    twain,
I gat his pardon and cut him down again."

82. " Of Horsadown."

" Hiredst thou not this horse at Horsa-
    down? "   " Yis ! "
" Where is Horsadown? "   " That mayest
    thou learn by this :   [field, town,
In high way, low way, fair way, foul way,
Wheresoever this horse is, there is Horsa-
    down ! "

83. " Of a Cock and a Capon."

A brave capon by a brag cock late being,
The proud cock thinking scorn, the same so
    seeing,
Said to the capon : " What thou barren
    bastard !
Perkest thou with me here as I were a haskard?
Where I—comely, combed, crowing, cocking
    cock—
Am husband or father to all this whole flock."
" What," (quoth the capon), " thou lewd
    lecherous wretch !
These chickens all for thine benefit thou this
    brag to stretch?   [alone !
As though there were but one treading cock

Yes, cock, yes! there be mo treading cocks
    than one;   [avaunt,
But since thou thus proudly dost make this
To repress thy pride, take this tale for a taunt.
I have of mine own—I treading hens never—
As many chickens as thou, treading thy hens
    ever."   [dead;
This strake the cock in a deep dump, dull and
Having a still tongue he had a busy head.
Two days after this, he trod not nor fed not,
His comb sore cut; but thanks to God! it bled
    not.

84. "Of Disdain."

" Is't mastery to disdain things by envy's
    school? "
" Nay, nay! no more mastery than to be a
    fool."

85. "Of Peter."

Peter the proud, and Peter the poor, in which,
Poor Peter oft as proud as Peter the rich.

86. "Of One in Newgate."

" Art thou in Newgate to stand to thy tack-
    ling? "   [ling."
" Nay; I am in Newgate to stand to my shack-

87. "Of Saving of Shoes."

Thou wearest, (to wear thy wit and thrift
    together),
Moils of velvet to save thy shoes of leather.
Oft have we seen moil men ride upon asses;
But to see asses go on moils: that passes.

88. "Of Hogstown."

The head man in Hogstown, hogherd is ex-
pressed;   [best.
Where hogs be parishioners, hogherd must be
Yet hogshead in Hogstown is no John-a-droin,
Pigs dare not quich there, if hogshead hang
    the groin.

89. "Of Cole-prophet."

Thy prophecy poisonly to the prick goeth:
Cole-prophet and cole-poison thou art both.

90. "Of Things Unlike."

Like will to like, men say; but not always so:
Contrary to contrary ofttimes doth go.
When folk be most open, their low parts most
    loose,
Then go they to stools that be made most close.

91. "Of the Gentleness of a Wife."

Thy wife is as gentle as a falcon: true!
And namely in this kind of gentleness: Hugh!
Being not hungry, lower falcons when ye list,
They will check oft, but never come to the fist.

92. "Of Catching a Fly."

A boy on his book clapped hand to catch a fly.
"Hast her?" cried his master. "Nay, God
    wot I."
"Then thou shalt drink!" "Master, I have
    her, I think."   [shalt drink."
"If thou have her," said the master, "thou
To furious masters, what helpeth fair speeches?
Flies caught, or not caught, up go boys'
    breeches!

93. "Of a Horse Wearing Great Breeches."

My horse to wear great breeches is now as-
     signed :
Why? to keep him from interfering behind.

94. "Of a Reckoning at a Shot."

" Give us a reckoning upon this pot filling :
What have we to pay in all?" "Ten
     shilling ! "
" What cometh our meat to?" "Four shil-
     lings, up and down ! "
" What is drink?" "Six shillings; that's to
     say a French crown."
" Why? Have we drunk more than we
     have eaten, knave?"
" Yea, as many other men, many times have."
Look wheresoever malt is above wheat,
There in shot ever drink is above meat.

95. "Of Use."

Use maketh mastery: this hath been said
     alway;
But all is not alway, as all men do say, [rote;
In April the cuckoo can sing her song by
In June, out of tune, she cannot sing a note :
At first, cuckoo, cuckoo, sing still can she do,
At last cuck, cuck, cuck—six cucks to one cu.

96. "Of One Asking for Sheep."

" Came there any sheep this way, you sheepish
     maids?" "Nay;   [way."
But even as you came, there came a calf this

97. "Of Walking and Talking."

Walk thou narrowly, walk thou nearly—
Walk as thy walk may end cheerily.
Talk thou basely, talk thou boldly—
In all thy talk, talk thou coldly.
Walk thou wetly, walk thou dryly—
In thy walk, walk not too highly.
Talk thou merrily, talk thou sadly—
Talk as thy talk may take end gladly.
Walk thou daily, walk thou weekly—
In all thy walk, walk thou meekly.
Talk thou softly, talk thou loudly—
In any talk, talk not proudly.
Walk thou firstly, walk thou lastly—
Walk in the walk that standeth fastly.
Talk or walk oldly or newly—
Talk and walk plainly and truly.

98. "Of Seeing and Feeling Money."

" Lacking spectacles, canst thou see money,
    John? "
" Yea : but having spectacles I can feel none."

99. "Of Taking Things Wrong."

" Perceived and taken things right, thou hast
    long,   [wrong :
But for one thing in thee long since taken
Thy credit is touched, and thou thereby the
    worse."
" What thing sayest thou have I taken
    wrong? "   " A purse."

100. " OF A NUMBER OF RATS MISTAKEN FOR
DEVILS IN A MAN'S SLOPS."

A big breeched man, fearing a dear year to
          come,   [bum.
Bestowed in his breech a cheese, hard by his
And, leaving off those hose for days two or
          three,   [be
Rats two or three crept into that breech; they
'Pointing themselves of that cheese to be
          keepers :   [sleepers.
In which ware watch be sure they were no
No wight riding men, from Sandwich to Sarum,
Could win that cheese from them without a
          larum.   [on,
At three days' end this man, putting these hose
Having tied his points, the rats began anon
To start and to stir that breech round about;
To seek and find some way, what way to get
          out.
But that breech was bolstered so with such
          broad bars,
Such cranks, such cony holes, such cuts and
          such stars,   [fast
With ward within ward, that the rats were as
As though they with thieves in Newgate had
          been cast.   [fumbling,
But this man, in his breech feeling such
Such rolling, such rumbling, joisting and
          jumbling,
He was therewith stricken in a frantic fear;
Thinking sure to himself that some sprites were
          there.
He ran out, he cried out, without coat or cloak,
Those rats in those rags whined like pigs in a
          poke.

" A conjuror," cried he, " in all haste I be-
    seech,   [breech ! "
To conjure the devil : the devil is in my
Running, and turning in and out as he flung,
One of the rats by the ribs he so wrung,
That the rat in rage to his buttock gat her ;
She set in her teeth, his eyes ran a-water.
She bote, he cried, dogs barked, the people
    shouted,   [doubted.
Horns blew, bells rang, the devil dreaded and
To be in his breech to bring him straight to
    hell—   [tell.
The woe and wonder whereof—too much to
At last to see what bugs in his breech frayed
    him,   [him.
Four or five manful men, manfully stayed
The rats hopping out at his hose pulling off,
All this sad matter turned to merry scoff.
When he saw these rats by this cheese brought
    this fear,
Rejoicing the 'scape he solemnly did swear
That in his breech should come no cheese after
    that,
Except in his breech he were sure of a cat.

FINIS.

Imprinted at London, in Fléeteftrete, by Thomas Powell.
                    Cum priuilegio.

A DESCRIPTION OF A
MOST NOBLE LADY

ADVIEWED BY JOHN HEYWOOD,
PRESENTLY; WHO ADVERTISING HER YEARS, AS
FACE, SAITH OF HER THUS, IN MUCH ELOQUENT
PHRASE:

Give place, ye ladies! all be gone;
Show not yourselves at all.
For why? behold! there cometh one
Whose face yours all blank shall.

The virtue of her looks
Excels the precious stone;
Ye need none other books
To read, or look upon.

In each of her two eyes
There smiles a naked boy;
It would you all suffice
To see those lamps of joy.

If all the world were sought full far,
Who could find such a wight?
Her beauty twinkleth like a star
Within the frosty night.

Her colour comes and goes—
With such a goodly grace,
More ruddy than the rose—
Within her lively face.

Amongst her youthful years
She triumphs over age;
And yet she still appears
Both witty, grave, and sage.

I think nature hath lost her mould
Where she her form did take;
Or else I doubt that nature could
So fair a creature make.

She may be well compared
Unto the phœnix kind;
Whose like hath not been heard
That any now can find.

In life a Dian chaste;
In truth Penelope;
In word and deed steadfast—
What need I more to say?

At Bacchus' feast none may her meet;
Or yet at any wanton play;
Nor gazing in the open street,
Or wandering, as astray.

The mirth that she doth use
Is mixed with shamefastness;
All vices she eschews,
And hateth idleness.

It is a world to see
How virtue can repair,
And deck such honesty
In her that is so fair.

Great suit to vice may some allure
That thinks to make no fault;
We see a fort had need be sure
Which many doth assault.

They seek an endless way
That think to win her love;
As well they may assay
The stony rock to move.

For she is none of those
That sets not by evil fame;
She will not lightly lose
Her truth and honest name.

How might we do to have a graff
Of this unspotted tree?
For all the rest they are but chaff
In praise of her to be.

She doth as far exceed
These women, nowadays,
As doth the flower the weed;

And more, a thousand ways.
This praise I shall her give
When Death doth what he can;
Her honest name shall live
Within the mouth of man.

This worthy lady to bewray—
A king's daughter was she—
Of whom John Heywood list to say,
In such worthy degree.

And Mary was her name, sweet ye,
With these graces indued;
At eighteen years so flourished she :
So doth his mean conclude.

A BALLAD OF THE GREEN WILLOW

All a green willow, willow;
All a green willow is my garland.

Alas! by what mean may I make ye to know
The unkindness for kindness that to me doth
    grow?   [bestow,
That one who most kind love on me should
Most unkind unkindness to me doth show?
   For all the green willow is my garland.

To have love, and hold love, where love is so
    sped,
Oh, delicate food to the lover so fed!
From love won to love lost where lovers be led,
Oh desperate dolour! the lover is dead;
   For all the green willow is my garland.

She said she did love me, and would love me
    still;
She sware above all men I had her good will;
She said and she sware she would my will
    fulfil—
The promise all good, the performance all ill;
   For all the green willow is my garland.

Now, woe worth the willow, and woe worth the
　　wight
That windeth willow, willow garland to dight;
That dole dealt in alms is all amiss quite,
Where lovers are beggars for alms in sight;
　　No lover doth beg for this willow garland.

Of this willow garland the burden seem'th
　　small,
But my break-neck burden I may it well call;
Like the sow of lead on my head it doth fall,
Break head, and break neck, back, bones, brain,
　　heart and all;
　　All parts pressed in pieces.

Too ill for her think I best things may be had;
Too good for me thinketh she things being
　　most bad;
All I do present her that may make her glad;
All she doth present me that make me sad;
　　This equity have I with this willow garland.

Could I forget thee as thou canst forget me,
That were my sound salve, which cannot nor
　　shall be;　　　　　　　　　　　　[flee,
Though thou like the soaring hawk every way
I will be the turtle most steadfast still to thee;
　　And patiently wear this green willow garland.

All ye that have had love, and have my like
　　wrong,　　　　　　　　　　　[among;
My like truth and patience plant still you
When feminine fancies for new love do long,
Old love cannot hold them, new love is so
　　strong
　　For all.

　　　　　　　　FINIS QD. HEYWOOD.

A BALLAD AGAINST
SLANDER AND DETRACTION

*Gar call him down, gar call him down, gar call
    him down, down a:
God send the faction, of all detraction, called
    down and cast away.*

Almighty God
Doth shake His rod
    Of justice, and all those
That unjustly,
Detractively,
    Detract their friends or foes.

He telleth each one:
Thou shalt judge none;
    And if thou judge unbidden,
Thyself, saith He,
Shall judged be;
    This lesson is not hidden.

To this now stirred,
This is concord,
    Which willeth us in each doubt;
To deem the best
That may be jest,
    Till time the truth try out.

Knowing by this,
That think amiss
   Against no man we may;
Much more must we
Ill language flee,
   And call it down, down a;
     Gar call him down, &c.

With sword or skain
To see babes slain,
   Abhorreth to look upon;
Attend to me,
And ye shall see
   Murder and slander one.

Like as a knife,
By rueing life,
   So slander fame hath slain;
And both once doon,
Both alike soon
   May be undone again.

Then what more ill,
With knife to kill,
   Or with the tongue to sting?
With knife or tongue
Strike old or young,
   Both in effect one thing.

These words are short,
But they import
   Sentence at length to way;
Of all which sense,
To flee offence,
   Call slander down I say;
     Gar call him down, &c.

When vice is fought
All vice is nought;
 But some vice worse than some;
And each man sees
Sundry degrees
 In each vice self doth come.

Now sins the least,
We should detest
 Vice or degree in vice;
If in the most
We show our boast,
 That showeth us most unwise.

If I in thee
Such faults once see,
 As no man else doth know;
To thee alone,
And other none,
 These faults I ought to show.

Then of intent
If I invent
 False tales, and them display;
That is most vile,
Which to exile,
 God calleth this down, down a.
  Gar call him down, &c.

Some count no charge
To talk at large
 Such ill as they do hear;
But God's account
Doth not amount
 To take such talkers here.

Of work ill wrought,
When it is fought,
　　In telling forth the same,
Though it be true,
The talk may brew
　　Drink of damnable blame.

To frame excuse
Of tongue's misuse,
　　We have no manner mean;
So that by this
No way there is
　　Ill tales to carry clean.

Which makes me call
Upon you all,
　　As calling call you may;
Tales false or true,
Me to ensue,
　　To call them down, down a.
　　　Gar call him down, &c.

Christ crieth out still:
Say good for ill;
　　But we say harm for harm;
Yea, ill for good
Ill tongues do brood—
　　Wrath is in them so warm.

Slander to fear,
And to forbear—
　　This text stands well in place;
Woe by the tongue,
Whereby is sprung
　　Slander in any case!

To slake this fire
Of slanders ire,
  Repentance must devise
To set all hands
To quench the brands
  With water of our eyes.

Which brand then blow
To make love glow,
  That love by grace may stay,
And by resort
Of good report,
  Call slander down I say.
    Gar call him down, &c.

FINIS QD. HEYWOOD.

A BRIEF BALLET

TOUCHING THE TRAITOROUS TAKING OF
SCARBOROUGH CASTLE

———

Imprinted at London, in Fleete-strete, by Tho. Powell.
Cum privilegio ad imprimendum solum.

———

Oh, valiant invaders! gallantly gay;
  Who, with your compeers, conquering the
    route,
Castles or tow'rs, all standing in your way;
  Ye take, controlling all estates most stout,
  Yet had it now been good to look about,
Scarborough castle to have let alone;
And take Scarborough warning everyone.

By Scarborough castle, not Scarborough
  I only mean—but further, understand,
Each haven, each hold, or other harborough
  That our good King and Queen do hold in
    hand:
  As due obedience bindeth us in band
Their Scarborough castles to let alone;
And take Scarborough warnings everyone.

The scalers of which castles evermore,
    In books of old, and in our eyes of new,
Have always lost themselves, and theirs there-
      fore;
    All this ye did forget in time to view,
    Which might have wrought both you and
      yours t'eschew,
Letting Scarborough castle now alone;
Taking Scarborough warning everyone.

This Scarborough castle simply standing,
    Yet could that castle slyly you beguile;
Ye thought ye took the castle at your landing,
    The castle taking you in the self while:
    Each stone within the castle wall did smile
That Scarborough castle ye let not alone;
And took Scarborough warning everyone.

Your putting now in ure your devilish dream,
    Hath made you see (and like enough to feel)
A few false traitors cannot win a ream;
    Good subjects be, and will be, true as steel
    To stand with you, the end they like no
      deal.
Scarborough castles they can let alone;
And take Scarborough warnings everyone.

They know God's law—to 'bey their King and
      Queen;
    Not take from them, but keep for them their
      own;
And give to them, when such traitors are seen,
    As ye are now, to bring all overthrow.
    They work your overthrow, by God's power
      grown.
God saith—let Scarborough castle alone;
Take Scarborough warning everyone.

Too late for you, and in time for the rest
   Of your most traitorous sect (if any be);
You are all spectacles at full witnessed,
    As other were to you—treason to flee,
    Which in you past, yet may the rest of ye
The said Scarborough castles let alone;
And take Scarborough warnings everyone.

This term, Scarborough warning grew, (some
    say),
   By hasty hanging, for rank robbery there.
Who that was met but suspect in that way,
    Straight was he truss'd up, whatever he
      wear.
    Whereupon, thieves thinking good to for-
      bear,
Scarborough robbing they let that alone;
And took Scarborough warning everyone.

If robbing in that way, bred hanging so,
   By theft to take way, town, castle, and so,
What Scarborough hanging craveth this, lo!
    Were yourselves herein judges capital,
    I think your judgments on these words **must**
      fall,
Scarborough robbing, who lett'th not alone,
Scarborough hanging deserve everyone.

We would to God that you, and all of you
   Had been considered, as well as ye knew
The end of all traitory, as you see it now,
    Long to have lived, loving subjects true.
    Alas! your loss we not rejoice, but rue
That Scarborough castle ye let not alone;
And took Scarborough warning everyone.

To crafts that ever thrive, wise men ever
   cleave;
  To crafts that seeld when thrive, wise men
    seeld when flee;
The crafts that never thrive a fool can learn
  to leave.
  This thriftless crafty craft then clear leave
   we,
  One God, one king, one queen, serve frank
   and free,
Their Scarborough castle let it alone;
Take we Scarborough warning everyone.

One sovereign lord and sovereign lady both,
  Laud we our Lord, for their prosperity;
Beseeching Him for it, as it now go'th,
  Continued so, in perpetuity;
We letting their Scarborough castles alone;
Taking Scarborough warnings everyone.

FINIS.

QUOD. J. HEYWOOD.

A BALLAD

SPECIFYING PARTLY THE MANNER, PARTLY THE
MATTER, IN THE MOST EXCELLENT MEETING
AND LIKE MARRIAGE BETWEEN OUR SOVEREIGN
LORD AND OUR SOVEREIGN LADY THE KING'S
AND QUEEN'S HIGHNESS

PENNED BY JOHN HEYWOOD

Imprinted at London by William Ryddell.

The eagle's bird hath spread his wings,
    And from far off hath taken flight,
In which mean way by no leverings
    On bough or branch this bird would light;
    Till on the rose, both red and white,
He 'lighteth now most lovingly,
And thereto most behovingly.

The month ensuing next to June,
    This bird this flower for perch doth take,
Rejoicingly himself to prune,
    He rouseth ripely to awake
    Upon this perch to those his make:
Concluding straight, for ripe right rest,
In the lion's bower to build his nest.

A bird, a beast, to make, to choose,
  Namely, the beast most furious,
It may seem strange, and so it does,
  And to this bird injurious;
  It seemeth a case right curious
To make construction in such sense,
As may stand for this bird's defence.

But mark, this lion so by name,
  Is properly a lamb t'assign,
No lion wild, a lion tame,
  No rampant lion masculine,
  The lamb-like lion feminine,
Whose mild meek property allureth
This bird to light, and him assureth.

The eagle's bird, the eagle's heir,
  All other birds far surmounting,
The crowned lion matcheth fair,
  Crown unto crown this bird doth bring;
  A queenly queen, a kingly king.
Thus, like to like here matched is—
What match may match more meet than this?

So meet a match in parentage,
  So meet a match in dignity,
So meet a match in patronage,
  So meet match in benignity,
  So matched from all malignity,
As, (thanks to God given for the same),
Seldom hath been seen; thus sayeth the fame.

This meet-met match, at first meeting,
  In their approach together near,
Lowly, lovely, lively greeting,

In each to other did so appear,
  That lookers-on, all must grant clear,
Their usage of such humane reach,
As all might learn, but none could teach.

Thou, in conjoining of these twain,
  Such sacred solemn solemnity,
Such fare in feast to entertain,
  Such notable nobility,
  Such honour with such honesty,
Such joy, all these to plat in plot,
Plat them who can, for I cannot.

But here one dainty president,
  Number so great in place so small,
Nations so many, so different,
  So suddenly met; so agree all,
  Without offensive word let fall;
Save sight of twain, for whom all met,
No one sight there, like this to get.

This lamb-like lion and lamb-like bird,
  To show effect as cause affords,
For that they lamb-like be concurred,
  The lamb of lambs, the lord of lords;
  Let us like lambs, as most accords,
Most meekly thank in humble wise,
As humble heart may most devise.

Which thanks full given most thankfully,
  To prayer fall we on our knees,
That it may like that Lord on high
  In health and wealth to prosper these,
  As faith for their most high degree:
And that all we, their subjects, may
Them and their laws love and obey.

And that between these twain and one,
   The three and one, one once to send.
In one to knit us everyone,
   And to that one such mo at end,
   As his will only shall extend.
Grant this, good God ! adding thy grace,
To make us meet to obtain this case.

FINIS.

A NOTE-BOOK, WORD-LIST, AND INDEX

INCLUDING

REFERENCES, NOTES, A COMPLETE INDEX TO ALL THE PROVERBS, PROVERBIAL SAYINGS, COLLOQUIALISMS, &c., together with a GLOSSARY OF WORDS AND PHRASES now Archaic or Obsolete; the whole arranged in ONE ALPHABET IN DICTIONARY FORM

A FOREWORD TO NOTE-BOOK, WORD-LIST, AND INDEX

Reference from text to Note-Book is copious, and as complete as may be; so also, conversely, from Note-Book to text. The following pages may, with almost absolute certainty, be consulted on any point that may occur in the course of reading.

The scheme of reference from Note-Book to text assumes the division, in the mind's eye, of each page into four horizontal sections; which, beginning at the top, are indicated in the Note-Book by the letters a, b, c, d following the page figure. In practice this will be found easy, and an enormous help to the eye over the usual reference to page alone in " fixing " the " catchword." Thus 126a = the first quarter of page 126; 40c = the third quarter of page 40; and so forth.

The Index to the Proverbs, Proverbial Sayings, Colloquialisms, &c. (specifically as an Index, and not as a Glossary, which indeed would be largely superfluous), is made with much completeness, careful attention being given, as an aid to reference, to Cross-entries. The more noteworthy Proverbs are, in the text, brought into prominence by the use of italics.

[FOR ERRATA SEE PAGE 466.]

INDEX, NOTE-BOOK, AND WORD-LIST

To John Heywood's Proverbs, Epigrams, and Miscellanies

ABJECT, " cast out as an abject " (100b), vagabond, ne'er-do-well, despicable person. " I deemed it better so to die, Than at my foeman's feet an abject lie."— *Mirrour for Magistrates* (1599), 20.

ABROOD, " weather meet to set paddocks abrood in " (50b), *i.e.* weather fit for toads or frogs to be abroad : cf. " fine weather for ducks."

ABSENTETH, " her presence absenteth all maladies " (10c), makes absent, expels, cures : now always with the reflective pronouns. " . . . or what change Absents thee or what chance detains? "—Milton, *Par. Lost* (bk. x.).

ACCOMPTE, " the full accompte " (8d), account : the old spelling. " *Smith.* The clerk of Chatham : he can write and read, and caste accompt."—Shakspeare, 2 *Henry VI.* (1594), iv. 2.

ACCOMPTED (125a), see previous entry.

ACCORDETH, see Rhymes.

ACHE (a) (140c), *i.e.* " aitch "=letter " H " : a play on *ache*=pain.
   (b), see Eye.

ADVIEWED (299b), considered.

ADVOUTRY, " in advoutry to catch him " (71b), adultery. " Calling this match advoutrie, as it was."—*Mirrour for Magistrates* (1599), 342.

HEY. II.   Y

AFLOAT, " thou art afloat " (176a), see also " at an ebb in Newgate . . . afloat at Tyburn " (176b).

AFTERCLAPS, " for fear of afterclaps " (114d), consequences : especially if unexpected or disagreeable ; now chiefly American. " He can give us an after-clap when we least ween."—Latimer, *Sermons* (1515), I. 27.

AGAINST, see Stream.

AGE, " age and appetite fell at a strong strife " (51d).

ALE, (a) " when ale is in wit is out " (200d).
   (b) " as sour ale mendeth in summer " (91b), that is, not at all.
   (c), " thy tales taste all of ale " (189b), i.e. are pot-house yarns ; stories " bemused in beer."

ALE-CLOUT, " wash her face in an ale-clout " (26d), get drunk.

ALL, see Bleed, Hear, Nought.

ALLOWED, " how his lie was allowed " (120c), *allow* = admit, approve, intend, think. " *Alowe*, to make good or allowable, to declare to be true."—Baret, *Alvearie* (1580), A. 297. The usage still survives in America.

ALMONRY, see God.

ALMS, " upon giving an alms " (109c ; 117a), *alms* is singular : the " s " = σ of the original Greek, though now used as a plural.

AM, " God taketh me as I am and not as I was " (90b).

AMATED, " all mirth was amated " (17d), paralysed, checked. " That I amazed and amated am, To see Great Brittaine turn'd to Amsterdam."—Taylor, *Mad Fashions* (1642).

AMEND, " he may soon amend for he cannot appair " (187c), *appair* = get worse : see Apaired.

AMENDED, see Said.

AMENDMENT, " let your amendment amend the matter " (77a).

AN, see And.

ANCHOR, (a) " I will straight weigh anchor and hoist up sail " (21c).

(b) " good riding at two anchors. . . . For if the tone fail, the t'other may hold " (92c), best to have more chances than one : cf. " two strings to one's bow."

AND, AN (*passim*), (a) if ; (b) on.

ANGRY, (a) " he that will be angry without cause, must be at one, without amends " (64c).

(b) " if she be angry, beshrew her angry heart " (44d).

ANOTHER, see Nail.

ANY, see Hear.

APAIR, see Amend.

APAIRED, " so apaired he " (88d), grew worse, degenerated. " I see the more that I them forbear, The worse they be from year to year : All that liveth appaireth fast."—*Everyman* (E.E.D.S., *Anon. Plays,* 1st Ser., 94d) : also Appaireth (131d).

APARTY, " choose we him aparty " (67c), aside, separate. " He that es verrayly meke, God sal safe hym of there, here aparty, and in tother worlde plenerly."—*MS. Coll. Eton.* 10, f. 40.

APE, (a) " she can no more harm than can a she ape " (27d).

(b) As a verb ape=to befool or dupe ; also to *make one an ape.*

APPAIRETH, see Apaired.

APPETITE, " age and appetite fell at a strong strife " (51d).

APPLE, " lost with an apple and won with a nut " (24b). " Nor woman true, but even as stories tell, Won with an egg, and lost again with shell."—Gascoigne, *Ferdinando* (d. 1577).

APPOSITION (281d), conjunction.

ARSE-SMART, " seeds of arse-smart " (289b), a popular name of *Polygonum persicaria.* " Arsmart . . . because if it [water pepper] touch the taile or other bare skinne, it maketh it smart, as often it doth, being laid into the bed greene to kill fleas."—Minsheu, Ductor (1617), 544.

ASCERTAINED, " the King was ascertained " (120*a*), made sure of, satisfied about. " *Mer.* But how shall I be *ascertained* that I also should be entertained? "—Bunyan, *Pilg. Prog.* pt. ii.

ASHES, " raked up in th' ashes and covered again " (58*b*).

ASK, see Thief.

ASPEN-LEAF, " thy tongue . . . that aspen-leaf " (85*c*).

ASS, " the dun ass hath trod on both thy feet " (181*d*) : see Black ox.

ASSAY, " I will assay to win some favour " (21*d*), endeavour, try, essay. " Yet wol I make assay."—Chaucer, *Cant. Tales* (1383), 13177. Also 139*b*.

ASSISH, " his assish stalking " (118*c*), foolish. " Passe not, therfore, though Midas prate, And assishe judgement give."—*Galfrido and Bernardo* (1570).

ASSOIL, " assoil thy question " (119*a*), solve, answer.

ASSURANCE, " words of assurance " (5*d*), affiance, betrothal. " This druge, diviner laid claim to me ; called me Dromio ; swore I was assured to her."—Shakspeare, *Comedy of Errors* (1593), iii. 2.

ATTACHETH (117*c*), attacketh. " I cannot blame thee ; Who am myself attach'd with weariness, To the dulling of my spirits."—Shakspeare, *Tempest* (1609), iii. 3.

ATTENDANCE, see Danceth.

AUDRY, see Saint Audry.

AUMBRY, see Cough.

AVAIL, (*a*) " avail, unhappy hook " (44*a*), *i.e.* Away ! Begone ! you are defeated in your purpose ; *hook* = a term of reproach. " That unhappy hook."—*Jack Juggler* (E.E.D.S., *Anon. Plays*, Ser. 3), 26*c* and 35*d*. (*b*) " vain avails " (261*d*), no purpose or profit.

AVANCED, " which should me much avanced " (22*a*), profited, advanced.

AXE, (*a*) " I send th' axe after helve away " (97*b*), *i.e.* I despair ; " in for a penny, in for a pound."

(b) " without ye axe me leave " (97c), ask : the word and also the construction, once literary, are now vulgar.

BABE, see Knave.

BABLE ; " how may bables be missed among fools " (189b), bauble (or bable)=a badge of office of the domestic fool : see other volumes of this series.

BACHELORS, (a) " bachelors boast how they will teach their wives good " (74d), hence bachelor's wife=an ideal wife : see *infra*.

(b) " bachelors' wives and maids' children be well taught " (75a). " The maid's child is ever best taught."—Latimer, *Sermons* (1562), v. " Ay, ay, bachelors' wives, indeed, are finely governed."—Vanbrugh, *Provoked Wife* (1726), i. 1.

BACK, see Clawed, Clothes, Horse.

BACKARE, " Backare, quoth Mortimer to his sow " (41c ; 208a and b), *i.e.* " Go back," " Give place," " Away " : the allusion is lost, though the phrase is common enough in old writers, the earliest dating about 1473.

BAG, (a) " he brought the bottom of the bag clean out " (98d), to make an end of things, to tell all, to lose all.

(b) " I know him as well as the beggar knoweth his bag " (38b ; 227a). " As well as the beggar knows his dish," is another form of this proverb found in *The Burning of Paules Church in London*, by Bishop Pilkington (1561).

BAKER, " so late met, that I fear we part not yet, quoth the baker to the pillory " (57b) : severe penalties for impurity of bread or shortness of weight were enforced against bakers from very early times ; they were frequently the subject of much sarcasm. " A pillorie for the punishment of bakers, offending in the assize of bread."—Stow, *Survey* (1598), 208. " They say the owl was a baker's daughter."—Shakspeare, *Hamlet* (1602), iv. 5. " Are not bakers' armes the skales of Iustice? yet is not their bread light."—Dekker, *Honest Whore* (1604). " Three dear years will raise a baker's daughter to a portion. 'Tis not the smallness of the bread, but the knavery of the baker."—Ray, *Proverbs.*

BALD, " bald as a coot " (13*d*), as bald as may be : the frontal plate of the coot is destitute of feathers. (See Tyndale, *Works*, 1530, ii. 224.)

BALE, (*a*) " this rather bringeth bale than boot " (63*d*), *bale*=trouble, sorrow ; *boot*=help, cure, relief. " God send every man boot of his bale."—Chaucer, *Cant. Tales* (1483), 13409.

(*b*), see Hekst.

BALL, " thou hast stricken the ball under the line " (42*b*), *i.e.* a line regarded as marking the limit of legitimate or successful play. " Poor mortals are so many balls, Toss'd some o'er line, some under fortune's walls."—Howell, *Letters* (1645).

BALLADS. See " John Heywood as a Ballad-monger " in " Terminal Essay " (Heywood's *Works* III).

BANKETS, " bonfires and bankets " (120*a*), banquets. " A great banket of meat."—Wever, *Lusty Juventers* (E.E.D.S. *Works* 28*b*).

BANNING, " be as be may is no banning " (53*b* ; 219*a*).

BARE, see Breech, Buckle, Leg.

BARGAINS, " some bargains dear bought good cheap would be sold " (19*c*), *cheap*=market : *good cheap*= bon marché. " He buys other men's cunning good cheap in London, and sells it deare in the country."— Dekker, *Belman's Night Walk* (1608).

BARGE, see Oar.

BARREL, (*a*) " in neither barrel better herring " (102*c*), not a pin to choose between, six of one and half a dozen of the other ; elliptical—no one barrel contains herrings better than another. " Lyke Lord, lyke chaplayne, neyther barrel better herynge."—Bale, *Kynge John*. " Begin where you will, you shall find them all alike, never a barrell the better herring."—Burton, *Anat. Melan.* (1621).

(*b*) see Beerpot.

BASS (70*c*), to cuddle, snuggle up to, give a smacking kiss : once literary. " I lye *bassing* with Besse."— More, *Works*, 557. " Thy knees bussing the stones." —Shakspeare, *Coriol.* (1610), iii. 2.

BASTETH, see Hog.

BAUBLE, see Bable.

BAUDRY, " suspicion of their baudry " (73*d*), wantonness, lechery.

BAYARD, " to have kept Bayard in the stable " (47*c*).
See Blind Bayard.

BE, (*a*) " be as be may is no banning " (53*b* ; 219*a*).
   (*b*) " that shall be, shall be " (53*b*).   See Shall.

BEAD-ROLL, " a bead-roll to unfold " (77*b*), a story,
narration ; specifically (as here) a catalogue of woes :
properly a list of those for whom a certain number
of prayers were offered, the count being kept by the
telling of beads.

BEAN, (*a*) " a bean in a monk's hood " (76*c* ; 204*a*).
   (*b*) " begging of her booteth not the worth of a
bean " (30*a*), a standard of the smallest value.
   (*c*) " the bigger eateth the bean " (68*d*).   " For I
am wery of this renning about, And yet alway I stand
in great doubt Least that the bigger wyll eate the
Been."—*XII Mery Jests of the Wyddow Edyth* (1525).

BEAR, (*a*) " bear with them that bear with you " (88*b*).
   (*b*) see Faces, Sow, Stake.

BEAR BUGS (261*c*), bugbears : *bug*=an object of terror,
a spectre, hobgoblin.

BEARDS, see Merry.

BEAT, see Bush.

BEAUTIFUL, " my beautiful marriage " (8*b*), *i.e.* marriage for beauty's sake.

BECK, " a beck as good as a dieu gard " (29*d*), nod,
salutation.   " Nods and becks and wreathèd smiles."
—Milton, *L'Allegro* (1637).

BED, see Ill, Leg.

BEDLAM, " after Bedlam sort " (78*a*), crazy, violently (or
madly) angry.

BEERPOT, " she was made like a beerpot or a barrel "
(52*a*), well rounded in the stomach, corpulent.

BEES, see Folk, Head, Quick.

BEFORNE (*passim*), before.

BEG, see Breech, Steal, Wrong.

BEGGAR, (a) " beggars should be no choosers " (29b; 170b). " Beggers must be no choosers ; In every place, I take it, but the stocks."—Beaumont and Fletcher, *Scornful Lady*, v. 3.

(b) see Bag, Lord, Thieves.

(c) " one beggar to beg of another " (100a).

BEGINNING, (a) " a hard beginning maketh a good ending (11a ; 170d).

(b) " of a good beginning there cometh a good end " (196c).

(c) see End, Fit, Ill.

BEHIND, see Best, Further, Worst.

BELL, (a) " Who shall tie the bell about the cat's neck " (38d ; 219c).

(b) " she beareth the bell " (27d), carries away the prize.

BELLY, " when the belly is full the bones would be at rest " (55b).

BELZABUB, " a baby of Belzabub's bower " (62c).

BENCH, " he must have the bench " (35b).

BENCHWHISTLER (37c ; 199a), loafer, idler on an ale-house bench.

BENT, see Bow, Break.

BESHREW, generally in imperative. " Beshrew your heart "=woe to you. " I beshrew all shrews."—Shakspeare, *Love's Labour's Lost* (1594), v. 2.

BESIDE, see Cushion.

BEST, (a) " the best is behind " (195b to d).

(b) " the plain fashion is best " (210a and b).

(c) see Truth, Wins.

(d) " the best is best cheap " (81b), the best is cheapest in the end.

BESTILL, " a good bestill is worth a groat " (68c), *bestail*=a law term for all kinds of cattle : Fr., *bétail*.

BETIMES, see Sharp thorn.

BETTER, see Bird, Break, Brim, Cap, Children, Fed, Horse, Late, Rule, Seldom, Sit, Unborn, Wish.

BETWEEN, see Stools.

BEWARE, see Fox, Had, Harms.

BEWRAYED, " things . . . might be bewrayed " (65b), spoilt, muddled, complicated.

BEYOND, see Moon.

BIBLIOGRAPHY. *The Dialogue of the Effectual Proverbs in the English language Concerning Marriage* seems to have been first printed, apart from the collected editions of *Heywood's Works* (*Proverbs and Epigrams*), in 1546 by T. Berthelet. A copy of this quarto appeared in the Roxburghe sale in 1812, and fetched £4 10s. Lowndes says this edition was reprinted in 1547, 1549, and 1556. Another edition, " newly overseen and somewhat corrected," appeared in 1561 in 8vo, an imperfect copy of which is preserved in the British Museum. In the following year it was appended to his *Epigrams*, and the whole was published as *John Heywoodes Woorkes*. This is the edition (collated with that of 1566) which forms the text of the present reprint. Another edition appeared in 1566, which Hazlitt erroneously says was " a reprint, without alterations, of the edition of 1562 " (see Variorum Readings). Further editions appeared in 1576, 1587 (? edited by Thomas Newton, of Cheshire) and 1598. Altogether, ten editions within the first fifty years : a record that is not often surpassed ! Moreover, it would appear from Dibdin (iv. 421) that the *Epigrams* were printed separately on flyleaves or broadsides ; as he states that he possessed two, printed on a long slip of paper, on one side only, and bearing an imprint—" Printed at London for Rowland Hall for James Rowbotham, and are to be sold at his shoppe under Bow Churche." Concerning the Ballads see the *Terminal Essay* [Works (E.E.D.S.) III.]. The text has been modernised except in cases where the rhyme or the interest attaching to a particular usage seemed to render desirable the retention of the old spelling. The punctuation has been altered only so far as to make intelligible what would otherwise be obscure.

BID, " his paternoster to bid " (136b), *to bid beads* originally = to pray prayers with or without a rosary, hence to count beads, each one dropped passing for a prayer.

BIG, see Body.

BILL, see Wing.

BIND, see Fast.

BIRD, (a) "better one bird in hand than ten in the wood" (36d ; 173d), possession is everything ; hazard of loss is not worth uncertain gain ; the modern "two in the *bush*," is not so exacting. Fr., "*Mieux vaux un tenez, que deux vous l'aurez.*" "An old proverb maketh with this which I take good. Better one bird in hand then ten in the wood."—Heywood, *Witty and Witless* (c. 1530), *Works* (E.E.D.S.) I., 213b.

(b) "it is a foul bird that fileth his own nest" (70d), *fileth*=defileth : the proverb occurs as early as 1250 in *The Owl and the Nightingale.* "Rede and lerne ye may, Howe olde proverbys say, that byrd ys nat honest, That fylyth hys owne nest."—Skelton, *Garnesche* (1520).

(c) "as bare as a bird's arse" (89a), as bare as may be.

(d) "the birds were flown" (47d ; 223d ; 224a).

(e) "when birds shall roost . . . who shall appoint their hour, the cock or hen?" (56b) ; compare "He who pays the piper may call the tune."

(f) "we shall catch birds to-morrow" (88c).

(g) "I hear by one bird that in mine ear was late chanting" (70a) ; modern, "a little bird told me."

(h) see Bush and Crow.

BIRDERS, BIRDING, "birders . . . in their birding" (151b), bird-catchers, bird-catching. "I do invite you to-morrow morning to my house to breakfast ; after we'll a birding together."—Shakspeare, *Merry Wives* (1596), iii. 3.

BIT, see Rough bit.

BITE, see Brain, Cat, Flies.

BLAB, "look what she knoweth, blab it wist and out it must" (24a), *i.e.* anything a blab knows must be told. "Labbe hyt whyste and owt yt muste."—*MS. Harleian* (c. 1490).

BLACK, "black will take none other hue" (92c).

BLACK OX, "black ox never trod on thy foot" (17c ;

181c), the black ox is the symbol of decrepitude or misfortune. " Venus waxeth old : and then she was a
pretie wench, when Juno was a young wife; now
crowes foote is on her eye, and the black oxe hath
trod on her foot."—Lyly, *Sapho* (1584).

BLE, " to cry ble " (34c), ble=bleat, as a sheep. One
of the *Hundred Mery Tales* (c. 1525) is entitled " Of
the husbande that cryed ble under the bed." " I hear
a young kid blea."—*Jacob and Esau* (1568), iv. 6.
(E.E.D.S. *Anon. Pl.* 2 Ser., 59c.)

BLEED, " here doth all lie and bleed " (68c ; 211c).

BLESS, " ye bless them all, but ye bass but one " (84d),
see Children.

BLESSING, " ye can give me your blessing in a clout "
(96b), *i.e.* the hoard (or talent) wrapped up in a
napkin, bag, or " stocking."

BLIND, (a) " who so deaf or so blind as is he that wilfully will never hear nor see? " (91a).
   (b) " the blind eat many flies " (73b ; 201b ; 220b).
" The blinde eateth many a flye : So doth the husband often, iwis, Father the childe that is not his."
—*Schole-house of Women* (1541), line 333.
   (c) " blind men should judge no colours " (73a ;
190a).
   (d) " as the blind man casts his staff or shoots the
crow " (96b).
   (e) " where the blind leadeth the blind both fall in
the dyke " (67b). " She hath hem in such wise
daunted, That they were, as who saith, enchaunted ;
And as the blinde an other ledeth, And till they falle
nothing dredeth."—Gower, *Confessio Amantis.*
   (f) " folk ofttimes are most blind in their own
cause " (73a), or, as in modern phrase, " blind to one's
own interests."
   (g) " the difference between staring and stark
blind, The wise man at all times to follow can find "
(82a).

BLIND BAYARD, " who so bold as blind Bayard is? "
(19d ; 185d), of persons who act without consideration
or reflection; generic for blindness, ignorance, and
recklessness. It occurs in *The Vision of Piers the
Ploughman* (1362), and in Chaucer's *Canterbury*

Tales (1383). *Bayard* originally=a grey horse; afterwards generic; and Skelton mentions a description of horse-loaf called "Bayard's bun." Bayard was a horse famous in old romances. See Bayard.

BLIND HARPERS, see Harpers.

BLISS, (*a*) " our Lord bliss me " (79*d*)—" not one penny to bliss him " (89*a*), bless.
    (*b*) see Branch.

BLISSING, " this busy blissing and nodding " (115*c*), *bliss*=to wave about, brandish, sway to and fro: probably from the lifting up of hands in consecration; " hardly (O.E.D.) an independent word."

BLIST, " by God's blist " (29*d*), bliss, joy, happiness.

BLOCK, see Straw.

BLOCKS, " I have more blocks in his way to lay " (70*a*). obstructions, hindrances, impediments.

BLOW, see Cold, Wind.

BOAST, (*a*) " this matter maketh boast of diminution " (101*a*), *to make boast*=to promise well, to seem very likely. " Nought trow I the triumphe of Julius, Of which that Lukan maketh moche bost."—Chaucer, *Cant. Tales* (1383), 4820-21.
    (*b*) " Great boast and small roast Maketh unsavoury mouths wherever men host " (36*c*), *i.e.* large promise and little performance is little to one's liking: *host*=lodge, abide.

BODKINS, " bodkins the tone " (206*c*), a mild imprecation.

BODY, (*a*) " the big part of her body is her bum " (24*c*).
    (*b*) see Leg.

BOLD, see Blind Bayard.

BOLT, (*a*) " mend, as the fletcher mends his bolt " (91*a*).
    (*b*) see Fool.

BONE, see Belly, Flesh and Tongue.

BONGRACE (52*a*), a forehead cloth, or covering for the head; a kind of veil attached to a hood: afterwards the hood itself. " Her bongrace which she wore."—Heywood, *Pardoner and Frere, Works* (E.E.D.S.), I. 7*c*.

BOOD, see Bud.

BOOK, see Cross.

BOORD, " in earnest or boord " (47d), jest, joke, mock, sport. " Speak but in bord."—Udall, *Roister Doister* (1550), 75d (E.E.D.S., *Works*). See also Bourd.

BOOT, (a) " it booteth not the worth of a bean " (30a), remedy, cure, help, advantage. " This knight thinketh his boot thou may'st be."—*Calisto and Melibœa* (E.E.D.S., *Anon Pl.*, 1st Ser.).

   (b) see Hekst.

BORAGE, " a leaf of borage might buy all the substance that they can sell " (25c), *i.e.* just such a trifle as would be a leaf of borage in a salad, as a pot-herb, or as an ingredient in cool tankards.

BORROW, (a) " not so good to borrow as to be able to lend " (25d).

   (b) " till liberty was borrow " (27c), pledged, mortgaged. " To borrow man's soul from blame."—*World and Child* (c. 1500), E.E.D.S., *Anon. Pl.*, Ser. I., 186 b. Also as *subs* (168d).

   (c) see Day.

BOSOM, " she speaketh as she would creep into your bosom " (23d).

BOTCHER, see God.

BOTE, " she bote, he cried " (297b), bit. " He bote his lippes."—*Piers Plow. Vis.*, v. 84.

BOTTOM, see Brim.

BOUGET, " in her bouget " (75b), budget, bag, (and figuratively) store. " With that out of his bouget forth he drew Great store of treasure, therewith him to tempt."—Spenser, *Fairy Queen* (1590), III. x. 29.

BOUGHT, see Dear, Wit.

BOUND, " they that are bound must obey " (68b).

BOURD, " sooth bourd is no bourd " (88a; 183b), a jest spoken in earnest is no jest at all; *sooth*=earnest, *bourd*=a jest: see Boord. " As the old saying is, sooth boord is no boord."—Harrington, *Briefe Apologie of Poetrie* (1591).

BOW, (a) " a bow long bent, at length must wear weak " (34c), *i.e.* a bow drawn back to the utmost and often : hence " to the top of one's bent " (see also the next line of text and the next entry).

(b) " the bent of your . . . bow " (37a ; 218a), inclination, tendency, disposition, course of action.

(c) " Many strings to the bow " (37a), alternatives, more resources than one. " I am wel pleased to take any coulor to defend your honor, and hope that you wyl remember, that who seaketh two stringes to one bowe, the may shute strong, but never strait."—*Letter of Queen Elizabeth to James VI.* (June, 1585).

(d) see Break.

BOWED SILVER (274b), crooked, bent money.

BOWL, " this seven years, day and night to watch a bowl " (71c), *seven years*=a long time (generic) : *i.e.* may watch his coming and going a long time without discovering anything.

BOX, " in the wrong box " (92a), mistaken, embarrassed, in jeopardy. " Sir, quoth I, if you will hear how St. Augustine expoundeth that place, you shall perceive that you are in a wrong box."—Ridley (" Foxe," 1838), vi. 438 (1554).

BOY ROPE, " haleth her by the boy rope " (78b), ? *bowrope*=(a) ox-bow ; (b) a rope of bow-string hemp ; or (c) bow-string. *Hale*, in Early English, is employed in various ways indicative of rapid movement.

BRAIN, " bitten to the brain " (45c), drunk : cf. " hair of the dog that bit one."

BRANCH, " ere . . . branch of bliss could reach any root the flower . . . faded " (17c).

BRAWLING, " brawling booteth not " (57c), *i.e.* tends to no advantage : *booteth*=profiteth.

BREAD, (a) " one . . . that would have better bread than is made of wheat " (81b).

(b) " know on which side bread is buttered " (86c), recognise one's interests : whence *to butter one's bread on both sides*=to seek advantages from more sides than one.

(c) " better is half a loaf than no bread " (37c), the earliest known example of this proverb.

(d) see Sheep's flesh.

(c) " within a hair bread " (135d).—" That he destroied this lond in brede & in length."—*R. Brunne*, p. 41.

BREAK, (*a*) " better is to bow than break " (22*a*; 199*c*). An early example is found in *The Morale Proverbs of Cristyne;* originally written in French about the year 1390 and of which a verse translation by Earl Rivers was printed by Caxton in 1478 : " Rather to bowe than breke is profitable, Humylite is a thing commendable."

   (*b*) " in that house . . . a man shall as soon break his neck as his fast " (40*c*).

BREAKETH, see Inch, Tongue.

BREATH, see Death.

BREECH, (*a*) " nothing more vain than . . . to beg a breech of a bare-arsed man " (20*c*).

   (*b*) " the master weareth no breech " (58*c*; also 208*c* *Epigrams*), is not master : *to wear the breeches*=to usurp a husband's prerogative (of women). " All women be suche, Thoughe the man bere the breeche, They wyll be ever checkemate."—*Boke of Mayd Emlyn* (1515).

BREED, see Pad.

BREEDETH, see Burr.

BRETCH, " in all that bretch " (93*b*), breach, quarrel, source of dissension.

BREW, " as I . . . brew, so must I . . . drink " (19*a*), in allusion to cause and effect. " If you have browen wel, you shal drinke the better."—Wodroephe, *Spared Houres of a Souldier* (1623).

BRIDAL (15*b*), a note as to the origin of the word may not be without interest. (*a*) " There were bride-ales, church-ales, clerk-ales, give-ales, lamb-ales, leet-ales, Midsummer-ales, Scot-ales, Whitsun-ales, and several more."—Brand's *Popular Antiquities*.

   (*b*) " it is meet that a man be at his own bridal " (15*b*), a variant of " every man must attend his own funeral."

BRIDLE, (*a*) " I gave her the bridle at beginning " (87*b*), let her have her own way.

   (*b*) " she taketh the bridle in the teeth and runneth

away with it " (87b), the modern version alters
" bridle " to " bit."

(c) see Rough Bit.

BRIDLED, " I should have bridled her first with rough
bit, To have made her chew on the bridle one fit "
(87b), fit=a portion or bout of anything—stanza of a
song, stave of a tune, scene of a play, round at fisti-
cuffs : here=a space of time.

BRIKE, " ye brike all from her, that brought all to you "
(76a), brike=breach, violation of, or injury done to,
anyone : hence deplete, " suck dry " (of money and
goods).

BRIM, " better spare at brim than at bottom " (66c),
i.e. at the beginning rather than at the end of one's
tether.

BROID, " better dissemble . . . than to broid him with
it " (69b), braid, abraid, reproach.

BROKEN, see Pot.

BROKER, see Knave.

BROOM, " the green new broom sweepeth clean " (54a),
still proverbial ; in the *Epigrams* " new broom sweepeth clean " is nearer the modern version (178a).

BROTHER, " I will not trust him though he were my
brother " (40c).

BUCKETS, see Well.

BUCKLE, " till he at length came to buckle and bare
thong " (89a), poverty, distress : thong=shoestring.

BUD, " This bood sheweth what fruit will follow "
(26b), bood=bud.

BUG, " bug's words " (66c), swaggering or threatening
language ; also " bugbear words " ; of " such bugbear
thoughts " (Locke). Bug=an object of terror, bogey.
" Matrimony hath euer been a blacke bugge in their
sinagoge and churche."—Bale, *Votaryes* (Pref.) : see
Bear bugs.

BUILT, see Rome.

BULL, see Cow calf.

BUM, see Body.

BURDEN, "light burden far heavy" (97*b*; 188*c* and *d*; 189*a*).

BURNT CHILD, see Child.

BURR, (*a*) "I take her for a rose, but she breedeth a burr" (26*b*).

(*b*) "they cleave together like burrs" (72*b*).

BUSH, (*a*) "while I . . . beat the bush . . . other men . . . catch the birds" (9*a*). Henry the Fifth is reported to have uttered this proverb at the siege of Orleans, when the citizens, besieged by the English, declared themselves willing to yield the town to the Duke of Burgundy, who was in the English camp. "Shall I beat the bush, and another take the bird?" said King Henry. The Duke was so offended that he withdrew his troops and concluded a peace. "I beat the bush, and others catch the bird, Reason exclaimes and sweares my hap is hard."—Pettowe, *Philochasander and Elanira* (1599).

(*b*) see Bird.

BUTTER, (*a*) "there will no butter cleave on my bread" (86*c*), *i.e.* nothing by which to profit or advantage.

(*b*) "it is not all butter that the cow shits" (94*d*).

(*c*) "she looketh as butter would not melt in her mouth" (27*b*), in contempt of persons of simple demeanour. "A cette parolle mist dame Mehault ses mains à ses costez et en grant couroux luy respondy que . . . et que, Dieu merci, aincores fondoit le burre en sa bouche, combien qu'elle ne peust croquier noisettes, car elle n'avoit que un seul dent."—*Les Evangiles des Quenouilles* (*c.* 1475).

(*d*) "As sure as it were sealed with butter" (86*c*; 189*d*), shaky, uncertain.

BUTTERED, see Bread.

BUTTERY, "thy buttery door" (125*c*), a larder for dairy stuff: hence (now chiefly at the universities and colleges) a pantry for provisions generally.

BUY, (*a*) "you to buy and sell" (23*d*), betray, impose upon, do for utterly.

(*b*) see Borage, Pig.

BY AND BY (50*a, et passim*), immediately, forthwith.

HEY. II.   Z

CAGE, see Cow.

CAKE, " would ye both eat your cake and have your cake? " (96a).

CALF, see Cow and Cow calf.

CALL, " things past my hands I cannot call again " (26a).

CALLET (70b), scold, drab, trull. " A wisp of straw were worth a thousand crowns, To make this shameless callet know herself—Helen of Greece was fairer far than thou."—Shakspeare, 3 *Henry VI.* (1592), ii. 2.

CALVES, " change of pasture maketh fat calves " (62a). " *Boniface.* You may see what change of pasture is able to do. *Honeysuckle.* It makes fat calves in Romney Marsh, and lean knaves in London, therefore, Boniface, keep your ground."—Dekker and Webster, *Westward Hoe* (1607).

CAMBERS, " gable ends, cambers, parlours " (239d), chambers.

CAMMOCK, " timely crooketh the tree that would a cammock be " (94a), *cammock* = a crooked tree or beam, a knee of timber : as used in shipbuilding. " Camocks must be bowed with sleight not strength."—Lyly, *Sappho and Phao* (1591).

CAN, (a) " can very good skill " (12a), know, able, possess. " Though he be ignorant and can little skill." —*Four Elements* (c. 1510), E.E.D.S., *Anon. Pl.*, Ser. I., 3c.
　(b) see Cup, Thank.

CANDLE, (a) " to set up a candle before [or hold a candle to] the devil " (24d ; 173b), propitiate through fear, to assist in, or wink at, wrong-doing. " Though not for hope of good, yet for the feare of euill, Thou maist find ease so proffering up a candell to the deuill."— Tusser, *Husbandrie* (1557), 148.
　(b) " upright as a candle standeth in the socket " (52b), as erect as may be.
　(c) " who that worst may shall hold the candle " (56d).
　(d) see Cat.

CANSTICK, " coll under canstick " (24b), coll = (a) kiss, embrace, or (b), deceit: see Coleprophet; canstick = candlestick, which was very generally pronounced thus. There was, however, a Christmas game called " coll (or coal) under canstick."—(Harsenet, Ded. Pop. Impost, 1603.)

CAP, " my cap is better at ease than my head " (85d; 177c).

CARDS, " tell thy cards and then tell me what thou hast won " (36b).

CARE, see Corner.

CARPENTER, " such carpenters, such chips " (80d), " like to its like." " New. By the faith of my body, such carpenter, such chips, And as the wise man said, such lettuce, such lips. For, like master, like man: like tutor, like scholar; And, like will to like, quoth the Devil to the Collier."—Fulwell, Like Will to Like (E.E.D.S.), 24d.

CARRAIN, " her carrain carcase " (56c), rotten, withered: a generic reproach.

CARRIER, " I will send it him by John Long the carrier " (35d), see John Long.

CARRON, " daws are carron " (151a), carrion.

CART, (a) " set the cart before the horse " (79a), to begin at the wrong end; to set things hind side before: Fr. " Il mettoyt la charette devant les beufz " (Rabelais). " He deemes that a preposterous government where the wife predominates, and the husband submits to her discretion, that is Hysterion and Proteron, the cart before the horse."—Harry White, his Humour.

(b) " the best cart may overthrow " (35c), " accidents may happen," " there's nothing certain save the unforeseen."

(c) " I am cast at cart's arse " (21b), in disgrace: offenders were formerly punished by being flogged when tied to the hinder part of a driven cart.

(d) " carts well driven go long upright " (35c), see section b supra.

CARTERLY, " carterly knave " (145d), " carterly collar " (258c), rough, unmannerly.

CARTWEAR, " cartwear of good horse " (186c), carter, driver.

CARVING, " he at meat carving her, and none else before, Now carved he to all but her, and her no more " (54b).

CASE, (a) " put case " (*passim*), to suppose or propose a hypothetical instance or illustration : an idiomatic expression formerly common in arguments. " Put case there be three brethren, John-a-Nokes, John-a-Nash, and John-a-Stile."—*Returne from Parnassus* (1606).

    (b) " clear out of the case " (32a), out of the running, beyond consideration.

CAST, (a) " privy nips or casts overthwart the shins " (24c)—" even the like cast hast thou " (33d)—" ye nother care nor wellnigh cast what ye pay " (81c), both as subs. and verb *cast* was in full work—throw, motion, turn, glance, blow, advice, counsel, plan, design, object of desire, attempt at flight, skill, art, trick, juggle, fashion, form, pattern, shade, colour, tinge, chance, venture, touch, stroke, and many more glosses beside, each with their corresponding verbal usages.

    (b) see Cart, Hog, Moon, Sheep's eye, Shoe, Turn.

CASTETH, see Moon.

CASTING, " far casting for commonwealth " (50d), roundabout search for joint benefit.

CAT, (a) " a cat may look on a king " (70c ; 189c), said of impertinent or misplaced interference ; there are certain things an inferior may do in the presence of a superior.

    (b) " the cat would (or will) eat fish and would (or will) not wet her feet " (34d ; 220a) ; cf. Shakspeare (*Macbeth*), " Letting, I dare not, wait upon, I would, Like the poor cat i' the adage." " Cat lufat visch, ac he nele his feth wete."—*MS. Trin. Coll. Camb.* (c. 1250).

    (c) " a woman hath nine lives like a cat " (60c ; 203b).

    (d) " let the cat wink and let the mouse run " (61b ; 213d ; 214a).

    (e) " it hath need to be a wily mouse that should

breed in the cat's ear " (71d). " A hardy mowse that
is bold to breede In cattis eeris."—*Order of Foles*,
MS. (*c.* 1450). " It is a wyly mouse That can build
his dwellinge house Within the cattes eare."—Skelton
(1520).

(*f*) " somewhat it is . . . when the cat winketh and
both her eyne out " (61a).

(*g*) " cat after kind, good mouse hunt " (33c).
" Cat after kind . . . sweet milk will lap."—*Jacob
and Esau* (1568), iv. 4 (E.E.D.S. *Anon. Pl.* 2 Ser.,
58a).

(*h*) " little and little the cat eateth the flickle " (82b).

(*i*) " no playing with a straw before an old cat "
(88a).

(*j*) " the cat knoweth whose lips she licketh " (98b).
" Li vilains reproche du chat Qu'il set bien qui barbes
il leche."—*Des trois Dames qui trouvèrent un Anel*
(*c.* 1300).

(*k*) " to turne the cat in the pan " (79a), to " rat ";
to reverse one's position through self-interest; to play
the turncoat; the derivation is absolutely unknown;
cat=" cate " or " cake " is historically (says Murray)
untenable. " Now am I true araid like a phesitien; I
am as very a turncote as the wethercoke of Poles;
For now I will calle my name Due Disporte. So, so,
finely I can turne the catt in the pane."—*Wit and
Wisdom* (E.E.D.S., *Anon. Pl.,* Ser. 4), 3 (*c.* 1559).
" As for Bernard, often tyme he turneth the cat in the
pan."—Shacklock, *Hatchet of Heresies* (1565).

(*l*) " my cat's leering look . . . showeth me that
my cat goeth a catterwawing " (70c), *i.e.* is given to
wantonness.

(*m*) " they two agreed like two cats in a gutter "
(54c).

(*n*) " by scratching and biting cats and dogs come
together " (54c).

(*o*) " when all candles be out cats be grey " (13c),
cf. " If you cannot kiss the mistress kiss the maid ";
" Joan in the dark is as good as my lady."

(*p*) see Bell.

CATCH, (*a*) " catch that catch may " (226d), in modern
form, " catch as catch can."

(*b*) see Hare.

CATTERWAWING, see Cat.

CAUSE, " cause causeth " (22*b*).

CHA, see Cham.

CHAD, see Cham.

CHAIR, " every man may not sit in the chair " (46*c*), it is not given to everyone to rule; all cannot be masters.

CHALK, (*a*) " to compare in taste, chalk and cheese " (63*c*), to compare (or mistake) things utterly different. The modern form is " to know chalk from cheese "=to have one's wits about one, to know what is worthless from what is of value. " Lo ! how they feignen chalk for cheese."—Gower, *Confessio Amantis* (1393). " Though I have no learning, yet I know chese from chalke."—*John Bon and Mast Person* (1548). " Do not these thynges differ as muche as chalcke and chese ? "—Shacklock, *Hatchet of Heresies* (1565). " To French and Scots so fayr a taell I tolde, That they beleeved whyt-chalk and chees was oen."—Churchyard, *Chippes* (1573).
(*b*) " alike in colour to deem ink and chalk " (63*c*), a variant of the foregoing entry.

CHAM, " cham ashamed " (136*b*), cham=I am : the conventional rustic speech of early plays is a mixture of southern and northern dialect, but chiefly the former. See other volumes of this series.

CHANGE, (*a*) " change be no robbery " (63*b* ; 204*b*), an excuse for a forced or jesting imposition ; a delicate way of making a present : now usually " fair exchange is no robbery."
(*b*) see Calves.

CHANGED, " would to God he and you had changed places " (80*c*).

CHAT, " no man may chat ought in ought of her charge " (24*b*), chat=talk. " Into a rapture lets her baby cry, While she chats him . . ."—Shakspeare, *Coriolanus* (1610), ii. 1.

CHATTING, " chatting to chiding is not worth a chute " (69*a*), it is hardly worth while to answer a scolding.

CHEAP, see Bargains, Best.

CHEAPEN, " cheapen a cony " (242*d*), price a rabbit.

CHECK, " checks and choking oysters " (43*c*; 122*c*; 135*b*; 244*c*), taunts, reproaches : see Choking oyster.

CHECKER, " not checker a-boord, all was not clear in the coast " (89*b*) ? *a-boord* = to jest, the prefix *a* being the old intensive. " Not as a checker, reprover, or despiser."—Coverdale, *Lewis's Hist. Bible into English*, 95.

CHEESE, (*a*) " ye may see no green cheese, but your teeth must water " (97*c*), *green cheese* = cream cheese.
    (*b*) see Chalk.

CHICKENS, (*a*) " there is a nest of chickens, which doth brood, That will sure make his hair grow through his hood " (66*b*), *i.e.* deceived, cuckolded as it were.

CHIDING, see Chatting.

CHIEVING (10*d* and 48*d*), doing, accomplishment.

CHIL, see Cham.

CHILD, " burnt child, fire dreadeth " (55*b*), once bit, twice shy. " So that child withdraweth is hond, From the fur ant the brond, That hath byfore bue brend, Brend child fur dredth, Quoth Hendyng."— *Proverbs of Hendyng*, MS. (*c*. 1320). " *Timon*. Why urge yee me? my hart doth boyle with heate, And will not stoope to any of your lures : A burnt childe dreads the ffyre."—*Timon* (*c*. 1590).

CHILDREN, (*a*) " children learn to creep ere they can learn to go " (37*b* ; 176*a*).
    (*b*) " children and fools cannot lie " (38*a*). "Master Constable says : You know neighbours 'tis an old saw, Children and fools speake true."—Lyly, *Endimion* (1591).
    (*c*) " better children weep than old men " (34*b* ; 175*c*). It is related in connection with the Gowrie conspiracy, that King James VI., about to depart from Gowrie Castle, was forcibly prevented by the Master of Glammis, and as the tears started to the eyes of the young king, " better bairns weep than bearded men " was the other's observation.
    (*d*) " ye have many godchildren to look upon, and ye bless them all, but ye bass but one " (84*d*).

CHIN, see Swim.

CHIP, (a) " who lacketh a stock his gain is not worth a chip " (94c).

    (b) " as merry as three chips " (17c), cf. Shakspeare's " dancing chips " (*Sonnets,* 128).

    (c) see Carpenters, Hew.

CHOKING OYSTERS, " checks and choking oysters " (43c), taunts and replies that put one to silence. " I have a stoppynge oyster in my poke."—Skelton, *Bowge of Court* (c. 1529), 477. " To a feloe laiyng to his rebuke that he was over deintie of his mouthe and diete, he did with this reason give a stopping oistre." —Udall, *Apoph.* (1542), 61.

CHOOSE, see Ill.

CHOOSERS, see Beggars.

CHOPPED, " chopped down empty candlesticks " (131c), " planked " down : *chop down* = to place with a sudden or violent motion.

CHURCH, " the nearer to the church, the further from God " (21a; 200a). " Qui est près de l'église est souvent loin de Dieu."—*Les Proverbes communs* (c. 1500).

CHURL, see Claw.

CHUTE, see Chatting.

CIRCUMQUAQUES (84d), far-fetched and roundabout stories.

CLARGY, " to put me to my clargy " (64b), see rhyme : *clergy* = learning, science, knowledge. " I rede how besy that he was Upon clergye, an hed of bras To forge and make it for to telle."—Gower, *MS. Soc. Antiq.*, 134, f. 104.

CLAW, (a) " thou makest me claw where it itcheth not " (85c).

    (b) " claw a churl by th' arse and he shitteth in my hand " (80c). " Claw a churl by the tail and he will file your hand."—*Jacob and Esau* (1568), ii. 3 (E.E.D.S. *Anon. Pl.* 2 Ser., 36a).

CLAWED, " I clawed her by the back " (24d).

CLEAN, see Broom.

CLEANSING, " in the cleansing week " (136d), Shrovetide : specifically from the evening of the Saturday before Quinquagesima Sunday and Ash Wednesday. On the Tuesday all Catholics were accustomed to confess.

CLEAR, see Case.

CLERKS, " the greatest clerks be not the wisest men " (67a ; 211a). " The greatest clerks ben not the wisest men, As whilom to the wolf this spake the mare."— Chaucer, *Cant. Tales* (1383), *Miller's Tale*. " Now I here wel, it is treue that I long syth have redde and herde, that the best clerkes ben not the wysest men." —*Historye of Reynard the Foxe* (1481).

CLIMBED, " he that never climbed never fell " (46d ; 220c).

CLIMME, " yes, climme " (242a), *i.e.* challenge me to say.

CLOAK, " what cloak for the rain soever ye bring me " (69d). " *Nicholas*. 'Tis good to have a cloake for the raine ; a bad shift is better then none at all ; Ile sit heere, as if I were as dead as a doore naile."—*Two Angry Women of Abingdon* (1599).

CLOCK, " and looked . . . what it was o'clock " (99b), saw how matters stood ; became aware of the facts : the phrase is still colloquial or slang. " To know what ys a clocke."—Skelton, *Works* (c. 1513), ii. 132 (Dyce).

CLOG, " where nought is to wed with, wise men flee the clog " (32a), originally *clog*=incumbrance ; hence a wife : this metaphor occurs very early. " *Science*. Ye have woon me for ever, dowghter, Although ye have woon a clog wyth all. *Wyt*. A clogg, sweete hart, what? *Science*. Such as doth fall To all men that joyne themselves in marriage."—*Wyt and Science* (c. 1540), *Anon. Plays*, 4 Ser. (E.E.D.S.). " The prince himself is about a piece of iniquity, Stealing away from his father with his clog at his heels."—Shakspeare, *Winter's Tale* (1604), iv. 4.

CLOTH, (a) " it is a bad cloth that will take no colour " (92d).
  (b) see Coat, Cut.

CLOTHES, (a) " to rent off my clothes fro my back "
(26b).

 (b) see God.

CLOUDS, " after clouds black we shall have **weather**
clear " (36c ; 173c).

COAL, see Cold.

COAT, " cut my coat after my cloth " (20b), to adapt oneself to circumstances ; to measure expense by income.
A relic of the sumptuary laws : an early allusion occurs
in the interlude of *Godly Queene Hestor* (c. 1530) :
" There is a cause why, That I go not gay : I tell you of
a word, Aman that new lord, Hath brought up all
good clothe, And hath so many gowns, as would
serve ten towns, Be ye never so loth : And any man in
the town, do buy him a good gown, He is very wroth.
And will him straight tell, the statute of apparel Shall
teach him good " (E.E.D.S., *Anon. Pl.*, 2nd Ser., 262a).

COCK, (a) " the young cock croweth as he the old
heareth " (23c), other readings are : " The young cock
learneth to crow of the old " (1509) ; " as the old cock
crows so does the chick " (1589).

 (b) " every cock is proud on his own dunghill "
(31b ; 217d), every man is a hero in his own circle ; one
fights best with friends and backers about him. " þet
fleshs is her et home, ase eorðe, þet is et eorðe : aut for
þui hit is cwointeˆt cwiuer, ᵉase me seið, þet coc is kene
on his owne mixenne."—*þe Ancren Riwle* (c. 1250).

 (c) " as oft change from hue to hue as doth **the**
cocks of Ind " (31a), ? *Ind*=indigo, the allusion being
to the changing sheen of the cock's bluish-black
feathers.

 (d) " he setteth cock on the hoop " (65d), gives way
to reckless enjoyment ; sets all by the ears ; is proud,
vaunting, and exultant. " You'll make a mutiny
among my guests ! You will set cock-a-hoop ! you'll
be the man ! "—Shakspeare, *Romeo and Juliet* (1595),
i. 5.

COCKNEY, (a) " he that cometh every day shall have a
cockney, He that cometh now and then shall have a
fat hen " (44a), Murray breaks up M.E. *cokeney* into
coken ey=cock's egg, and defines the word when used
by Langland as " egg," a rendering which seems

confirmed in the present instance. " I have no salt
bacon, Ne no cokeney, by Crist, coloppes for to make."
—Langland, *P. Plowman* (1363), 4370.

(b) " a good cockney coke " (97d), *i.e.* a cockney
cook : in derision and contempt, with perhaps a play
on *cokes*=fool. The origin of *cockney* (=one born
within the sound of Bow Bells) has been much debated ;
but, says Dr. Murray, in the course of an exhaustive
statement (*Academy,* May 10, 1890, p. 320), " the history
of the word, so far as it means a person, is very clear
and simple. We have the senses (1) ' cockered or pet
child,' ' nestle-cock,' ' mother's darling,' ' milksop,'
primarily the child, but continued to the squeamish
and effeminate man into which he grows up. (2) A
nickname applied by country people to the inhabitants
of great towns, whom they considered ' milksops,' from
their daintier habits and incapacity for rough work.
York, London, Perugia, were, according to Harman,
all nests of cockneys. (3) By about 1600 the name
began to be attached especially to Londoners, as the
representatives *par excellence* of the city milksop.
One understands the disgust with which a cavalier in
1641 wrote that he was ' obliged to quit Oxford at the
approach of Essex and Waller with their prodigious
number of cockneys.' "

COCKSCOMB, " to wear a cockscomb " (67d), the comb of
a cock was one of the ensigns or tokens of a profes-
sional fool.

COIN, " when coin is not common, commons must be
scant " (51b).

COLD, (a) " let them that be a-cold, blow at the coal "
(29d). " Our talwod is all brent, Our faggottes are
all spent, We may blow at the cole."—Skelton, *Why
come ye not to Court* (c. 1520).
    (b) see God, Hot, Key.

COLEPROPHET, " ye play coleprophet (quoth I) who taketh
in hand To know his answer before he do his errand "
(21a), *coleprophet*=a false prophet or cheat. " Cole-
prophet and cole-poyson, thou art both."—Heywood,
Ep., 89, *Cent.* vi.

COLL, " coll under canstick she can play both hands "
(24b), see Canstick.

COLLOP, " it is a dear collop that is cut out of th' own flesh " (28d). " God knows thou art a colup of my flesh."—Shakspeare, 1 *Henry VI.* (1592), v. 5.

COLOURS, see Blind, Cloth.

COLT, (a) " of a ragged colt there cometh a good horse " (33b). " *Touchstone.* This cannot be fained, sure. Heaven pardon my severitie! ' The ragged colt may prove a good horse.' "—Jonson, &c., *Eastward Hoe* (1605).
(b) " colts may prove well with tatches ill " (33b), *tache* (or *tatch*)=spot, blemish.

COME, (a) " come what, come would " (44b).
(b) " you come to your cost " (34a).
(c) see Come, Light, Thieves.

COMETH, (a) " all cometh to one " (50b), in modern phrase, " all cometh to him that waits."
(b) see Eggs, Goeth, Last, Seldom, Time.

COMING, " it is ill coming . . . to th' end of a shot and beginning of a fray " (79c).

COMMODITIES (10b), matters of advantage or convenience (also 120b; 125a).

COMMON, see Jack.

COMMONS, " the commons common so " (243b), " people say."

COMMONWEALTH, see Casting.

CONSITHER (5b; 278c), consider.

CONSTANTINE (193c), Constantinople.

CONSTER (13d), construe, explain.

CONTENTATION, " rich by his contentation " (144c), satisfaction, content.

CONVERSION, " join this conversion " (208d). " Conversion is the changing or altering of words in a proposition. . . ."—Wilson (1551), *The Arte of Logike*, fol. 21.

CONVEY (48b), steal. The classical quotation is of

course from Shakspeare, and from the same authority I give illustrations of derivatives: the rendering was popular. " *Nym*. The good humour is, to steal at a minute's rest. *Pist*. Convey, the wise it call."— Shakspeare, *Merry Wives of Windsor* (1596), Act i., Sc. 3. " Since Henry's death, I fear there is conveyance."—Shakspeare, 1 *Henry VI.* (1592), i. 3. " O good ! convey? Conveyers are you all, That rise thus nimbly by a true king's fall."—Shakspeare, *Richard II.* 1597), iv. 315.

Cony mop, " sweet cony mop " (242c), an endearment.

Cook, " a poor cook that may not lick his own fingers " (89b). " He is an evyll coke y^t can not lycke his owne lippes."—*Vulgaria Stambrigi* (c. 1510). " *Capulet*. Sirrah, go hire me twenty cunning cooks. 2 *Servant*. You shall have none ill, sir ; for I 'll try if they can lick their fingers."—Shakspeare, *Romeo and Juliet* (1595), iv. 2.

Cookquean, see Cuckquean.

Cope, " segging is good cope " (94a), sedge is good covering.

Cord, " would to our lord ye had . . . hanged both in one cord " (80b).

Corner, " the corner of our care (quoth he) I you tell " (20b), *corner*=gist, the furthest point of probing.

Corse, " my comely corse " (85a), body.

Cotsold lion, see Lion.

Couch, (a) " couch malt and water in house together " (242b), lay, place.

(b) " couch a hogshead " (58b), go to sleep : *hogshead*=head. " I couched a hogshead in a skypper this darkmans."—Harman, *Caveat* (1567), 66 (1814).

Cough, " thou canst cough in the aumbry " (82d), *aumbry*=cupboard, pantry. " Some slovens from sleeping no sooner be up, But hand is in aumbrie, and nose in the cup."—Tusser, *Five Hundred Points* (1573), ii. 5.

Counsel, see Court, Mum, Three.

Counterpoise, " whether they counterpoise or outweigh " (10a).

COURT, " I was neither of court nor of counsel made "
(43*b*), *i.e.* neither approached for advice, nor invited
to express an opinion.

COURTESY, " so courtesy, so kind " (255*a*), polished,
courteous.

COVET, " all covet, all lose " (97*c*; 184*a*).

COVETISE (12*c*), covetousness.

COW, (*a*) " the cow is wood " (78*a*), *wood* = mad, furious.
    (*b*) " God sendeth the shrewd cow short horns "
(27*c*), *shrewd* = malicious, badly disposed.   " The Bishop of Sarum sayd, That he trusted ere Christmas
Day to visit and cleanse a good part of the kingdom.
But most commonly God sendeth a shrewd cow short
horns, or else many a thousand in England had
smarted."—Foxe, *Acts and Manuments.*
    (*c*) " as comely as is a cow in a cage " (52*d*).
    (*d*) " Margery, good cow, gave a good meal, but
then she cast it down again with her heel " (86*a*).
    (*e*) " every man as he loveth, Quoth the good man,
when that he kissed his cow " (53*a*).
    (*f*) " many a good cow hath an evil calf " (28*a*).

COW-CALF, " as well for the cow-calf as for the bull "
(62*a*).

COY, " as coy as a croker's mare " (52*b*), *croker* =
saffron-dealer.

CRABS, " the greatest crabs be not all the best meat "
(40*d*).

CREED, see Paternoster.

CREEP, see Children, Kind.

CRIPPLE, " it is hard halting before a cripple " (71*d*).
" I perceyve (quod she) it is evill to halte before a
creple . . . and it is evill to hop before them that
runne for the bell."—Gascoigne, *Fable of Ferdinando
Jeronimi and Leonora de Valases* (1575).

CROKER'S MARE, see Coy.

CROOK, see Hook.

CROSS, (a) " now will I make a cross on this gate "
(43d; 226b), the cross as the emblem of disappoint-
ment and misfortune, and the fact that many pieces
of money were stamped on one side with a cross gave
rise to many quibbles : see b and c infra, and 226a. " I
will make a cross upon his gate ; yea, cross on, Thy
crosses be on gates all, in thy purse none."

(b) " I cross thee quite out of my book " (44a).

(c) " since thou art cross failed, avail, unhappy
hook " (44a), *cross*=money (see *a* supra); *unhappy
hook*=a commiserating address. " Now I have never
a crose to blesse me, Now I goe a-mumming, Like a
poore pennilesse spirit, Without pipe or druming."—
Marriage of Witt and Wisdome, 1579 (E.E.D.S.,
Anon. Plays, Ser. 4, 227a). " Not a penny, not a
penny ; you are too impatient to bear crosses."—Shakspeare, 2 *Henry IV.* (1598), i. 2.

CROSS ROW, " worst among letters in the cross row "
(140b), *cross row*=Christ-cross row, *i.e.* the alphabet ;
from a cross placed at either end ; or from an old
practice of writing the alphabet in the form of a cross
by way of a charm. Note the difference between the
old and modern girds at the letter " H "—" aitch "
v " ache."

CROW, (a) " we have a crow to pull " (70d), complaint
to make, quarrel, a bone to pick. " *Abelle.* Dere
brother, I will fayre On feld ther our bestes ar, To
looke if they be holgh or fulle. *Cayn.* Na, na, abide,
we have a craw to pulle."—Mactacio Abel, in *Towneley Mysteries* (c. 1420).

(b) " the crow thinketh her own birds fairest in the
wood " (61c). " It must needs be good ground that
brings forth such good corne ; When I look on him,
methinks him to be evill favoured, Yet the crowe
thinkes her black birds of all other the fairest."—
Lupton, *All for Money* (1578).

(c) " as good then to say, the crow is white " (69a ;
203b, and c), " You're talking nonsense, or worse, telling lies."

(d) see High.

CROWETH, see Cock.

CRUMMETH, " cracketh and crummeth " (79a), crumbleth.

CRY A LEISON (78b), *i.e.* Kyrie eleison (" Lord, have mercy "), a short petition used at the beginning of the Roman Mass. The phrase was early the subject of punning allusions. Tyndale uses it in the sense of a complaint or scolding (*Obed. Chr. Man*, 130b, 1528) ; and Heywood, in the present instance, apparently means something of the same kind, with an added sarcasm in his corrupted orthography, " cry a leison " (=a cry à [*la*] Alison, which appears (89b) to be the name of the wife of whom the husband is speaking).

CUCKQUEAN, " ye make her a cookquean " (76b), a female cuckold : here possibly also a play on " cook."

CUMBRETH, " the kitchen cumbreth not by heat " (125c), is not a trouble, source of annoyance.

CUNNING, " that cunning man " (66d), orig. knowledge, skill, learning, no bad sense being implied : as early as the time of Lord Bacon, however, the word was on the down-grade in meaning, influenced, no doubt, by the mundane truth that skill in the hands of the unscrupulous is used to defraud those less gifted. " If I forget thee, O Jerusalem, let my right hand forget her cunning."—*Bible*, Auth. Vers. (1611), *Psalm* cxxxvii. 5. " The cunning manner of our flight, Determined of."—Shakspeare, *Two Gent.*, ii. 4.

CUP, " merry . . . as cup and can could hold " (60a).

CUPSHOTTEN, " somewhat cupshotten " (31a), drunk.

CURRIED, see Horse.

CURRYFAVEL, " they can curryfavel and make fair weather " (66b), *curryfavel* = flatter.

CUSHION, (a) " ye missed the cushion, for all your haste " (97c), idiomatic : from the practice of archery = to fail in an attempt, to miss the point. " Trulie, Euphues, you have mist the cushion, for I was neither angrie with your long absence, neither am I well pleased at your presence."—Lyly, *Euphues* (1581).

(b) " I may set you beside the cushion " (97c), *i.e.* pass over with contempt, ignore, shelve. " Thus is he set beside the cushion, for his sincerity and forwardness in the good cause."—Spalding, *Hist.* i. 291.

CUT, see Coat.

DAGGER, (a) " he beareth a dagger in his sleeve " (35b),
i.e. hidden, in reserve, ready for use.

(b) " it be ill playing with short daggers " (47c),
in modern phrase, " edged tools."

DAIMENT, " sufferancee is no quittance in this daiment "
(64d), ? judgment, settlement : cf. *daysman*=umpire,
arbitrator. *Day* (in legal sense)=return of a writ,
appearance.

DAINTIES, see Dear.

DAME, " he that will not be ruled by his own dame shall
be ruled by his stepdame " (92d).

DANCE, " sufferance is your dance " (68b), *rôle,* lot :
cf. " to lead one a dance."

DANCETH, " he danceth attendance " (219d), to wait
upon constantly and obsequiously.

DARK, see Fair.

DARLING, " it is better to be an old man's darling than
a young man's warling " (80a), *wawl* as verb=to
wrangle ; hence as subs. (it occurs only in this proverb)
it probably=an object of nagging or bad temper.
" Leave this brawling and wawling."—*Misogonus,
Anon. Plays,* 2 Ser. 227a.

DAW (*passim*), an empty-headed, foolish fellow. " He
that for commyn welth bysyly Studyeth and laboryth,
and lyveth by Goddes law, Except he waxe ryche,
men count hym but a daw ! "—*Four Elements (c.*
1510), *Anon. Plays,* Ser. 1 (E.E.D.S.), 4d. " Good
faith, I am no wiser than a daw."—Shakspeare,
1 *Henry VI.* (1592), ii. 4.

DAY, (a) " one day was three till liberty was borrow "
(27c), *borrow*=pledged, mortgaged.

(b) " I see day at this little hole " (26b), in modern
phrase, " daylight "; an echo, possibly, of another
proverbial saying—" It is always darkest before the
dawn."

(c) " Say no more till the day be longer " (202b).

(d) " be the day never so long, evermore at last they
ring to evensong " (82b). " For though the day be
never so long At last the bell rings for evensong."—
Hawes, *Pastime of Pleasure.*

(e) " the day of doom shall be done " (85a).

HEY. II.   A A

(f) " farewell, my good days, they will be soon gone " (57a).

(g) see Dog, Fair, Rome.

DAYMENT (281d), judgment.

DEAD, (a) " for gain (he) is dead and laid in tomb " (66a).

(b) " I have . . . a dead man's head in my dish " (80b), the " dear departed " of modern phrase. " As bold-fac'd women, when they wed another, Banquet their husbands with their dead love's heads."—Marston, *Insatiate Countess*.

(c) see Devil, Shoes.

DEAF, (a) " then were ye deaf, ye could not hear on that side " (90d), *i.e.* wilfully deaf.

(b) " who is so deaf as he that will not hear? " (186d).

DEAR, (a) " whoso that knew what would be dear, should need be a merchant but one year " (4b ; 171a).

(b) " dear bought and far fet are dainties for ladies " (38d), *fet*=fetched. " Some far fet trick, trick good for ladies, some stale toy or other."—Marston, *Malcontent* (1604). " *Niece.* Ay, marry, sir, this was a rich conceit indeed. *Pompey.* And far fetched; therefore good for you, lady."—Beaumont and Fletcher, *Wit at Several Weapons* (1614).

DEAREST, " to buy the dearest for the best alway " (81c), cf. " cheap and nasty."

DEATH, (a) " death ! . . . take me that time, to take a breath " (45a), waiting for dead men's shoes profiteth little.

(b) " though love decree departure death to be " (48c).

DEED, " deed without words " (71b).

DENAY (222d), deny : note the rhyme.

DEPARTURE, see Death.

DESART (238c), desert : note the rhyme.

DESERT, " desert and reward be ofttimes things far odd " (42a).

DESTINY, see Wedding.

DEVIL, (*a*) " the devil hath cast a bone to set strife "
(57*c*).

(*b*) " young saint, old devil " (27*c*; 177*a*), this
occurs in *MS. Harleian* (*c.* 1490).

(*c*) " he must have a long spoon that would sup
(or eat) with the devil " (71*d*). " Therefore behoveth
him a ful long spone, That shal ete with a fend : thus
herd I say."—Chaucer, *Squieres Tale* (*Cant. Tales, c.*
1383). " *Courtesan.* Will you go with me? *Dromio.*
Master, if you do, expect spoonmeat or bespeak a long
spoon. *Antipholus.* Why, Dromio? *Dromio.* Marry,
he must have a long spoon that must eat with the
devil."—Shakspeare, *Comedy of Errors* (1593), iv. 3.

(*d*) " like as the devil looked over Lincoln " (91*c*).
" The middle or Rood tower of Lincoln Cathedral is
the highest in the whole kingdom, and when the spire
was standing on it, it must, in proportion to the
height of the tower, have exceeded that of old St.
Paul's, which was five hundred and twenty feet. The
monks were so proud of this structure, that they
would have it that the devil looked upon it with an
envious eye : whence the proverb of a man who looks
invidious and malignant, ' he looks as the devil over
Lincoln.' "—*Tour through England and Wales* (1742).
Ray gives another account : " It is probable that it
took its rise from a small image of the devil standing
on the top of Lincoln College, in Oxford."—*Proverbs*
(1737).

(*e*) " he must needs go when the devil doth drive "
(78*c*). " There is a proverb which trewe now preveth,
He must nedes go that the dyvell dryveth."—Heywood, *Johan Johan, Tyb, and Syr Jhan.*

(*f*) " the devil is no falser than is he " (71*d*).

(*g*) " the devil go with thee down the lane "
(83*d*).

(*h*) " meet to set the devil on sale " (77*b*).

(*i*) " the devil in th' orloge " (63*d*; 195*a* and *b*).
" Some for a tryfull pley the devyll in the orloge."—
Harman, *Vulgaria* (1530).

(*j*) " the devil is dead " (91*c*; 184*c* and *d*; 185*a*
and *b*).

(*k*) " the devil with his dam hath more rest in hell
than I . . . with thee " (85*b*).

A A 2

(*l*) " the devil's good grace might have given a greeting " (99*c*).

(*m*) " I will not bear the devil's sack " (73*d*), compound a wrong.

(*n*) " what change may compare to the devil's life like his that have chosen a devil to his wife? " (74*c*).

(*o*) see Candle.

DIEU-GARD, " a beck as good as a dieu-gard " (29*d*), a salutation, " God save you! " still in use in Scots Masonic lodges as a salute. " Each beck of yours shall be in stead of a diew garde unto me."—Florio, *Second Frutes* (1591), 81.

DINERS, " dinners cannot be long, where dainties want " (51*b*); the old spelling, by an oversight, is retained in the text.

DIRTY PUDDINGS, see Dogs.

DISCOMMODITIES (135*c*), disadvantages : see Commodities.

DISCRIVE (16*a*), describe.

DISEASED, " more diseased by early lying down " (55*c*), *disease* formerly was generic for " absence of ease."

DISGUISE, " three cups full at once shall oft disguise thee " (247*b*), make drunk. " *Harp.* I am a prince disguised. *Hir.* Disguised! How? Drunk ! "—Massinger, *Virgin Martyr* (1622), iii. 3.

DISH, (*a*) " I may break a dish there " (38*d*), have a meal, take pot-luck, ply knife and fork.

(*b*) " as well as the beggar knoweth his dish (or bag)," see Bag.

DISTAFF, see Tow.

DITCH, see Blind.

Do, (*a*) " it is as folk do and not as folk say " (73*b*).

(*b*) " nought can she do and what can she have then " (26*c*).

DOCK, " in dock, out nettle " (54*d*), a charm for a nettle sting which early passed into a proverb expressive of inconstancy. " Ye wete well Ladie eke (quoth I) that I have not plaid racket, Nettle in, Docke out, and with this the weathercocke waved."—Chaucer, *Testament of Love*. " Is this my in dock,

out nettle? "—Middleton, *More Dissemblers besides
Women* (1623).

DOE, " when he hunteth a doe that he cannot avow all
dogs bark not at him " (72*a*).

DOG, (*a*) " a man may handle his dog so that he may
make him bite him " (85*c*).

   (*b*) " when he hunteth a doe that he cannot avow
all dogs bark not at him " (72*a*).

   (*c*) " it is . . . a poor dog that is not worth the whistling " (43*b*).

   (*d*) " unable to give a dog a loaf " (81*b*).

   (*e*) " a dog will bark ere he bite " (85*b*).

   (*f*) " she will lie as fast as a dog will lick a dish "
(78*a*).

   (*g*) " a dog hath a day " (36*d*), or, in modern
phrase, " every dog has its day "; *i.e.* a period during
which he is in his prime.

   (*h*) " an old dog biteth sore " (75*b*).   " Olde dogges
bite sore."—Churchyard, *Handeful of Gladsome Verses*
(1592).

   (*i*) " it is hard to make an old dog stoop " (85*c*).

   (*j*) " to help a dog over a stile " (39*b*), the modern
version has " lame dog ": to give a hand, to assist
in difficulty.   " Here is a stile so high as a man
cannot help a dog over it."—Marston, *Insatiate Countess* (1605), ii. 2.

   (*k*) " a hair of the dog that bit us last night "
(45*c*), a pick-me-up after a debauch : apparently a
memory of the superstition, which was and still is
common, that, being bitten by a dog, one cannot do
better than pluck a handful of hair from him, and lay
it on the wound.   Old receipt books advise that an
inebriate should drink sparingly in the morning some
of the same liquor which he had drunk to excess over-
night.

   (*l*) " it is ill waking of a sleeping dog " (30*a* ; 172*c*),
cf. " let sleeping dogs lie."

   (*m*) " at every dog's bark, seem not to awake "
(68*d*).

   (*n*) " hungry dogs will eat dirty puddings " (14*a*),
another proverb declares that a hungry man will eat
anything, except Suffolk cheese.

   (*o*) see Cat, Love.

DOING, see Saying.

DOLE, (a) " his dole is soon done " (37d), lot, share. *Happy man be your dole*=a general wish for success. " Happy man be his dole that misses her."—*Grim the Collier of Croydon.*

(b) " ye deal this dole out at a wrong door " (9d), your charity is ill bestowed.

DONE, (a) " as good undone as do it too soon " (74a).

(b) " things done cannot be undone " (26a).

(c) " better it be done than wish it had been done " (74a).

DOOM, see Day.

DOON (30c), done.

DOOR, (a) " it is good to have a hatch before the door " (32c), *hatch*=a wooden partition coming over the lower half of a doorway and leaving open the upper half.

(b) see Dole, Wrong.

(c) " he turned her out of doors to graze on the plain " (99d).

DORTER, " the mouth is the tongue's dorter " (274a), a dormitory or sleeping room. " Slepe as monke in his dortoure."—Langtoft, p. 256.

DOTING, " after a doting and drunken deed, let submission obtain some mercy or meed " (28c), *doting*= foolish, silly.

DOYT (80c), doth.

DRAFF, " the still sow eats up all the draf " (27c ; 196d), " draf is your errand, but drink ye would " (31d), *draff*=dregs, dirt, refuse, anything thrown away as unfit for food. " 'Tis old but true, Still swine eat all the draff."—Shakspeare, *Merry Wives* (1596), iv. 2.

DRAWLATCH, see John Drawlatch.

DREDE (73b), fear : in a lesser degree than is usually conveyed by the word.

DRINK, (a) " I drink (quoth she) ; quoth he, I will not pledge " (60d).

(b) see Brew, Draff.

(c) " then thou shalt drink " (293d), a play on the

two meanings of *drink* (=(*a*) imbibe and (*b*) suffer punishment) was common in old writers. " I hold a penny ye will drink without a cup."—Udall, *Roister Doister* (E.E.D.S. 18*d*), i. 3.

(*d*) see Horse.

DRIVEL, " drivel and drudge " (83*b*), *drivel*=sērvant. " To encourage the husband to use his wife as a vile dreuell."—Udall, *Corinth.*, ch. xi.

DRIVETH, see Nail.

DROPPETH, see Hunger.

DRUDGE, see Drivel.

DRUNK, (*a*) " drunk in the good ale glass " (45*c*), *i.e.* in a state of " alecie."

(*b*) " he that killeth a man when he is drunk shall be hanged when he is sober " (28*c*).

DUCK, " like a duke? like a duck ! " (86*b*), a play on words.

DUMP, " which dumb dump " (132*d*), a melancholy strain. " To their instruments Tune a deploring dump."—Shakspeare, *Two Gent.* (1595), iii. 2.

DUN ASS, see Ass.

DUNGHILL, see Cock.

DUNSTABLE, " as plain as Dunstable highway " (69*b*), *plain Dunstable*=anything homely, plain, simple— why, is not clear : sometimes *byeway*. " These men walked by-wayes, and the saying is, many by-walkers, many balkes, many balkes, much stumbling, and where much stumbling is, there is sometime a fall ; howbeit there were some good walkers among them, that walked in the king's high way ordinarily, up-right, plaine Dunstable way."—Latimer, *Sermons* (*d.* 1555).

DUR (9*d*, 20*c*, 26*b*, 32*c*, &c.), door (A.S.).

DYKE, (*a*) " my beautiful marriage lieth in the dyke " (8*b*), see Beautiful.

(*b*) see Blind.

EAR, (a) " in at the tone ear and out of the tother "
(92*d* ; 183*b*). " Troilus, that nigh for sorrow deide,
Tooke little hede of all that ever he ment ; One **eare**
it heard, at the other out it went."—Chaucer, *Troilus
and Creseide* (1369).

(b) " her ears might well glow, for all the **town**
talked of her " (52*c* ; 218*d*), that the ears burn when
talked of by someone absent is still a prevalent superstition.

(c) " you had on your harvest ears, thick of hearing " (91*a*). " Thine eares be on pilgrimage, or in
the wildernes, as they say commonly, thou hast on
thy harvest eares, *vestræ peregrinantur aures*."—
Withal, *Dictionary* (1608), 46.

(d) " he must both tell you a tale and find you **ears** "
(91*a*).

(e) " by the ears " (54*d*), quarrelling, at strife.
" Were half to half the world by the ears, and **he**
Upon my party, I'd revolt."—Shakspeare, *Coriolanus*
(1610), i. 1.

(f) " thy ear groweth through thy hood " (198*a*),
as the mark of an ass or a cuckold.

(g) see Bird, Pitchers, Sow.

EARLY " early up and never the near " (6*d*), **near** =
nearer. " Better far off than near, be ne'er the
near."—Shakspeare, *Richard II.* (1597), v. 1.

EASE, see Cap, Inn, Nothing, Sufferance.

EAST, " the longer east, the shorter west " (50*b*).

EAT, see Blind, Cat.

EATETH, see Sow.

EBB, (a) " he was at an ebb, though he be now afloat "
(38*b*), in difficulties or hard up, but now in better
circumstances.

(b) " thou art at an ebb in Newgate " (176*b*).

EEL, " as sure to hold as an eel by the tail " (24*c*), *i.e.*
slippery, unreliable. " Cauda tenes anguillam : you
have an eele by the taile."—Withal, *Dictionary* (ed.
1634), 554. " Paulo momento huc illuc impellitur.
Hee is as wavering as a wethercocke. He is heere
and their all in a moment. Theirs as much holde to
his word, as to take a wet eele by the taile."—
Terence in English (1614).

EEL-SKINS, " we shall see him prove a merchant of eel-skins " (66c).

EGGS, " in came the third, with his V eggs " (52c; 220c), to interfere, meddle, put in one's spoke. " What, come you in with your seven eggs? "—*Misogonus, Anon. Pl.*, 2 Ser., 1888b (E.E.D.S.).

END, (a) " some loose or odd end will come . . . some . . . day " (45a).
    (b) " such beginning, such end " (94b).
    (c) " the game from beginning sheweth what end is meant " (75d).
    (d) see Beginning, Good.

ENOUGH, (a) " enough is enough " (103a). " And of enough enough, and nowe no more, Bycause my braynes no better can devise . . . It is enough and as good as a feast."—Gascoigne, *Memories* (1575).
    (b) " enough is as good as a feast " (103a; 209d). " It is an olde proverb He is well at ese y^t hath enough and can say ho."—*Dives and Pauper* (1493)
    (c) " he that knoweth when he hath enough is no fool " (81c).
    (d) " here is enough and too much " (82c).

ENVIED, " better be envied than pitied " (32a).

EPIGRAMS, see Bibliography.

ERRAND, (a) " thus is thine errand sped " (79d).
    (b) " I am sped of mine errand " (101d).
    (c) see Draff, Sleeveless, Errand.

ERRATA, see page 466.

EVEN, " I shall be even with him " (31c), on equality with, quits with : now chiefly colloquial.

EVEN RECKONING, see Reckoners.

EVENSONG, see Day.

EVERYCHONE (5d), everyone.

EWE, " she can wink on the ewe and worry the lamb " (24a).

EXIGENT, " brought . . . an exigent " (260a), extremity, situation of difficulty. " Hath driv'n her to some desperate exigent."—*Wisdome of Dr. Dodypole* (1600). E.E.D.S. *Anon. Pl.*, 7 Ser., s.v. Exigent.

EXTREMITIES, " flee th' attempting of extremities " (68c),
i.e. avoid the harshest measures.

EYE, (a) " I might put my winning in mine eye and
see never the worse " (42a). " You have had conferences and conferences again at Poissy and other
places, and gained by them just as much as you
might put in your eye, and see never the worse."—
Bramhall, *Works*, i. 68. " Bating Namure, he might
have put all the glorious harvests he yearly reap'd
there into his eye, and not have prejudic'd his royal
sight in the least."—T. Brown, *Works* (d. 1682),
ii. 329.

(b) " better eye out than alway ache " (19d; 170b).

(c) " he winketh with the tone eye and looketh with
the tother " (40b).

(d) " that the eye seeth not, the heart reweth not "
(78c). " The blinde eats many a flie, and much water
runnes by the mill that the miller never knowes of:
the evill that the eye sees not, the hart rues not."—
Greene, *Never too Late* (1590).

(e) " blame me not too haste for fear mine eyes be
bleared " (8d), *haste*=hastily.

(f) see Fields.

EYESORE, " but an eye sore " (13b; 173a). " Quod the
Barbour, but a lytell eye sore."—*Merry Jests of the
Wyddow Edyth* (1525).

FABLETH (121b), see next entry.

FABLING, " without fabling " (15b), exaggeration, the
long bow, lie. " Without fable or guile."—*Four
Elements* (c. 1500), E.E.D.S., *Anon. Plays*, Ser. 1.

FACE, (a) " I did set a good face on the matter "
(187d), make the best of things.

(b) " two faces in one hood " (23d; 180d), double-
dealing, shuffling. " *Alberto*. Not play two parts
in one? away, away, 'tis common fashion. Nay, if
you cannot bear two subtle fronts under one hood;
ideot, goe by, goe by; off this world's stage! O
times impuritie ! "—*Antonio and Mellida* (1602).

(c) " their faces told toys " (17d), told tales: **see**
Toy.

(d) " thy face is shorn against the wool " (198d).

Fain, see Fool.

Fair, (a) " the fair lasteth all the year " (57*b* ; 177*b*), any time or every day is meet for the purpose : see next entry.

(b) " a day after the fair " (20*a*), too late, when everything is over.

(c) " fair words did fet " (53*c*), politeness costs nothing : *fet*=fetch.

(d) " the grace of God is worth a fair " (46*d*), a matter or affair to remember.

(e) " the fair and the foul by dark are like store " (13*c*), comparisons are not always possible ; under some circumstances quality is no matter ; in the dark all cats are grey.

(f) see Thread.

Fair and well (96*d*), farewell.

Fair words, see Fool, Tongue.

Fall, (a) " to fall in and not to fall out " (31*a*), to concur and agree, and not to disagree, quarrel, or fall at odds with.

(b) see Sit.

Falleth, see Sheaf, Sky.

False, (a) " I fear false measures " (73*d*).

(b) " as false as fair " (94*c*).

(c) " as false as God is true " (78*a*).

(d) see Knave.

Falsehood, " falsehood in fellowship " (69*c* ; 211*b*), *fellowship*=companionship.

False measures, see Measure.

Fancy, " fancy may bolt bran and make ye take it flour " (62*c*), make-believe counts for much.

Far, (a) " I have seen as far come as nigh " (34*a* ; 216*a*), the drip of water wears away the stone.

(b) " things erst so far off, were now so far on " (96*d*).

(c) see Runneth.

Fardle, " best fardle in my pack " (151*d*), article, item, piece, property ; a burden of any kind.

FARE, (a) " ye see your fare, set your heart at rest "
(43*d* ; 227*c*), business, conduct, goings on, course, path.
   (b) " fare ye well how ever I fare " (43*d*).
   (c) " her time to take up to show my fare at best "
(43*d*), see supra *a*.
   (d) " well mote ye fare " (43*d*).

FAREN, " have gone further and have faren worse "
(62*c*), *faren*=fared.

FAREWELL, (a) " farewell and feed full—that love ye well
to do, but you lust not to do that longeth thereto "
(34*c*), *i.e.* like to live well without the right to do so.
   (b) see Day.

FART, (a) " I shall get a fart of a dead man as soon as
a farthing " (37*d*).
   (b) " they that will be afraid of every fart must go
far to piss " (69*c*).
   (c) " the tone cannot piss but the tother must let a
fart " (67*c*).

FARTHER, see Church.

FARTHING, (a) " she thinketh her farthing good silver "
(26*d* ; 217*c*). " Take example at me . . . I thought
my halfpeny good silver within these few yeares past,
and no man esteemeth me unlesse it be for counsell."
—Gascoigne, *Glasse of Government* (1575).
   (b) " but for a farthing who ever did sell you might
boast you to be better sold than bought " (27*a*).
   (c) " one farthing worth of good " (26*b*), a low
standard of value.

FASHION, (a) " every man after his fashion " (38*c*), probably a pun (a common one at the time) on *fashion*=
farcy. " *Sh.* What shall we learn by travel? *An.*
Fashions. *Sh.* That's a beastly disease."—*Old For-
tunatus* (1600).
   (b) see Best.

FAST, (a) " fast bind, fast find " (8*d* ; 224*c*). " Wherefore a plaine bargain is best, and in bargaines
making ; fast bind, fast find."—*Jests of Scogin* (1565).
   (b) see Goeth, Hold, Last, Weed.

FASTER LANE (284*b*), Foster Lane.

FAT, (a) " the fat is in the fire " (8*b* ; 217*d*), all is confusion, all has failed : of failures and the results of

sudden and unexpected revelations and disappointments. " Faith, Doricus, thy braine boils ; keele it, keele it, or all the fatt's in the fire."—Marston, *What You Will* (1607).

(*b*) " a swine over-fat is cause of his own bane " (81*d*).

(*c*) " little knoweth the fat sow what the lean doth mean " (30*a*).

(*d*) " the fat clean flit from my beard " (9*a*).

(*e*) see Hog.

FAULT, (*a*) " he hath but one fault, he is nought " (35*c*).

(*b*) " hard is for any man all faults to mend " (35*c*).

FAULTLESS, " he is lifeless that is faultless " (35*c*), *i.e.* perfection is not attained during life.

FAVER (5*a*), favour : see the rhyme " have her " in next line.

FEAKED, " the fool was feaked for this " (148*b*), beaten, whipped.

FEAR, see False.

FEAST, see Enough.

FEAT, " handling of things feat " (133*b*)—" frame in feat " (137*b*), neat, dextrous, elegant. " And look how well my garments sit upon me, Much feater than before."—*Temp.*, ii. 1.

FEATHER, (*a*) " she may not bear a feather but she must breathe " (26*d*), *i.e.* much ado about nothing, mountains made of molehills.

(*b*) " if your meet-mate and you meet together, then shall we see two men bear a feather " (42*c*), of means employed altogether disproportionate to the end in view.

(*c*) " I gat not so much . . . as a good hen's feather or a poor eggshell " (44*b*), said of altogether inadequate results.

(*d*) " he would fain flee, but he wanteth feathers " (35*c*), condition, substance : compare the modern " not a feather to fly with."

(*e*) see Goose.

FED, (*a*) " better fed than taught " (25*b* ; 174*a*).

(b) " he that gapeth till he be fed may fortune to fast and famish for hunger " (21c), " if you want a thing done, do it yourself," " God helps those who help themselves," " he that will not work cannot eat."

(c) see Tun.

FEED, " feed by measure and defy the physician " (81d), *i.e.* use and do not abuse things; temperance bringeth health.

FEET, (a) " he thinketh his feet be where his head shall never come " (35c).

(b) " here is since thou camest too many feet abed " (79d), *i.e.* you are not wanted, are *de trop*; your room is desired more than your company.

(c) see Cat.

FELL, (a) " too fell " (129d), irritating, sharp, keen.

(b) see Climbed.

(c) " they fell out and . . . they fell in " (55a).

FELLOW, see Thief.

FELLOWSHIP, see Falsehood, Poverty.

FERDER, " the ferder thou art " (216a), further: still in vulgar use.

FERNE, " old ferne years " (5d), long ago, bygone.

FET, (a) " fet him in some stay " (32a)—" ye can fet as much " (95c), fetch. " From thence we fet a compass."—*Bible*, Author. Ver. (1611), *Acts* xxviii. 13. [Such archaisms in the Scriptures were not completely changed until well into the eighteenth century.]

(b) see Fair.

FETTERS, (a) " no man loveth his fetters be they made of gold " (19c). " Who would weare fetters though they were all of gold? Or to be sicke, though his faint browes, for wearing night-cap, wore a crown."—Webster, *Sir T. Wyatt* (1607).

(b) " were I loose from the lovely links of my chain I would not dance in such fair fetters again " (19c).

FEW, (a) " few know and fewer care " (100b).

(b) see Kinsfolk.

FEWER, " the fewer, the better fare " (79c).

FIELDS, (a) " fields have eyes and woods have ears "
(70b), now usually " walls have ears." " The were
bettur be still; Wode has erys felde has si3t Were
the forster here now right, Thy wordis shuld like the
ille."—*King Edward and the Shepherd,* MS. (c. 1300).
  (b) " bidding me welcome strangely over the fields "
(40d).

FIEND, see Devil.

FIERCE, see Lion.

FILTH, " a false flattering filth " (23d), a generic term
of contempt—slut, slattern, or worse. " If the filth
be in doubt."—*Gammer Gurton's Needle* (c. 1562),
E.E.D.S., *Anon. Plays,* Ser. 3, 136d.

FIND, (a) " ye seek to find things ere they be lost "
(34a), *i.e.* " too previous."
  (b) see Fast, Seek.

FINDETH, " he findeth that seeks " (25b).

FINE, " in fine " (45d), in conclusion, finally, to sum up.
" In fine, delivers me to fill the time, Herself most
chastely absent."—Shakspeare, *All's Well that Ends
Well* (1598), iii. 7.

FINGER, (a) " [folly] to put my finger too far in the fire "
(57d), *i.e.* to meddle or interfere too much.
  (b) " to make me put my finger in a hole " (73c).
  (c) " with a wet finger ye can fet as much as
may easily all this matter ease " (95c), *i.e.* easily,
readily : as easy as turning over the leaf of a book,
or rubbing out writing on a slate. " He darting an
eye upon them, able to confound a thousand conjurers
in their own circles, though with a wet finger they
could fetch up a little divell."—Dekker, *A Strange
Horse-Race* (1613), sig. D 3. See Wet finger.
  (d) " each finger is a thumb " (66a), of clumsy
handling. " Each finger is a thumb to-day, methinks."
—Udall, *Roister Doister* (1534), i. 3. (E.E.D.S.,
Works, 20d).
  (e) " I suck not this out of my own finger's end "
(43a).
  (f) " I perfectly feel even at my finger's end "
(14c), *i.e.* know perfectly, am fully familiar with.

FIRE, (a) " where fire is, smoke will appear " (70a), there
is no effect without a cause : see *infra*.

(b) " there is no fire without some smoke " (69d),
see *supra*.

(c) " make no fire, raise no smoke " (69d), see *supra*.

(d) " soft fire maketh sweet malt " (6c ; 170a),
gentle means are best ; take things quietly. " O
Maister Philip, forbeare ; you must not leape over the
stile before you come at it ; haste makes waste ; soft
fire makes sweet malt ; not too far for falling ; there's
no hast to hang true men."—Haughton, *Two Angry
Women of Abington* (1599).

(e) " fire in the tone hand and water in the tother "
(24a).

(f) " to lay fire and tow together " (73c), to court
danger or disaster.

(g) see Child, Fat, Frying pan.

FISH, (a) " fish is cast away that is cast in dry pools "
(34c).

(b) " she is neither fish nor flesh nor good red
herring " (24d), nondescript ; neither one thing nor
another ; neither hay nor grass. " Wone that is nether
flesshe nor fisshe."—Roy, *Rede me and be nott Wrothe*
(1528), i. iij. b. " *Prince Henry*. An otter, sir John !
why an otter ? *Falstaff*. Why ? she is neither fish nor
flesh ; a man knows not where to have her."—Shakspeare, 2 *Henry IV.* (1598), iv. 3.

(c) " old fish and young flesh doth men best feed "
(61d), *i.e.* mature fish and young womanhood.

(d) " all is fish that cometh to net " (39c), all serves
the purpose. " But now (aye me) the glasing christal
glasse Doth make us thinke that realmes and townes
are rych, Where favour sways the sentence of the law,
Where al is fishe that cometh to net."—Gascoigne,
Steele Glas (1575).

(e) see Cat.

FISHED, " he hath well fished and caught a frog " (32a).
" Well I have fished and caught a frog, Brought little
to pass with much ado."—Latimer, *Remains*.

FISHING, " it is ill fishing before the net " (38d ; 221b).

FIT, (a) " by that surfeit . . . I feel a little fit " (55c),
disordered, out of sorts.

(b) " for a beginning this was a feat fit " (57c), a round of a contest, struggle, or fight.

FIVE, see Eggs.

FLEA, " a flea in his ear " (35a), an annoying suggestion or experience, a good scolding.

FLEABITING, " a fleabiting " (57c ; 208c), a trifle, anything of little or no moment. " Their miseries are but fleabitings to thine."—Burton, *Anat. Melan.* (1621).

FLEBERGEBET (25b ; 286c), =sycophant, smooth-tongued talker. " And when these flatterers and flibbergibbes another day shall come and claw you by the back."— Latimer, *Sermons* (d. 1555), fol. 39.

FLEE, (a) " flee charge and find ease " (34c), *charge*= business, matters, affairs, anxieties, cares, responsibility.
(b) " worst part to flee " (69c).

FLEET, see Afloat.

FLEK, " flek and his make " (70a), *flek*=a generic reproach (of man or woman), specifically in contempt as of something altogether insignificant ; *make*=companion. " Fie upon me ! 'tis well known I am the mother Of children, scurvy fleak ! 'tis not for nought You boil eggs in your gruel."—Davenant, *Wits* (1636).

FLESH, (a) " it will not out of the flesh that is bred in the bone " (87c), *i.e.* cannot be eradicated ; in modern phrase, " What's bred in the bone will come out in the flesh." " He values me at a crack'd three farthings, for aught I see. It will never out of the flesh that's bred in the bone. I have told him enough, one would think, if that would serve ; but counsel to him is as good as a shoulder of mutton to a sick horse."— Jonson, *Every Man in his Humour* (1596).
(b) see Fish.

FLETCHER, " mend as the fletcher mends his bolt " (91a), *i.e.* not at all. " Her mind runs sure upon a fletcher, or a bowyer ; however, I'll inform against both ; the fletcher for taking whole money for pieced arrows ; the bowyer for horning the headmen of his parish, and taking money for his pains."—Rowley, *Match at Midn., O. Pl.* (Reed), vii. 378.

FLIBERGIBET, see Flebergebet.

HEY. II.   B B

FLIES, (*a*) " hungry flies bite sore " (91*c* ; 182*b*).
(*b*) see Blind.

FLIM-FLAM (24*b*), a lie, imposition.

FLINGING, " by flinging from your folks at home "
(91*b*), *flinging*=departing hastily, " rushing off."

FLOUNDER, see Frying pan.

FLOWER, " she is not only the fairest flower in your
garland, but also . . . all the fair flower thereof " (88*b*).

FLOWN, see Bird.

FLUNG, " he . . . flung away amain " (133*a*).

FLY, see Blind.

FOAL, " how can the foal amble if the horse and mare
trot? " (33*c*).

FOLK, " as folk ring bees with basins " (78*b*).

FOLLOW, " the wise man at all times to follow can find "
(82*a*).

FOLLY, see Hog, Wall.

FOND, " to wed with me fond are " (4*d*), *fond*=pleased.

FOOL, (*a*) " No fool to the old fool " (56*b* ; 203*d*).
" Comedie upon comedie he shall have ; a morall, a his-
torie, a tragedie, or what he will. One shal be called
the Doctor's dumpe . . . and last *a pleasant Enterlude
of No Foole to the Olde Foole*, with a jigge at the
latter end in English hexameters of *O Neighbour
Gabriel!! and his wooing of Kate Cotton.*"—Nash,
Have with you to Saffron Walden (1596).
(*b*) " a fool's bolt soon shot " (58*d* ; 205*d*), in quot.
sot=fool. " Sot is sot, and that is sene ; For he wel
speke wordes grene, Er ther hue buen rype. ' Sottes
bolt is sone shote,' Quoth Hendyng."—*Proverbs of
Hendyng*, MS. (*c*. 1320).
(*c*) " fair words make fools fain " (69*b* ; 204*c* and
d). " When thou art become one of that courtlie
trayne, Thinke on this proverbe olde, quod he, that
faire woordes make fools faine."—*Paradyse of Dayn-
tie Devises* (1578).
(*d*) " God sendeth fortune to fools " (75*d* ; 190*c*) ;
cf. " God watches over children, drunkards, and
fools."
(*e*) see Children.

FOOT, (a) " he loveth her better at the sole of the foot than ever he loved me at the heart root " (70d).

(b) " wrap it in the cloth and tread it under foot " (63d).

(c) " folk shew much folly, when things should be sped, to run to the foot, that may go to the head " (67b). " Thou that stondys so sure on sete, Ware lest thy hede falle to thy fete."—*The Boke of Curtasye,* MS. (c. 1350).

(d) see Black ox.

(e) " set in foot " (224b and c).

FOOTMANSHIP, " swift footmanship " (118d), pedestrianism.

FORBODDEN, " these hens be forbodden your sight " (116b), forbidden.

FORGAVE, " he forgave her, as he forgiven would be " (90a).

FORGETTETH, see Parish priest.

FORGIVE, " to forgive and forget " (90a).

FORGIVEN, " forgiven and forgotten " (59b).

FORGO, see Nought.

FORSPEAK, " forspeak not your fortune " (38c), gainsay.

FORTHINK, " better foresee than forthink " (148d), grieve, vex, repent.

FORTUNE, see God.

FOSTER, " no longer foster, no longer lemman " (96c), *foster* = to cherish, indulge, harbour ; *lemman* = darling, beloved one.

FOUGHTEN, " a hard foughten field where no man scapeth unkilled " (45d).

FOUL, (a) " foul water as soon as fair will quench hot fire " (13c).

(b) " though her mouth be foul she hath a fair tail " (13d), *i.e.* though she be shrewish yet her person is desirable.

(c) see Fair.

FOUL BIRD, see Bird.

FOUR QUARTERS, " since my four quarters in four quarters shall stand " (131*a*), quartering and drawing after hanging was once the punishment of treason.

FOX, (*a*) " be a man never so greedy to win, He can have no more of the fox but the skin " (96*a*; 189*d*).
  (*b*) " when the fox preacheth, then beware your geese " (82*c*; 201*c*).

'FRAID, " more 'fraid than hurt " (11*c*).

FRAY, " fray babes . . . from dugs " (261*c*), frighten, terrify. " Whenne Jacob was moost in fray, God him counfortide, that al do may."—*Cursor Mundi, MS. Coll. Trin. Cantab.* f. 30.

FREE, see Thought.

FRENCH, see Gentleman, Tott'n'am.

FRIDAY, " he may his part on Good Friday eat and fast never the worse " (36*a*), *i.e.* have nothing, Good Friday being a " black " or total fast.

FRIEND, (*a*) " a friend is never known till a man hath need " (46*a*; 218*b*).
  (*b*) " prove thy friend ere thou have need " (46*a*; 172*a*).
  (*c*) " ye may write to your friends that ye are in health " (62*b*; 210*d*).
  (*d*) " even reckoning maketh long friends " (213*a*).
  (*e*) see Kinsfolk.

FRO (*passim*), from.

FROG, see Fished.

FRYING PAN, " out of the frying pan into the fire " (72*c*), from bad to worse.

FULL, see Tun.

FURDER (192*d*), further : now dialectal or vulgar : see Wall.

FURTHER, (*a*) " might have gone further and have faren worse " (62*c*), see next entry.
  (*b*) " the further ye go, the further behind " (88*b*; 183*c*), see previous entry.

GAINS, see Light.

GALL, " rub him on the gall " (71*b*), *gall*=a sore, a rubbed place. " Enough, you rubbed the guiltie on the gaule."—*Mirr. for Mag.* (1559), 463.

GALLED, (*a*) " Gup ! with a galled back, Gill " (52*d*).
(*b*) see Horse.

GANDER, " not a more gaggling gander hence to Chester " (30*d*), cackling goose, a woman given to immoderate laughter and idle talk. " But when the priest is at seruice no man sitteth, but gagle and ducke like so many geese."—Hackluyt, *Voyages* (1582), i. 241.

GAPS, (*a*) " to stop two gaps with one bush " (95*a*), to do (or achieve) a double purpose : cf. " to kill two birds with one stone."
(*b*) " to stop gaps with rushes " (95*a*), a simile of futile effort.

GARDS, " broidered gards " (243*c*), trimmings, facings, ornaments on dress. " Nay, mock not, mock not ; the body of your discourse is sometimes guarded with fragments ; and the guards are but slightly basted on neither."—Shakspeare, *Much Ado* (1600), iii. 4. " On rhimes are guards on wanton Cupid's hose."—Shakspeare, *Love's L. L.* (1594), iv. 3.

GARSONS, " small wages maketh poor garsons " (226*c*), youth, page : Fr., *garcon*. " Ther sone was a prowde garson, Men hym clepyd syr Befown."—*MS. Cantab.*, Ff. ii. 38, f. 115.

GAT, " she gat a husband " (25*d*), got : an old preterite.

GATE, see Cross.

GAY, (*a*) " all thing is gay that is green " (54*a*), *green*=fresh, new, recent : cf. a green memory.
(*b*) " as we may we love to go gay " (27*a*).

GEAN, see Triacle.

GEAR, " ware that gear " (71*d*), *i.e.* be careful of that matter : *gear* formerly did service for not only dress or ornament, but for outfit of all kinds, goods, and property generally ; also matter, business, affair, &c. " I will remedy this gear ere long ! "—Shakspeare, 2 *Henry VI.* (1594), iii. 1.

GEAT, " nor nought we can geat " (11a), get : see the rhyme with " meat " in next line. Another example occurs (151b), where " geat me " rhymes with " eat me."

GEESE, see Fox.

GENTLE, " farewell, gentle Geoffrey " (36b).

GENTLEMAN, " Jack would be a gentleman if he could speak French " (35b) is obviously a relic of the Norman subversion of England. Speaking of the rule of the Anglo-Norman kings, the elder Disraeli writes :— " This was the time when it was held a shame among Englishmen to appear English. It became proverbial to describe a Saxon who ambitioned some distinguished rank, that ' he would be a gentleman if he could but talk French.' "—*Amenities of Literature.*

GERMAN'S LIPS, see Jerman.

GID, " such a gid did her head take " (40c), properly a disease in sheep, now known as " sturdy," marked by staggers, stupor, &c., and which is caused by an insect in the brain : hence *gid* here=" maggot," fancy, " bee in bonnet."

GIFT, (a) " throw no gift again at the giver's head " (37c; 17c), cf. " look no gift horse in the teeth."
(b) " as free of gift as a poor man of his eye " (37d).

GIFT HORSE, see Horse.

GILL, (a) wanton, strumpet : but the word, a common female name, does not always carry a bad meaning.
(b) see Jack.

GINIFINEE, see Nycebecetur.

GIRDLE, see Head, Key.

GIVE, " better to give than to take " (13b ; 169b), a later form is " better to give than to receive."

GIVER'S HEAD, see Gift.

GLEANING, " thou goest a-gleaning ere the cart have carried " (34b), *i.e.* you are " too previous "; you seek a thing before it is lost.

GLISTERS (GLITTERS or GLISTENS), see Gold.

GLOME, GLOMED, " did lower and glome " (23*c*)—" folks
  glomed on me too " (23*c*), lour, look gloomy.

GLOW, see Ear.

Go, see Children, Come, Further, Light, Run.

GOD, (*a*) " she is one of them to whom God bad ho ! "
  (39*d* ; 199*b*), *ho* = stop : a common exclamation to
  arrest attention, and more particularly a call to cessa-
  tion of action : " *There is no ho with him* " = he is
  not to be restrained.
    (*b*) " God is where he was " (46*d* ; 218*a*).
    (*c*) " here is God in th' aumbry " (63*d* ; 194*d*), (*a*)
  aumbry = cupboard, pantry, almonry ; specifically a
  room in which alms were distributed ; and (*b*) *ambry*
  = a niche or cupboard near the altar in a church in
  which were kept the utensils used for public worship ;
  a slight confusion exists between the two forms which,
  however, is of little moment.
    (*d*) " every man for himself and God for us all "
  (96*d* ; 184*b*).
    (*e*) " God is no botcher " (53*a* ; 177*a*).
    (*f*) " alway the grace of God is worth a fair " (46*c*),
  see Fair.
    (*g*) " out of God's blessing into the warm sun "
  (67*a*), from bad to worse ; " to jump out of the fry-
  ing-pan into the fire " : and conversely, " I am too
  much i' the sun " (*Hamlet,* i. 2) = unfortunate, un-
  blessed. " Therefore if thou wilt follow my advice, and
  prosecute thine own determination, thou shalt come
  out of a warme Sunne into God's blessing."—Lyly,
  Euphues (1579), 23*b*. " Pray God they bring us not,
  when all is done, Out of God's blessing into this
  warm sun."—Harrington, *Epig.* (*d.* 1612), ii. 56.
    (*h*) " God sendeth cold after clothes " (11*b*). " Dieu
  donne le froid selon la robbe," is the French form of
  this proverb, found in *Les Prémices* (1594), by Henry
  Estienne.
    (*i*) " God never sendeth mouth but he sendeth
  meat " (11*a*).
    (*j*) " there was God . . . when all is done " (17*c*).
    (*k*) " who hopeth in God's help his help cannot
  start " (11*c*), *start* = change, put aside, alter.
    (*l*) " God stint all strife " (88*d*).
    (*m*) " God have mercy, brother " (88*d*).

(*n*) " spend and God shall send " (66*d*).

(*o*) " God will send time to provide for time " (47*b*).

(*p*) " God and Saint Luke save you " (43*a*).

(*q*) " God sendeth fortune to fools " (75*d* ; 190*c*).

(*r*) see Church, Cow, Horse.

GODCHILDREN, see Children.

GODFREY, see Gentle.

GOETH, (*a*) " as fast as one goeth another cometh " (188*a*).

(*b*) see Hare, Pot.

GOLD, (*a*) " all is not gold that glitters " (27*c*). " Uns proverbes dit et raconte Que tout n'est pas ors c'on voit luire."—*Li Diz de freire Denise cordelier* (*c.* 1300). "All things that shineth is not by and by pure gold."—Udall, *Ralph Roister Doister* (1566). See also Chaucer, *Chanones Yemannes Tale,* and Lydgate, *On the Mutability of Human Affairs.*

(*b*) " a man may buy gold too dear " (81*c*).

(*c*) " in words gold and whole " (77*d*), words of wisdom and import : the simile of golden speech is common, and on the other hand we have, " Speech is silvern, but silence is golden."

(*d*) see Fetters.

GOOD, (*a*) " of a good beginning cometh a good end " (25*d*). " But in proverbe I have herde saie, That who that well his warke beginneth, The rather a good ende he winneth."—Gower, *Confessio Amantis* (1393).

(*b*) " a man far from his good is nigh his harm " (91*c* ; 193*a*).

(*c*) " they know no end of their good nor beginning of any goodness " (39*c*) : see *d*.

(*d*) " he knoweth none end of his good " (221*b*).

(*e*) " to do me, not the more good, but the less harm " (24*d*).

(*f*) " may do her good and you no harm " (29*a*).

(*g*) " if he be good now, of his ill past no force " (33*b*), by repentance and well-doing forgiveness is won.

(*h*) " with many conditions good, one that is ill Defaceth the flower of all, and doth all spill " (76*d*), *i.e.* " the strength of a chain is that of its weakest link."

(*i*) " evil gotten good never proveth well " (42*d*).

(*j*) " her good be laid up so, lest thieves might spy it, that n'other she could, nor he can, come by it " (100*c*).

(*k*) " he that hath plenty of goods shall have more ; He that hath but little, he shall have less ; He that hath right nought, right nought shall possess " (46*b*).

(*l*) " I hope good hap be not all outworn " (93*d*).

(*m*) " she . . . for love . . . he . . . for good . . . to wed " (128*c*), *good* (as in *c, d, i, j*)=property.

(*n*) see Beginning, Enough, Farthing, Feast, Good, Horse, Merry, Play, Wind, Wit.

GOOD CHEAP, see Bargains, Best.

GOODWIN SANDS, " set up shop upon Goodwin's sands " (92*c*), properly Godwin Sands, from Godwin Earl of Kent, the father of King Harold II. The land now represented by these quicksands (off the east coast of Kent) was given to the monastery of St. Augustin at Canterbury, but the abbot neglecting to keep the sea wall in repair, the tract was submerged about 1100.

GOOSE, (*a*) " the pure penitent that stale a goose and stuck down a feather " (42*c* ; 201*a*), otherwise " to steal a goose and give the giblets in alms."

(*b*) " as deep drinketh the goose as the gander " (82*d*), " what is good for the goose is good for the gander " is the modern version. " Gentlewoman, either you thought my wits very short, that a sip of wine could alter me, or else yours very sharp, to cut me off so roundly, when as I (without offence be it spoken) have heard, that as deepe drinketh the goose as the gander."—Lyly, *Euphues and his England.*

GOOSE GIBLET, see Hare.

GOSLING, " who meddleth in all things may shoe the gosling " (59*d* ; 209*c*), undertake a work of supererogation, engage in a foolish or profitless task. " Whoso melles of wat men dos, Let hym cum hier and shoo the ghos."—*Inscrip.* in Whalley Church (*c.* 1434). " What hath lay men to do The gray goose for to sho ! "—Skelton, *Colin Clout* (*c.* 1510). Compare " It is as great pyte to se a woman wepe as a gose to go barefote."—*Hundred Mery Talys* (*c.* 1525).

GOSPEL, " all is not gospel that thou dost speak " (57*a*), the exact truth.

GOTTEN, (*a*) " soon gotten, soon spent " (76*a*).
    (*b*) " ill gotten, ill spent " (76*a*).

GRACE, (*a*) " in space cometh grace " (11*a*; 171*a*), in time a condition of mind and conduct that embellishes character and commands favour and esteem : cf. *past grace* = devoid of shame.
    (*b*) see Heart.

GRAFFS (228*d*), grafts, slips, cuttings, young plants.

GRAFT, " then graft we a green graft on a rotten root " (45*a*).

GRASS, (*a*) " while the grass groweth the horse sterveth " (36*d*). " Whylst grass doth growe, oft sterves the seely steede."—Whetstone, *Promos and Cassandra* (1578). " Ay, sir, but, While the grass grows,—The proverb is something musty."—Shakspeare, *Hamlet* (1596), iii. 2.
    (*b*) see Heart.

GRATETH, " where this . . . gravely grateth " (6*b*), touches, concerns, disturbs. " Grating so harshly all his days of quiet."—Shakspeare, *Hamlet* (1596), iii. 1.

GREASE, " she fryeth in her own grease " (44*d*), to be left vindictively or resentfully alone : also " stew in one's own juice." " But certeynly I made folk such chere That in his owne grees I made him frie."—Chaucer, *Prologue of Wyf of Bathe.*

GREAT, see Small.

GREATEST, see Clerks.

GREEDY, " they be both greedy guts all given to get " (39*c*), gluttons. " *Edace*, an eater, a devourer, a greedigut."—Florio, *Worlde of Wordes* (1598).

GREEN, see Cheese, Moon, Rushes.

GREEVES, (*a*) " lamenting their greeves " (47*a*), here shin shackles or the stocks, with an eye on the old plural of grief. An iron foot was formerly so called (see *Mir. Mag.* 46).
    (*b*) see 180*b*, Epigram 69. " On Theft and Receipt."

GRIEVES, see Greeves.

GRINDSTONE, see Nose.

GROANING, " a groaning horse and a groaning wife never fail their master " (60c), *groaning-wife*=a woman ready to lie-in. " As smoothe as a groaning-wive's bellie."—Nashe, *Unf. Trav.* (1594), 92 (Chiswick Press, 1892).

GROAT, (a) see Bestill.
    (b) " not worth a groat " (33d, 38b), a small standard of value; *grey groat*=something of no value, a " brass farthing." " I 'll not leave him worth a grey groat."—Marlowe, *Jew of Malta* (1586), iv. 4.
    (c) " who can sing so merry a note As may he that cannot change a groat? " (47a).

GROIN, " like a hog hangeth the groin on her husband " (74c), *groin* (A.N.) = to grumble, and as subs. = grumbler, malcontent : usually " groiner."

GROMWELL SEED, " fair words did fet gromwell seed plenty " (53c), possibly with an eye on *gravelled*= worried, vexed ; gromwell seed being anciently administered for the cure of gravel.

GROUND, (a) " these lovers . . . think the ground bear them not " (25c), *i.e.* in modern phrase, are " up in the skies," have neither eyes nor ears for aught but their mutual endearments.
    (b) see Stools.

GROWETH, see Grass, Weed.

GUEST, (a) " an unbidden guest knoweth not where to sit " (21b).
    (b) " I bid you to dinner as no guest " (59a), *i.e.* without formality, to take " pot-luck," as we now have it. Or, it may be elliptical=" as we have no invited guests."

GUNSTONE, see Pith.

GUTTER, see Cat.

GYLES, " dread of such gyles " (48c), guiles, deceits. " Many on trowyn on here wylys, And many tymes the pye hem gylys."—*MS. Harl.* (1701), f. 3.

HAB OR NAB (9b), have or have not, without order, by fair means or foul.

HACKNEY-MEN (40b), originally proprietors of horses let for hire : *hackney*=a saddle horse. It was not until the reign of Charles I. that the title was transferred to the drivers of vehicles, the year 1625 being the date of the first appearance of hackney coaches in the streets of London. They were then only twenty in number, but the innovation occasioned an outcry (Sharman) : " The world runs on wheels. The hackney-men, who were wont to have furnished travellers in all places with fitting and serviceable horses for any journey, (by the multitude of coaches) are undone by the dozens, and the whole commonwealth most abominably jaded, that in many places a man had as good to ride on a wooden post, as to poast it upon one of those hunger-starv'd hirelings."—Taylor, *Works* (1630).

HAD, (a) " had I wist " (6c ; 219d), had I known : a common exclamation in old writers, who also used it substantively. " But, out alas, I wretch too late did sorrowe my amys, Unless lord Promos graunt me grace, in vayne is had-y-wist."—Whetstone, *Promos and Cassandra* (1578), ii. 2. " His pallid feares, his sorrows, his affrightings, His late-wisht had-I-wists, remorcefull bitings."—Browne, *Brit. Past.* (1613), I., ii. 57.
   (b) " who had that he hath not would do that he doeth not " (95d).

HADDOCK, (a) " not worth a haddock " (99d), of small value : cf. " as witty as a haddock "=downright foolish (*Hickscorner* [*c.* 1550], E.E.D.S., *Anon. Plays,* Ser. 1, 153b).
   (b) " thus had he brought haddock to paddock " (99d), outrun the constable : *haddock=cod=*purse (" the fish we call a hadock, or a cod " [Florio])— the meaning thus being, a purse or bag of money has melted as if cast to the paddocks (frogs).

HAIR, (a) " make his hair grow through his hood " (66b ; 198a), go-betweens will become rivals : usually the phrase means " to cuckold." " It will make his hair grow through his hood."—Ingelend, *Disobedient Child* (*c.* 1550), *Works* (E.E.D.S.), 74b. " French hood,

French hood, I will make your hair grow thorough."
—Middleton, *Anything for a Quiet Life* (1662).

(*b*) " long hair and short wit " (82*d*). " Hair ! 'tis
the basest stubble ; in scorn of it The proverb sprung,
—He has more hair than wit."—Decker, *Satiromastix*
(1602). " More hair than wit,—it may be ; I'll prove
it : The cover of the salt hides the salt, and therefore
it is more than the salt : the hair, that covers the
wit, is more than the wit, for the greater hides the
less."—Shakspeare, *Two Gentlemen of Verona* (1595),
iii. 2.

(*c*) " take a hair from his beard " (78*d*).

(*d*) see Chickens, Dog.

HALF, (*a*) " this half sheweth what the whole meaneth "
(84*d*).

(*b*) " that's just if the half shall judge the whole "
(50*a*).

(*c*) " half warned, half armed " (77*a*), the modern
version is " forewarned, forearmed."

HALFPENNY, see Hand.

HALL, " it is merry in hall when beards wag all " (79*d*),
an extremely popular saying in olden times. " 'It is
merry in hall when beards wag all.' Husband, for
this, these words to mind I call : This is meant by
men, in their merry eating, Not to wag their beards
in brawling and threating.—Wife, the meaning hereof
differeth not two pins, Between wagging of men's
beards and women's chins " (167*b*).

HALTING, see Cripple.

HALTER, " thy taking of thine halter in thine arms
teacheth other to beware of their harms by thine "
(42*b*).

HALVES, " as for that, reason runneth to halves—As
well for the cow calf as for the bull " (62*a*), see
Cow-calf.

HAND, (*a*) " so hard is your hand set on your halfpenny " (14*c* ; 174*b*), eye on main chance, attention
on self-interest. " *Ri.* Dromio, looke heere, now is
my hand on my half-peny. *Half.* Thou liest, thou
hast not a farthing to lay thy hands on."—Lyly,
Mother Bombie (1594).

(b) " lay your hand on your heart " (101c), as a symbol of sincerity.

(c) " glad is he that hath her in hand " (52d), under control.

(d) " many hands make light wark " (66b ; 221d). " The werke is the soner done that hathe many handes : Many handys make light werke : my leve child."—*How the Goode Wif Thaught hir Doughter* (c. 1471), 113.

(e) " both their hands full " (73c).

(f) " she can play on both hands " (24b), is expert, " wide."

(g) see Bird, Call, Claw.

HANG, (a) " he that hangeth himself a Sunday, Shall hang still uncut down a Monday for me " (33b).

(b) " hang the bell about the cat's neck " (38d), see *infra*. " But they are loth to mell, and loth to hang the bell about the cat's neck, for dread to have a check."—Skelton, *Colin Clout* (c. 1518), 165. " But, quoth one Mouse unto the rest, Which of us all dare be so stout To hang the bell cat's neck about? If here be any, let him speake. Then all replide, We are too weake : The stoutest Mouse and tallest Rat Doe tremble at a grim-fac'd Cat."—*Diogines Lanthorne* (1607).

(c) see Keys.

HANGED, (a) " he that hath an ill name is half hanged " (77a), or modern, " give a dog a bad name and hang him."

(b) see Cord, Hatchet.

HANGING, see Wedding.

HAP, (a) " such hap here hapt " (48c)—" brought by good hap " (75c), chance, fortune : subs. or verb.

(b) " in hope of good hap " (100c), see *supra*.

HAPPETH, " it happeth in an hour that happeth not in seven year " (38c ; 172c).

HAPPY, (a) " happy man, happy dole " (9d ; 224d), a generic wish for success. " Wherein, happy man be his dole, I trust that I Shall not speede worst, and that very quickly."—Edwards, *Damon and Pith.*, *O. Pl.* (Reed), i. 177.

(b) " better be happy then wise " (75c ; 190b).

HARBOROUGH, " good harborough " (223*d*), shelter, harbour, refuge. " Ah pleasant harborough of my heart's thought ! Ah sweet delight, the quick'ner of my soul." —Wilmot and others, *Tancred and Gism.*

HARD, (*a*) " ill believed and worse hard " (91*b*), heard : note the rhyme.
  (*b*) see Cripple.

HARDLY, " hardly if ye can " (59*c*), boldly, certainly. " And hardly, aungel, trust therto, For doughtles it shal be do."—*MS. Coll. Trin. Dubl.* D. iv. 18.

HARD WALL, see Wall.

HARDY, " ye be hardy " (135*d*), courageous, bold.

HARE, (*a*) " there goeth the hare away " (73*a* ; 190*a*), " that's the gist, trend, secret, why and wherefore of the matter." " *Man.* By my fayth a lytell season I folowd the counsell and dyet of reason. *Gets.* There went the hare away."—Medwall, *Nature* (1510).
  (*b*) " to hold with the hare and run with the hound " (24*a* ; 180*c*), play a double game, keep on good terms with two contending parties.
  (*c*) " mad as March hare " (73*a* ; 184*b*), a proverbial type of madness ; but Skelton has it differently. " Thanne they begynne to swere and to stare, And be as braynles as a Marshe hare."—*Blowbol's Test* (14—?). " As mery as a Marche hare."—Skelton, *Magn.* (1526), 930. " I saye, thou madde Marche hare."—Skelton, *Replycation Against Certayne Yong Scolers* (1520).
  (*d*) " catch (or hunt for) a hare with a taber " (21*a*), to engage in or attempt a hopeless task : the taber was a shallow drum beaten with the fingers. " The poore man that gives but his bare fee, or perhaps pleads *in formâ pauperis,* he hunteth for hares with a taber, and gropeth in the darke to find a needle in a botle of hay."—Greene, *Quip for an Upstart Courtier* (1592), *Harl. Misc.,* v. 407. " One day after the set of this comet men shall catch hares with tabers." —Simon Smel-knave, *Fearefull and Lamentable Effects of Two Dangerous Comets* (1591).
  (*e*) " set the hare's head against the goose jiblet "

(64*a*). " Ide set mine old debts against my new
driblets, And the hare's foot against the goose giblets."—Decker, *Shomakers Holiday* (1600).

HARM, (*a*) " there is no harm done in all this fray,
Neither pot broken nor water spilt " (44*c*).

> (*b*) " thou art so wood thou knowest not who doth
> thee harm, who doth thee good " (86*c*).

> (*c*) " it is good to beware by other men's harms "
> (42*b*).

HARP, (*a*) " ye harp on the string that giveth no
melody " (63*d*), dwell persistently : see *infra.*

> (*b*) " harp no more on that string " (96*d* ; 184*c*),
> *supra.*

HARPERS, " have among you blind harpers " (79*b*), a
proverbial pledge in drinking.   Macaulay observes
that in the old ballad poetry, all the gold is " red "
and all the ladies " gay."   So, also, the harpers are
blind.   *The Poet's Blind Man's Bough: or, Have
among you blinde Harpers,* was the title of a tract
by Martin Parker, printed in 1651.   " *Leoc.* Have
towards thee, Philotas.   *Phil.* To thee, Archippus.
Arch. To thee, Molops.   *Molops.* Have among you,
blind fiddlers."—Cartwright, *Royall Slave* (1651).

HARVEST, " a long harvest for a little corn " (46*c*).

HARVEST EARS, see Ears.

HASKARD, " as I were a haskard " (291*d*), a sloven.

HASTE, (*a*) " haste maketh waste " (60*c* ; 169*d*).

> (*b*) " the more haste the less speed " (7*a*).

> (*c*) " in more haste than good speed " (20*b*).

> (*d*) " no haste but good " (97*c*).

> (*e*) " then seeth he haste and wisdom things far
> odd " (7*a*).

> (*f*) " ye had like haste to waste " (95*b*).

HASTY, " hasty man never wanteth woe " (7*b* ; 167*d*),
" Thou wert afire to be a ladie, and now your ladi-
ship and you may both blowe at the cole, for aught I
know. ' Selfe doe, selfe have.' ' The hastie man
never wanteth woe,' they say."—Jonson, &c., *Eastward Hoe* (1605), v. 1.

HAT, " mine old hat must have a new band " (52*d*).

HATCH, see Door.

HATCHET, " I have hanged up my hatchet " (33*b* ; 197*d*).

HATH BEEN, " ye know what he hath been . . . ye know not what he is " (37*d*).

HAUT, " men haut or high " (81*d*), *haut*=proud. " No lord of thine, thou haught insulting man."—Shakspeare, *Richard II.* (1597), iv. 1.

HAVE, see Harpers, Hold, Nought, Wind, Wish.

HAVOC, " he maketh havoc " (65*d*).

HAWK, (*a*) " she hath one point of a good hawk, she is hardy " (64*b*), bold, stubborn.
(*b*) " he hath his hawks in the mew, but With empty hands men may no hawks allure " (66*b*), *mew* =a place where falcons were kept.

HAWKING, (*a*) " the first point of hawking is hold fast " (64*b*).
(*b*) " hawking upon me, his mind herein to break " (18*a*), spluttering, spitting : *hawk* is from Welsh " hochi," apparently an imitative word (Skeat).

HEAD, (*a*) " then have you his head fast under your girdle " (71*b* ; 205*b*), on the hip, " in chancery."
(*b*) " break my head and give me a plaster " (95*b*).
(*c*) " a scald head is soon broken " (60*b*).
(*d*) " my aching head to ease I will couch a hogshead " (58*b*), see Couch.
(*e*) " when the head acheth, all the body is the worse " (85*d*).
(*f*) " their heads be full of bees " (47*c*), projects : usually denotive, however, of crazy crotchets. " But, Wyll, my maister hath bees in his head."—Edwards, *Damon and Pithias* (1571).
(*g*) see Nail.
(*h*) " to-morrow I will to my beads to pray that as ye both will, so ache your heads " (58*a*).
(*i*) " so many heads, so many wits " (9*c* ; 168*d*). " Quot homines tot sententiæ " (Terence). " For amonge feaders are alwayes sondry appetytes, and in great assemblyes of people, dyuurse, and varyaunt judgements ; as the saynge is, so many heades, so many wyttes."—Queen Elizabeth, *Godly Meditacyon of the Christen Sowle* (1548). " Ah, sirha, I see wel

HEY. II.   C C

the olde proverbe is true, which saith : so many men so many mindes."—Gascoigne, *Glasse of Government* (1575).

(*k*) " two heads are better than one " (23*a*).

(*l*) see Cap, Dead, Foot, Gift.

HEALING, " It is ill healing of an old sore " (87*c*).

HEALTH, " ye may write to your friends that ye are in health " (62*b* ; 210*d*).

HEAR, (*a*) " a man should hear all parts, ere he judge any " (49*b* ; 202*d*).

(*b*) " I cannot hear on that side " (187*c*), an excuse for wilful deafness.

HEART, (*a*) " to set at my heart that thou settest at thy heel " (34*b* ; 175*a* and *b*).

(*b*) " she taketh such heart of grace " (87*c*), to pick up courage, some thinking it was originally " to take heart at grass " : in the *Epigrams on Proverbs* (183*d*) both forms occur—" thou takest heart of grass . . . not heart of grace." " He came within the castle wall to-day, His absence gave him so much heart of grace, Where had my husband been but in the way, He durst not," &c.—Harington, *Ariost.* (1591), xxi. 39. " Seeing she would take no warning, on a day took heart at grasse, and belabour'd her well with a cudgel."—Tarlton, *News out of Purgatory* (1590).

(*c*) " your heart is in your hose " (36*d* ; 175*d*), a simile of fear or trepidation : modern, " heart in mouth " or " shoes." " Be your hearts in your hose? "— *Thersites, Anon. Pl.,* Ser. 1 (E.E.D.S.), 208*a*.

(*d*) see Eye, Hose.

HEAVEN, (*a*) " she made us cheer heaven high " (60*a*), heartily, " sky-high," " raise the roof."

(*b*) see Hell.

HEAVY, see Burden, Hot, Light.

HEDGE, (*a*) " where the hedge is lowest, men may soonest over " (68*d*). " Where hedge is lowe, there every man treads downe, And friendship failes, when Fortune list to frowne."—Gascoigne, *Posies* (1575).

(*b*) see Stake.

HEED, " take heed is a fair thing " (88*c*).

HEELS, (a) " show (or take to) a fair pair of heels "
(78b), to take flight, run away. " Darest thou be so
valiant as to play the coward with thy indenture and
show it a fair pair of heels? "—Shakspeare, 1 *Henry
IV.* (1598), ii. 4.

　(b) see Cow, Heart.

HEINSBY (38a), upstart, " nouveau riche "; a generic
reproach of any person in an inferior grade of society,
or of low origin : cf. *rudesby* = an impertinent.

HEKST, " when bale is hekst, boot is next " (46c ;
225d), things when at worst begin to mend. " When
bale is greatest, then is bote a nie bore."—Chaucer,
Testament of Love.

HELL, (a) " uphill to heavenward, downhill to hell "
(274d).

　(b) " they that be in hell ween there is none other
heaven " (40a).

HEN, (a) " as nice as a nun's hen " (52c), a very ancient
proverbial simile : ? *nun* = (a) a variety of pigeon
having its head almost covered with a veil of feathers ;
(b) the smew ; or (c) the blue titmouse—most likely
the last. " Women, women, love of women, Make
bare purs with some men. Some be nyse as a nonne
hene, Yet al thei be not soo ; Some be lewde, some
all be schrewde, Go schrewes wher thei goo."—
Satirical Verses on Women (1462). " I have the
taught dyvysyon between Frende of effect, and frende
of countenaunce ; The nedeth not the gall of none hen
That cureth eyen."—Lydgate, *Proverbes* (c. 1520).
" I knewe a priest that was as nice as a Nonnes
Henne."—Wilson, *Arte of Rhetorique* (1562).

　(b) see Cockney.

HEPT, " this hall hept with gold " (36a), heaped.

HERBENGERS, " their horses be their herbengers " (119d),
harbinger : properly *herberger*, or *herbergeour*, originally one who not only announced the approaching
arrival of a guest, but who made all ready for his
reception ; hence a messenger.

HERE, see Some.

HEREAFTER, " though hereafter come not yit " (82a).

HERRING, see Fish.

HEW, " hew not too high lest the chips fall in thine eye " (82a). " For an old proverbe it is ledged ' he that heweth to hie, with chips he may lose his sight.' " —Chaucer, *Testament of Love.*

HEYWOOD (JOHN), see Terminal Essay, Vol. III.

HIGH, (a) " not too high for the pye, nor too low for the crow " (82a ; 214b).
 (b) see Hew.
 (c) " her heart is full high when her eye is full low " (28a).
 (d) " high in t' instep " (216a), haughty, proud, arrogant. " Now the gentleman was growne higher in the instep, as appeared by the insolent conditions he required."—Moryson, *Itin.* (1617), II. 26.

HILT, " I will as soon be hilt " (44c), probably =cudgelled : *hilt*=cudgel.

HIP, " then have ye him on the hip or on the hurdle " (71b), at an advantage : probably from hunting (Nares) ; the hurdle in old law was a frame or sledge on which criminals were drawn from the prison to the place of execution, and designed to preserve the offender from the extreme torment of being dragged on the ground. " I'll have our Michael Cassio on the hip."—Shakspeare, *Othello* (1602), ii. 7.

HO, " to whom God bade Ho ! " (39d), originally a call or exclamation ; hence a stop or limit, and whence many idioms—*out of all ho*=out of all bounds ; *no ho with him*=not to be restrained ; *Let us ho*=stop. " Howbeit they would not crie hoa here, but sent in post some of their covent to Rome? "—Stanihurst, *Description of Ireland,* 26.

HODDYPEAK (121c), fool, craven : a generic reproach. " They counte peace to be cause of ydelnes, and that it maketh men hodipekes and cowardes."—Christopherson, *Exh. against Rebel* (1554).

HOG, (a) " routing like a hog " (30a), *rout*=snore. " Hark, my pygg, how the knave dooth rowte ! Well, whyle he sleepth in Idlenes lappe, Idlenes marke on hym shall I cappe."—*Wit and Science* (E.E.D.S., Anon. Pl. Ser. 4).

(*b*) " every man basteth the fat hog, but the lean shall burn ere he basted be " (46*a* ; 225*c* and *d*).

(*c*) " cast precious stones before hogs " (93*a* ; 182*d*), a variant of " to cast pearls before swine."

HOGSTOWN (293*a*), ? Hoxton : play on *hog* (=churl, clown) in connection with place names was common. The classical instance is, " I think thou wast born at Hogs-Norton (a village in Oxfordshire, and properly Hoch, or High Norton, neighbouring towns or hamlets being Chipping Norton, Over Norton, &c.) where pigs play upon the organs," and applied to clownish behaviour. Then " over a Hogsdon cask " (=hurriedly, unceremoniously); " a hog in armour " (of a rustic or lout in fine apparel); " hog-rabbler " (=a churl, clown, clodhopper); " hog-in-togs " (=a well-dressed loafer : American ; cf. " hog in armour "); " hog-age " (=hobbledehoyhood) ; " hog-grubber " (= a niggard) ; and so forth.

HOLD, (*a*) " hold fast when ye have it " (29*c* ; 226*d*), " sit tight," " freeze on to."

(*b*) " hold ye fast . . . lest ye be cast " (64*b*).

(*c*) " who may hold that will away " (75*d*).

(*d*) [She will] "let fall her hold [rather] than be too bold " (64*b*).

(*e*) see Hare, Nose, Shoe.

HOLE, see Day.

HOLY DAY, (*a*) " this gear was gotten on a holy day " (75*d*).

(*b*) " he laid her up for holy days " (100*c*).

HOME, (*a*) " home is homely though it be poor " (11*b* ; 169*a*).

(*b*) " thou gossipest at home to meet me at land's end " (83*a*).

HONESTY, " the flower of honesty " (28*b*), cf. " flower of chivalry," " flower of the flock," &c.

HONEY, " where words seemed honey . . . now are they mustard " (54*b*).

HONEY MOON, " it was yet but honey moon " (17*c*).

HOOD, (*a*) " by my hood " (102*d*), formerly, as now, the

commonest as well as the most sacred things were convenient pegs upon which to hang a " cussword."

(*b*) see Bean, Chickens, Ear, Face.

HOOK, (*a*) " avale, unhappy hook " (44*a*), adieu : *hook* = a term of reproach, here equivalent to " miserable failure." " That unhappy hook."—Heywood, *Works* (E.E.D.S.), I., 26*c* and 35*d*.

(*b*) " by hook or crook " (44*a*), by some means or other, by fair means or foul, at all hazards : a term derived from old forestry. " Nor will suffer this boke, By hooke or by crooke, Prynted for to be."— Skelton, *Colin Clout* (1520). " Dynmure Wood was ever open and common to the . . . inhabitants of Bodmin . . . to bear away upon their backs a burden of lop, crop, hook, crook, and bag wood."—*Bodmin Register* (1525).

(*c*) see Cross.

HOP-ON-MY-THUMB, " it is a small hop on my thumb " (31*b*), a small, insignificant person : in derision. " Plain friend hop o' my thumb, know you who we are? "—Shakspeare, *Taming of the Shrew* (1593).

HOPPETH, " when wooers hop in and out, long time may bring him that hoppeth best at last to have the ring " (9*a*).

HORNS, see Cow.

HORN WOOD (99*c*), *i.e.* horn-mad, stark staring mad, originally because cuckolded ; see Wood. " Sure my mistress is horn-mad."—Shakspeare, *Comedy of Errors* (1593), ii. 1.

HOROLOGE, see Devil.

HORSADOWN (291*b*), ? Horsleydown.

HORSE, (*a*) " rub a galled horse on the back and he will kick " (196*c*), see next entry.

(*b*) " I rub the galled horse back till he winch " (84*c*), *winch* = wince.

(*c*) " a scald horse is good enough for a scabb'd squire " (40*b*), *i.e.* like to like ; a mangy screw is good enough for a disreputable rider : " scald " and " scabb'd " are synonymous, and both are used in contempt of anything shabby, disgusting, or paltry. " Like lettuce like lips, a scabb'd horse for a scald squire."—*New Custom, Anon. Pl.*, Ser. 1 (E.E.D.S.),

174*d*. In the *Epigrams* (200*c*), the identity of
" scald " and " scabb'd " is shown by the wording
of the proverb being reversed.

(*d*) " a short horse is soon curried " (23*b* ; 174*c*).

(*e*) " a man may well lead a horse to the water, but
he cannot make him drink " (33*a* ; 175*b*).

(*f*) " a good horse that never stumbleth " (20*a* ;
187*a*). " A good horse that trippeth not once in a
journey."—*Three Proper and Wittie Familiar Letters*
(1580).

(*g*) " some man may steal a horse better than some
other may stand and look " (91*d* ; 203*a*). " Good Epi,
let mee take a nap ; for as some man may better
steale a horse then another looke over a hedge ; so
divers shall be sleepie when they would fainest take
rest."—Lyly, *Endimion* (1591).

(*h*) " it is . . . a proud horse that will not bear
his own provender " (98*b*). " Sir, hee's a proud horse
that will not carry his own provander, I warrant yee."
—Porter, *Two Angry Women of Abingdon* (1599).

(*i*) " recover the horse, or lese the saddle too "
(95*a*).

(*j*) " no man ought to look a given horse in the
mouth " (13*c*). " A gyven hors may not be loked in
the tethe."—*Vulgaria Stambrigi* (*c.* 1510). " It is
certainly as old as Jerome, a Latin father of the fourth
century ; who when found fault with . . . quoted the
proverb, that it did not behove to look a gift horse
in the mouth."—Trench, *Proverbs and their Lessons*.

(*k*) " as shortly as a horse will lick his ear " (93*d*).

(*l*) " it would have made a horse break his halter "
(53*d*).

(*m*) " God have mercy, horse " (78*c*), *i.e.* God help
us ; according to *Tarlton's Jests* (1611), this arose from
an adventure of Richard Tarlton, the player, with
Banks's performing horse, Morocco, the phrase being
a retort that tickled the ears of the assembled crowd
and " caught on."

(*n*) " the grey mare is the better horse " (64*a*), the
wife is master : a tradition, perhaps, of the time when
priests were forbidden to carry arms or ride on a
male horse : *Non enim licuerate pontificem sacrorum
vel arma ferre, vel praeter quam in equuâ equitare.*—
Beda, *Hist. Eccl.* ii. 13. Cf. Fr. *Mariage d'épervier*=a

hawk's marriage; the female hawk being the larger
and stronger bird. Lord Macaulay's explanation (pre-
ference given to the grey mares of Flanders over the
finest coach horses of England) is the merest guess-
work. "What! shall the graye mayre be the better
horse, And the wanton styll at home?"—*Pryde and
Abuse of Women Now a Dayes* (*c.* 1550).

(*o*) "evermore the common horse is worst shod"
(42*a*), cf↓ "the shoemaker's wife is worst shod."

(*p*) "folk call on the horse that will carry alway"
(42*a*), in modern phrase, "the willing horse is always
most ridden."

(*q*) "as wholesome a morsel for my comely corse
as a shoulder of mutton for a sick horse" (85*a*),
utterly worthless, distasteful. "Counsel to him is as
good as a shoulder of mutton to a sick horse."—
Jonson, *Every Man in his Humour* (1596), ii. 1.

(*r*) see Cart, Colt, Galled, Grass.

HORSE LOAVES, "as high as two horse loaves her person
is" (24*c*), a jocular standard of measurement (sometimes three horse loaves): compare the phrase, still
current, which says that diminutive persons must
stand on three penny loaves to look over the back of
a goat, or a duck. The horse-loaf was made of beans
and wheat. "Her stature scant three horse loaves
did exceed."—Harington, *Ariosto.*

HORSE PLUM, "purple ruddy like a horse plum" (24*c*),
horse, a generic qualificative=coarse, large.

HOSE, "your heart is in your hose" (36*d*; 175*d*).
"*Primus Pastor.* Breck outt youre voce, yet se as ye
yelp. *Tercius Pastor.* I may not for the pose bot I
have help. *Secundus Pastor.* A, thy hert is in thy
hose."—*Towneley Mysteries* (*c.* 1430).

HOST, see Oste, Reckoners.

HOT, (*a*) "hot love soon cold" (6*d*). "Dowghter, in
this I can thinke none oother But that it is true thys
proverbe old, Hastye love is soone hot and soone
cold!"—*Wyt and Science* (*c.* 1540), *Anon. Pl.,* Ser. 4.

(*b*) "when th' iron is hot, strike" (8*c*), act at the
right moment, seize an opportunity. Fr. "Messieurs,
ce pendant que le fer est chauld il le fault battre"

(Rabelais, II. 31). " *Birdlime*. Strike whilst the iron is hot. A woman, when there be roses in her cheeks, cherries on her lips, civet in her breath, ivory in her teeth, lilies in her hand, and liquorice in her heart, why, she's like a play : if new, very good company ; but if stale, like old Jeronimo, go by, go by, therefore, as I said before, strike."—Webster, *Westward Ho* (1607). See Iron.

(c) " little pot soon hot," see Pot.

(d) " neither too heavy nor too hot " (48b).

(e) " soon hot, soon cold " (88b).

HOUND, see Hare.

HOUR, see Happeth.

HOUSE, (a) " a man may love his house well though he ride not on the ridge " (61a).

(b) see Mend.

HOUSEBAND (281c), husband : originally the head or master of a house ; also a farmer, tiller of the soil.

HOUSEHOLDERS, see Wishers.

HOUSEWIFE, " a clean-fingered housewife and an idle " (26c), *i.e.* if a mistress does her duty she cannot ever have clean hands.

HUM, " bearers of the hum " (247b), old, mellow, and very strong ale. " Hum, Meath, and Obarni."—Jonson, *Devil's an Ass* (1616), I. I.

HUNDRED, " what ye won in the hundred ye lost in the shire " (92b), *hundred*=a division of a county in England, supposed to be named from originally containing one hundred families of freemen.

HUNGER, (a) " hunger droppeth even out of both their noses " (39d ; 207d).

(b) " hunger pierceth stone wall " (47a). " They said, they were an-hungry ; sigh'd forth proverbs ;— That, hunger broke stone walls ; that, dogs must eat ; That, meat was made for mouths ; that, the gods sent not corn for the rich man only."—Shakspeare, *Coriolanus* (1610), i. 1.

(c) " hunger maketh hard beans sweet " (29b), cf. " hunger is the best sauce."

(d) " they must hunger in frost that will not work in heat " (34d).

HUNGRY, (a) see Dogs, Flies.

    (b) " two hungry meals made the third a glutton "
(45b).

HUNTER, " close hunting the good hunter alloweth "
(72a).

HUSBANDS, " husbands are in heaven whose wives scold
not " (85c).

HUSWIFE (25a), primarily a housewife: whence (a)
domestic servant; (b) a wanton or a gad-about wench;
and (c) a comic endearment. Hence, too, " house-
wifery " and " housewife's tricks "=the habit of
wantonness. " A gude husy-wife ay rinning in the
toun."—Gawain and Gologras, " Ballade " (1508),
Pinkerton, Scottish Poems (1792), iii. " Half lost for
lack of a good huswife's looking to."—Puttenham,
English Poesie (1589), ii. 16 (ed. Arber, 148). " Huswife, I'll have you whipped for slandering me."—
Look About You (1600), sc. 28 (Dodsley, Old Plays,
4th ed., 1875, vii. 476).

ICH, " Ich said " (136b), I.

IGNORANCY, " cometh not of ignorancy " (73b), ignorance. " Rocked in blyndnes and ignorauncy."—Tyn-
dall, Workes, 157.

ILES, see Out isles.

ILL, (a) " from ill to worse and worse " (89a), the
modern version is " bad to worse."

    (b) " of two ills choose the least " (12d; 211d).
" Of harmes two the lesse is for to cheese."—
Chaucer, Troilus and Creseide.

    (c) " turn . . . ill beginning to a good end " (89c).

    (d) " ill believed and worse hard " (91b).

    (e) " they that think none ill are soonest beguiled "
(73d).

    (f) " all be not a-bed that shall have ill rest " (86d).

    (g) " an ill wind that bloweth no man to good "
(93c; 183a).

    (h) see Dagger, Dog, Fishing, Run, Stake, Weed.

ILLGOTTEN, " ill gotten, ill spent " (190d), cf. " lightly
come, lightly go."

IMPORTABLE, " may grow importable " (82b), unendur-
able, insupportable. " Beware of the importable burdens of the high-mynded pharisees."—Bale, *English
Votaries,* pt. i.

IN, " in by the week " (84b ; 176d).

INCH, (a) " as good is an inch as an ell " (95c), *ell=*
a cloth measure (in England 45 inches) : cf. " it is the
first step that counts."
    (b) " when I gave you an inch ye took an ell, till
both ell and inch be gone " (95c), see *supra* (a).
    (c) " better an inch of your will than an ell of your
thrift " (95b), see *supra* (a).
    (d) " an inch breaketh no square " (167d ; 168a).
    (e) " may I be holp forth an inch at a pinch " (95c).

INDE, see Cock.

INIONS, " ropes of inions " (281a), now vulgar. It
occurs also in Heywood's *Spider and the Fly*
(E.E.D.S., *Works,* III.) : " Not worth an inion."

INK, " ink is all black and hath an ill smack, No man
will it drink or eat " (63a).

INN, " take mine ease in mine inn " (12d ; 171d), enjoy
oneself as if one were at home. " Shall I not take
mine ease in mine inn, but I shall have my pocket
picked ? "—Shakspeare, 1 *Henry IV.* (1598), iii. 3.

INOWE (*passim*), enough.

INSTEP, " high in th' instep " (37d ; 216a), haughty,
proud. " The gentleman was grown higher in the
instep, as appeared by the insolent conditions he required."—Moryson, *Itin.* (1617), ii. 26. " He was
too high in the instep to wear another man's shoes."
—Fuller, *Holy War* (1639), II. viii. (1647), 53.

IRON, " when the iron is hot strike " (8c ; 221c), act at
the appropriate time. " Right so as while that iron
is hot, men should strike."—Chaucer, *Melib.* (c. 1386),
70. See Hot.

ISSUES, " lost'st a mark in issues " (279c), *issues=*
fines ; *mark=*money of account, value 13s. 4d. : as a
coin it was never used in England, though in Scotland
marks were current in the 15th and 16th centuries.

ITCH, "itch and ease can no man please" (62*b*).

ITCHING, "he whom in itching no scratching will forbear, he must bear the smarting that shall follow there" (28*c*).

ITCHETH, see Claw.

IWYS (*passim*), certainly, indeed, truly : often no more than a metrical tag.

JACK, (*a*) "jack out of office" (58*d*; 213*c*), one dismissed or out of employment. "For liberalitie is tourned Jacke out of office, and others appointed to have the custodie."—Rich, *Farewell to Militarie Profession* (1581).

(*b*) "all . . . well, Jack shall have Jill" (58*c*; 169*b*), Jack and Jill (or Gill) are generic for "man" and "woman" : specifically of the common people. "For Jok nor for Gyll will I turne my face."—*Towneley Myst.* (*c.* 1460), iii. 336.

(*c*) "I have been common Jack to all that whole flock" (41*d*), in disparagement; *i.e.* at everyone's beck and call : cf. "a twangling jack" (*Taming of the Shrew*), and "silken, sly, insinuating jacks" (*Richard III.*).

(*d*) see Gentleman.

JERMAN, "just as Jerman's lips" (56*b*). "As just as German's lips, which came not together by nine mile."—Latimer, *Remaines.* "Agree like Dogge and Catte, and meete as just as German's lippes."—Gosson, *Schole of Abuse.*

JESTS, "such jests could not juggle her were ought amiss" (88*a*).

JESTING, "it is ill jesting on the sooth" (88*a*), *i.e.* true jesting is no jest at all : *sooth*=truth.

JET, *subs.* and *verb* (*passim*), strut, swagger, pose. "O peace ! Contemplation makes a rare turkey-cock of him ; how he jets under his advanc'd plumes !"—Shakspeare, *Twelfth Night* (1602), ii. 5.

JIS, "by Jis" (136*b*), Jesus : a common contraction.

JOAN (or JONE), "ye should have none for Jone" (96*c*), *Joan*=a generic name for a female rustic. "Some men must love my lady, and some Joan."—Shakspeare, *Love's Labour's Lost* (1588), iii. 1. 207.

JOHN-A-DROIN (293*a*), the exact meaning is unknown: another example is found in Nash (*Saffron Walden* P j b).—"That poor Iohn a Droynes his man, . . . a great big-board thresher."

JOHN DRAWLATCH (88*c*), a thief; also idle fellow, loafer, ne'er-do-well. "Well, phisitian, attend in my chamber heere, till Stilt and I returne; and if I pepper him not, say I am not worthy to be cald a duke, but a drawlatch."—Chettle, *Hoffman* (1602).

JOHN LONG THE CARRIER (254*b*), proverbial for delay and postponement.

JOY, (*a*) "for one month's joy, to bring her whole life's sorrow" (27*c*), in allusion to the honeymoon.
   (*b*) "poverty brought that joy to joyfail" (100*c*).
   (*c*) "with all your joy join all your jeopardy" (101*c*).

JOYFAIL, "poverty brought that joy to joyfail" (100*c*), *joyfail* = a nonce word intended as a pun.

JUDGE, see Blind, Hear.

JUDICARE, "to know how Judicare came into the Creed" (20*b*).

KA, "ka me, ka thee" (41*c*), a phrase implying mutual help, service, flattery and the like; to "logroll."

KAY, see Key.

KEEP, see Three, Wise.

KEY, (*a*) "cold as a kay" (54*b*), as cold as may be, spec. cold as in death: usually "key-cold." "With quaikard voce and hart cald as a key."—Douglas, *Pal. Hon.* (1501), 674.
   (*b*) "the keys hang not all by one man's girdle" (37*a*; 216*c*).

KIBED, "kibed heels . . . kibed hearts" (175*b*), *kibed heels* = heels affected with chilblains. "No wonder yf he halted, for kybed were his helys."—*How Plowman Learned Pater-Noster* (c. 1500).

KICK, see Horse, Wall.

KID, "a piece of a kid is worth two of a cat" (86*a*).

KILL, see Mustard.

KIND, " kind will creep where it may not go " (33c), *kind*=human nature, kinship. " He . . . rode in poste to his kynsman . . . verefiying the old proverbe : kynne will crepe, where it maie not go."— Hall, *Chron.* (c. 1548), *Edw. IV.*, 190. " Ay, gentle Thurio ; for you know that love Will creep in service when it cannot go."—Shakspeare, *Two Gentlemen of Verona* (1595), iv. 2.

KING, see Cat, Nothing.

KINSFOLK, " many kinsfolk, few friends " (45d ; 218b).

KIRTLE, " though nigh be my kirtle yet near is my smock " (28d), *kirtle*=originally a man's garment reaching to the knees or lower, sometimes the only body garment, but more usually worn with a shirt (or smock) beneath, and a cloak or mantle above ; also (as here) a woman's gown : both forms became archaic long since. " Beside, there is a antiquitie a proverb no lesse practised then common, which is, Nearer untò mee is my shirt then my coate ; by following of which, every man commonly loveth his owne profit more than others."—*The Contention betweene Three Brethren ; the Whore-monger, the Drunkard, and the Dice Player* (1608). *Near*=nearer.

KISS, (a) " many kiss the child for the nurse's sake " (84d).
(b) " how can she give a kiss, sour or sweet? Her chin and her nose within half an inch meet " (53a).

KISSED, see Cow.

KIT CALLOT (29c). Kit Callot and Giles Hather are said to have been the first English persons who took up the occupation of gipsies (Sharman) : hence *calot* (callet, calot, calet, or caillot)=a scold, infamous woman : a generic term of abuse. " Gogs bread ! and thinkes the callet thus to keep the neele me fro."—*Gammer Gurtons Needle* (1560).

KITE, see Leg.

KNACKS, " such knacks in her bouget " (75b), see Bouget. *Knacks*=tricks, fancies, " bees in bonnet."

KNAPPISH, " I am knappish to see " (244d), rude, vexed, testy. " A certaine saucie or knappishe young springall."—Udall, *Erasmus Apoph.* (1542), 165 (1877).

KNAVE, (a) " two false knaves need no broker " (35d; 175d), broker=a go-between. " Some will say, A crafty knave need no broker, But here's a craftie knave and a broker too."—*Knacke to Knowe a Knave* (1594). " As two false knaves need no Broker, for they can easily enough agree in wickednesse . . . so among true and faithfull men, there need no others."—*A Sword against Swearers* (1611).

(b) " an old knave is no child " (58a), see *infra*. " Thus the English proverb saith, No knave to the learned knave."—Moryson, *Itin.* (1627), iii. 5.

(c) " an old knave is no babe " (198a), see *supra*.

(d) " the one knave now croucheth while th' other craveth " (36a).

(e) " it is merry when knaves meet " (35d). " No more of Cocke now I wryte, But mery it is when knaves done mete."—*Cocke Lorelles Bote* (c. 1510). " Merrie meeting? why that Title is stale. There's a Boke cald Tis merry when knaves meete, and there's a Ballad Tis merry when Malt-men meete; and besides there's an old Proverbe The more the merrier."—Samuel Rowlands, *Tis Merrie when Gossips meete* (1602).

(f) " the more knaves the worse company " (36a).

KNOT, " mark this knot " (138d), problem, point, gist of a matter. " The knotte why þat every tale is toold."—Chaucer, *Cant. Tales* (c. 1386), *Sq. Tale*, 393.

KNOW, see Bag.

KNOWETH, see Good.

KNOWLEDGE, " I know and knowledge " (26a), own, acknowledge, confess. " They knowledge thee to be the Father of an infinite majesty."—*Goodly Primer* (1535), 82 (1834).

KNOWN, see Friend.

KNUCKLEBONEYARD, " he is a knuckleboneyard " (40b), a clumsy fellow. " A knokylbonyarde wyll counterfete a clarke, He wolde trotte gentylly, but he is to stark."—Skelton, *Magn.* (1526), 485.

KYX, " light as a kyx " (135a), a dry hollow stalk:
also " kex."

LABOUR, " ye shall never labour younger " (21c), become, grow: cf. *to labour on*=to go on.

LABOURETH, " reason laboureth will " (13b), cultivates.

LACK, (a) " lack is the loss of these two young fools "
(49b).
(b) " no lack to lack a wife " (103a).
(c) " ye had been lost to lack your lust " (32c),
lust=wish, desire.
(d) see Love.

LADY, " there is nothing that agree'th worse than doth a
lady's heart and a beggar's purse " (27b).

LAID, see Water.

LAMB, " look like a lamb " (91c).

LAMBSKIN, (a) " as soon goeth the young lamb's skin to
the market as th' old ewe's " (60c). " It is a common saying, there do come as many skins of calves
to the market as there do of bulls or kine."—Barclay,
Ship of Fools (1509).
(b) " a lambskin . . . to lap her in " (76c), *i.e.*
beat, trounce her: *lambskin*=stroke, blow; *lap*=
coil, wind round, wrap up (cf. " The Wife Lapped in
Morelles Skin," *Earl. Pop. Poet.*, iv. 179). " And
because therof, I did give her three or four lamb-
skines with the yerd. Thou servedst her well ynough,
said he."—*MS. Ashmol.*, 208.

LAP, see Lambskin (b).

LARK, see Leg, Sky.

LARUM (a) (78b), hubbub, uproar. " Then the crye and
larum began."—Berners, *Huon* (c. 1533), cxxix. 472.
(b) see Ringeth.

LAST, " he that cometh last make all fast " (210b).

LATE, (a) " better late than never " (26b ; 227d). " Far
bet than never is late."—Chaucer, *Can. Yeom. Prol.
and T.* (c. 1386), 857. Also in Tusser's *Five Hundred Points of Good Husbandry*.
(b) " too late . . . repentance shewed is " (26b).

LAUGH, " they laugh that win " (12*d* and 215*b* and *c*), the adage occurs in various forms : " they win that laugh " ; " they laugh best that laugh last " ; " give losers leave to talk," &c. " Give loosers leave to talke : it is no matter what *sic probo* and his pennilesse companions prate, whilst we have the gold in our coffers."—Nash, *Pierce Penilesse* (1592). " Let them laugh that win the prize."—May, *Heir* (1622), iii. 1. See Laughter and Win.

LAUGHED, see Sleeve.

LAUGHING, " from laughing to lowering " (54*c*).

LAUGHTER, " better is the last smile then the first laughter " (94*d*), see Laugh.

LAW, see Need.

LAWN, " he that will sell lawn before he can fold it, he shall repent him before he have sold it " (19*b*). Another " lawn " proverb says, " No piece of lawn so pure but hath some fret " (Barnefield, *Pecunia*, 1598, xxxvi.).

LAY, (*a*) " reason for reason ye so stiffly lay by proverb for proverb " (14*d*), " cap " by, compare with. " They conferre the one with the other, and lay them with the lawe."—Tr. *Bullinger's Decades* (1577), II. viii. 192.
   (*b*) " the trial thereof we will lay a water till we try more " (10*a*), put aside, defer judgment concerning, render nugatory : see Water. " If he had broke his arme . . . either Apollo must have played Bonesetter, or every occupation beene laide a water."— Gosson, *Schoole of Abuse* (1579).

LEAD, see Horse.

LEAF, " she will turn the leaf " (64*b*), adopt a different line of conduct : now, always in a good sense. " He must turn the leaf and take out a new lesson."— Holinshed, *Chron.* (1577), I. 21, 2.

LEAP, " look or ye leap " (7*c* ; 168*b*). " He that leaps before he look . . . may leap in the mire."—*Marr. Wit and Science* (*c.* 1570), *Anon. Plays* (E.E.D.S.), Ser. 4.

LEAST, see Ill.

LEATHER, " they cut !arge thongs of other men's leather " (66b), cf. " to steal another man's thunder." " Men cut large thongs here of other men's leather." —Mary Paston, *Paston Letters* (1460), III. 372. " D'autrui cuir font large curoie."—*C'est li Mariages des Filles au Dyable,* MS. (c. 1300).

LEAVE, (a) " leave it or it leave you " (224b).

(b) " better leave than lack " (12c). " A worthy work (wherein the Reader may rather leave then lack)."—Fuller, *Holy and Prof. State* (1642), IV. xiv. 310.

(c) " leave is light " (25a; 194c and d).

LECTOUR, " a wiser lectour " (84a), a college or university " reader " or lecturer.

LEG, (a) " while the leg warmeth the boot harmeth " (56a).

(b) " a leg of a lark is better than is the body of a kite " (11b). " *Gyrtrude.* I would not change husbands with my sister; I. ' The legge of a larke is better than the body of a kite.' *Mistress Touchstone.* Know that; but—— *Gyrtrude.* What, sweet mother, what? *Mistress Touchstone.* It's but ill food when nothing's left but the claw."—Chapman, Marston, and Jonson, *Eastward Hoe* (1605).

(c) " in house to keep household, when folks will needs wed, mo things belong than four bare legs in a bed " (19c). " Furthermore it shall be lawful for him that marries without money to find four bare legs in a bed : and he that is too prodigal in spending, shall die a beggar by the statute."—*Pennilesse Parliament of Threadbare Poets* (1608).

LEMAN, " as tender as a parson's leman " (26c; 217b), mistress, concubine : also a gallant or lover. " They founde greater gaines by priestes lemmans then they were like to haue by priestes wives."—T. Wilson, *Rhet.* (1553), 28b.

LENGTH, " yourself to length it taketh direct trade " (14c), prolong, lengthen, spin out. " Thought must length it."—Daniel, *Zethys Festiv.* (1610), F. 3b.

LESE (24c, 39b, 51b, 67c, *et passim*), lose.

LESS, " who will do less than they that may do most " (39d).

LET (*passim*), objections, hindrances.

LEVERINGS (315c), apparently a verb. subs. from *laveer*
=to beat to windward, to tack : obviously, if so, on
account of the rhyme, and hence the coinage is noteworthy. Clarendon (*Essays*) speaks of schoolmen as
" the best laveerers in the world."

LIBERTY, see Day.

LIBET, " baste ye well with a libet " (286d), a stick to
beat with, or throw at anything.

LICK, see Cat, Cook.

LIE, (a) " lies laid on by load " (78d).
   (b) see Bleed, Children.

LIEVER, " had I not liever " (151b), rather.

LIFE, " what is life where living is extinct clear? "
(90c).

LIGER DE MAINE (143a), sleight of hand, jugglery,
legerdemain.

LIGHT, (a) " light come, light go " (93c ; 193d ; 194a).
" Wyte thou wele it schall be so, That lyghtly cum
schall lyghtly go."—*Debate of the Carpenter's Tools.*
   (b) " light gains make heavy purses " (37b ; 198b
and c).
   (c) " ye stand in your own light " (62c), injure your
own interests. " Take counsel and do not stand in
your own light."—Jonson, *Tale of a Tub* (1633), ii. 1.
   (d) see Burden, Hands, Leave, Lips.

LIKE, " like will to like " (11a), a typical proverbial
formula, with many variants—" like master, like
man "; " like lord, like chaplain "; " like carpenter,
like chips "; " like men, like manners," &c. : Fulwell's *Like Will to Like* is the title of an early play.

LIME-FINGERED (26c), given to pilfering. " They are
light-footed and lime-fingered."—Purchas, *Pilgrimage*
(1613), VIII. iv. 629.

LINE, (a) " as right as a line " (33d), in a direct course,
straightforwardly, immediately : also line-right.
" Streyt as lyne he com."—Chaucer, *Troilus* (c. 1374),
II. 1412 (1461).

(b) " we drew both in one line " (80b), were unanimous, in complete accord. " The Senat thus drawing all in a line."—Holland, *Livy* (1600), XLII. xxi. 1127.

LINGEL, " without last or lingel " (139c), a shoemaker's waxed thread. " The cobler of Caunterburie, armde with his aul, his lingel, and his last, presents himselfe a judiciall censor of other mens writinges."— *The Cobler of Caunterburie* (1590).

LION, " as fierce as a lion of Cotsolde " (44d), a sheep: cf. *Essex* (or *Rumford*) *lion*=a calf. " Carlus is as furious as a lyon of Cotsold."—Davies, *Epigrams* (1596). " You stale old ruffian, you lion of Cotsolde."—*Sir John Oldcastle*.

LION'S BOWER (315d), the lion as emblematic of the sovereign power of England : here of Queen Mary.

LIPS, (a) " such lips, such lettuce " (80d), like to like. " Every lip has its lettuce to himself : the lob has his lass, the collier his dowdy, the western-man his punk, the student his nun in Whitefriars, the puritan his sister, and the lord his lady ; which worshipful vocation may fall upon you, if you'll but strike whilst the iron is hot."—Webster, *Westward Hoe* (1607). See Like.
(b) " your lips hang in your light " (62b), *i.e.* hanging your lips in vexation is against your interests.
(c) see Light.

LIPWORT SEED (288d), idle talk, " jaw ": a nonce word.

LIST, " which me list " (8a), like, wish, desire.

LISTENING, " I have learned in listening " (43b), cf. " listeners hear no good of themselves."

LITHER, (a) " too lither " (48a; also 73c), bad, rascally inclined.
(b) " be he lusty or lither " (242b), ill-conditioned, sorry.

LITTER, " the litter is like to the sire and the dam " (33c), see Like.

LITTLE, see Nothing, Said.

LOGIC, " she choppeth logic " (64b), argues a point, is contentious, answers sharply. " If he heare you thus

play choploge."—Udall, *Roister Doister* (E.E.D.S.),
iii. 2.

LONG, (a) " long be thy legs and short be thy life " (82d).
(b) see Day, Devil, Offering, Stake.

LONGER, see Day.

LONGETH, " that longeth thereto " (34d), is appropriate
to, that pertains to; often written " 'longeth," as if
=" belong." " With such austerity as longeth to a
father."—Shakspeare, *Taming of the Shrew* (1596),
iv. 4. 6.

LOOK, (a) " look or ye leap " (7c), see Leap.
(b) " look as ye list " (91c), *list*=like, wish, desire.
(c) see Cat, Horse, Lamb.

LORD, (a) " there is no good accord where every man
would be a lord " (74d).
(b) " there is nothing in this world that agreeth
worse than doth a lord's heart and a beggar's purse "
(174d), see Lady.

LORNE, " the corn is lorne " (27d), injured, ruined,
spoilt.

LOSE, (a) " lose both living and love of all their
kin " (25d).
(b) see Covet, Nothing.

LOSERS, " let the losers have their words " (76b; 190d).

LOST, (a) " as good lost as found " (28a).
(b) " it is lost that is unsought " (38c).
(c) " like one half lost till greedy grasping gat it "
(97d).

LOST'ST, " thou lost'st a mark " (279c), a noteworthy
inflection: see Issues.

LOTHE, " the lothe stake " (60d; 222a and b), ugly,
misshapen.

LOUGH, " his master lough " (137d), laughed.

LOVE, (a) " in love is no lack " (10d; 168d; 169a).
(b) " love me, love my dog " (93a; 182c), a proverb
in the time of Saint Bernard. " *Cudora.* Love me?
—love my dog! *Tharsalis.* I am bound to that by the
proverb, madam."—Chapman, *Widow's Tears* (1612).
(c) " love me little, love me long " (57b). " *Bella-*

mira. Come, gentle Ithamore, lie in my lap. *Itha-more.* Love me little, love me long ; let music rumble, Whilst I in thy incony lap do tumble.''—Marlowe, *Jew of Malta* (1586), iv.

(*d*) " by love, without regard of living, these twain have wrought each other ill chieving " (48*c*).

(*e*) " love hath lost them the love of their friends " (48*d*).

(*f*) " we could live by love " (10*c*).

(*g*) " lovers live by love . . . as larks live by leeks " (25*c*).

(*h*) " what need we lump out love " (57*a*).

(*i*) see Hot.

LOVEDAY, " break a loveday " (69*b*), an agreement for the amicable settlement of a dispute. " He is more redy to make a fraye than a loue day.''—Horman, *Vulg.* (1519), vii. 66 b.

Low, see High.

MACKABROINE, " such a mackabroine " (74*c*), old hag : from Fr. *machabree* ; Murray marks it " rare," and gives only the present instance.

MAD, see Hare.

MADE, see Much, Mocked.

MAIDS, see Malkin.

MAISTER, " maister promotion saieth " (13*a*), master.

MAISTRY, " use maketh maistry " (55*d* ; 219*a*), gives power, skill, the knowledge and experience which constitutes a master.

MAKE, (*a*) " make or mar I will " (173*c*).

(*b*) " how flek and his make " (70*a*), *make*=com-panion. " This is no season To seek new makes in." —Jonson, *Tale of a Tub* (1633), i. 1.

(*c*) see Cross, Last, Small, Sorrow.

MAKEBATE (24*a*), breeder of strife. " Such a malicious makebate.''—More, *Suppl. Soulys* (1529), *Wks.,* 296. 2.

MAKETH, see Havoc, Offering, Use.

MALE, " males and male horses " (258*d*), *male*=bag, pack : now Scots and American.

MALKIN, " mo maids but Malkin " (32*c*; 200*b*), *Malkin* (=Mary) is generic for a woman of low birth, country wench, servant : frequently used proverbially to signify drab, wanton. " There are more houses then Parishe Churches, more maydes than Maulkin." —Gosson, *Sch. of Abuses* (1597), 37 (Arber).

MALT, (*a*) " soft fire maketh sweet malt " (6*c*), an ad-monition to be gentle or merciful : see Fire.
(*b*) " malt is above wheat with him " (31*a*), *i.e.* " he is under the influence of drink." " Malt is now aboue wheat with a number of mad people."—Breton, *Fantastickes* (1626), B3.

MAN, see God, Good, Happy, Haste, Hog, Horse, Mend, Mustard, Oar, Tide, True, Wind.

MANY, see Hands, Kinsfolk, Small.

MAR, see Make.

MARCH HARE, " as mad as a March hare " (73*a*), see Hare.

MARE, (*a*) " mine old mare would have a new crupper " (52*d*).
(*b*) " the grey mare is the better horse " (64*a*), see Horse.
(*c*) " well nigh every day a new mare or a moil " (81*a*), *mare*=a woman (contemptuously) ; *moil*=mule ; also contemptuously of a trull, for the sake of the rhyme.
(*d*) see Coy.

MARJORUM GENTLE (288*a*). " Marierome is called . . . in English Sweete Marierome, Fine Marierome, and Marierome gentle ; of the best sort Maiorane."—Gerarde, *Herbal* (1597), II. ccvii. 539.

MARK (279*c*), see Issues.

MARKET, " the market goeth by the market men " (38*a*), *i.e.* prices, rates of purchase and sale.

MARKS, " yet have ye other marks to rove at hand " (37*a*), *rove*=to shoot at.

MARMASAT, " a minion marmasat " (141*c*), of a man= a term of abuse or contempt ; " ape," " fool," &c. *Minion* apparently=servile, unworthy ; as in one sense of the subs.

MARRIAGE, " a goodly marriage she is . . . were the woman away " (52d), *i.e.* her money is desirable if her person is not.

MARRY, " when men will needs marry . . . wisdom and haste may vary " (49a).

MARRYING, " marrying or marring " (18c), in slightly different guise still proverbial.

MARYBONES, " on your marybones crouch to the ground " (22a), the knees. " Down he fel vpon his maribones."—More, *Confut. Tindale* (1532), *Wks.*, 727/2.

MASE, " nother muse nor mase " (135a), *mase*=perplexity, doubt, abashment.

MASTER, see Breech.

MASTERSHIP, " would your mastership " (139a, *et passim*), a respectful address.

MASTERY, see Maistry.

MATE, " I am mad to see thee mate thy husband " (244c), puzzle, browbeat, withstand.

MATINS, " if it be morn we have a pair of matins " (78a).

MATTER, see Face, Water.

MAUGRE, " maugre her head " (48a), in spite of : Fr., *malgré*.

MAY, (a) " that one may not another may " (55d).
(b) " he that will not when he may, when he would he shall have nay " (8a ; 168c), in Burton, *Melanch.* (1621).
(c) see Catch.

MEAL, see Cow.

MEALMOUTH (23d), a person of soft, carneying words, of hypocritical delicacy of speech : now surviving in " mealy-mouthed."

MEALS, " better are meals many than one too merry " (84a).

MEASURE, (a) " measure is a merry mean " (82a ; 191a to d ; 192a to c), moderation. " *Magn.* Yet mesure is a mery mene. *Fan.* Yea, syr, a blaunched almonde is no bene, Measure is mete for a marchauntes hall."—*Magnyfycence* (*c.* 1520). " There is measure in everything."—Shakspeare, *Much Ado* (1600), ii. 1.

    (*b*) " thou fearest false measures " (178*a*).

MEAT, (*a*) " look not on the meat but look on the man " (62*a*).

    (*b*) " that one loveth not, another doth ; which hath sped All meats to be eaten and all maids to be wed " (55*d*).

    (*c*) see Crabs, Sweet.

MEDDLE, see Gosling.

MEDDLING, " of little meddling cometh great rest " (57*d*). " Grete reste stande in lytell besynesse, Beware also to sporne against a wall."—Lydgate, *Proverbes.*

MEET, see Sow.

MEET-MATE (42*c*), helpmate : cf. *meet-help* = help-meet, a wife. " In my discoveries of him and his meet-help." —Spratt, *Relation of Young's Contrivance.*

MELANCHOLY, " turn melancholy to mirth " (88*a*).

MELT, see Butter.

MEN, see Blind, Clerks.

MEND, (*a*) " if every man mend one, all shall be mended " (167*b*), many hands make light work.

    (*b*) " I will mend this house and pair another " (88*d* ; 182*a*), *pair* = impair, neglect. " He bulde newe citees and amended citees þat were i-peyred."— Trevisa, *Higden* (Rolls), vi. 399 (1387).

MERCHANT, (*a*) " ye merchant " (31*c* ; also 66*c*), a familiar address—" fellow," " chap." " I would have so scourged my marchant, that his breech should ake." —*New Custom* (*c.* 1550), *Anon. Plays* (E.E.D.S.), Ser. 3, 162*b*.

    (*b*) " a merchant without either money or ware " (66*c* ; 206*a*).

    (*c*) see Dear, Eel-skins.

MERRIER, " the more the merrier " (79*c*). " Store makes no sore : loe this seemes contrarye, And mo the merier is a Proverbe eke, But store of sores maye make a maladye, And one to many maketh some to seeke,

When two be mette that bankette with a leche."—
Gaiscoigne, *Posies* (1575).

MERRY, (*a*) " good to be merry and wise " (6*d* ; 172*d*).
" I . . . garnished my shop, for want of plate, with
good wholesome, thriftie sentences ; as, ' Touchstone,
keepe thy shoppe, and thy shoppe will keepe thee.'
' Light gaines make heavie purses.' ' Tis good to be
merry and wise.' "—*Eastward Hoe* (1605).

  (*b*) " merry as a cricket " (31*b*)—" merry as a pie "
(60*a*). " By the Lord of Ludgate, my Liege, I'll be as
merrie as a Pie."—Decker, *Shomakers Holiday* (1600).

  (*c*) " it is merry in hall when beards wag all "
(79*d*), see Hall. " Swithe mury hit is in halle When
burdes wawen alle."—*Life of Alexander* (1312).
" Be merry, be merry, my wife has all ; For women
are shrews, both short and tall, 'Tis merry in hall
when beards wag all."—Shakspeare, 2 *Henry IV.*
(1598), v. 3.

  (*d*) see Chip, Measure.

MESS, (*a*) " to keep yet one mess . . . in store " (89*b*),
" put by something for a rainy day."

  (*b*) see Mustard.

MESSENGER, " to come . . . before the messenger "
(31*c*), to be " previous," be one's own postman.

MEVE (15*c*, 59*b*, 84*d*, *et passim*), move.

MEW, " hawks in the mew " (66*b*), properly a cage for
hawks : figuratively a place where anything is in
keeping.

MIDS, MIDDES (186*b*), midst : note rhyme with " bids."

MIGHT, " might overcometh right " (69*a* ; 197*c*), in
modern phrase, " might is right."

MILESTONE, see Millstone.

MILK, " milk is white, And lieth not in the dike, But
all men know it good meat " (62*d*).

MILL, " much water goeth by the mill that the miller
knoweth not of " (73*d*). " What, man ; more water
glideth by the mill Than wots the miller of, and easy
it is Of a cut loaf to steal a shive."—Shakspeare,
Titus Andronicus (1593), ii. 7.

MILLSTONE, " seen far in a millstone " (25*d* ; 176*c*) :
" to look (or see) into a millstone "=to fathom a
secret ; to be far or sharp sighted. " Your eies are
so sharp that you cannot onely looke through· a mil-
stone, but cleane through the minde, and so cunning
that you can levell at the dispositions of women whom
you never knew."—Lyly, *Euphues and his England*.

MILNER, " the milner tolleth corn " (149*b*), miller : see
Tolleth.

MIND, see Sight.

MINION (40*b*), " a creature " : here a debased sense of
minion=favourite ; *i.e.* an unworthy or unseemly
favourite : also as adj. (141*c*)=servile, unworthy.

MINISH, MINISHETH (99*a*, 76*a*), diminish. " To abbridge
his power, and to minishe his authoritie."—Hall,
Henry VI. f. 81.

MIRE, " lay my credence in the mire " (57*d*), compare
" to drag one's reputation through the mud."

MISCELLANIES, see Terminal Essay, *Heywood's Works*
(E.E.D.S.), III.

MISERY, " misery may be mother where one beggar is
driven to beg of another " (100*a*).

MISRECKONING, " misreckoning is no payment " (64*d* ;
212*d*).

MISSED, see Cushion.

MO (12*c*, 19*a*), more.

MOCK, " he mocked much of her " (53*c*), feigned, pretended to make. " He mocks the pauses that he
makes."—Shakspeare, *Antony and Cleopatra* (1608),
v. I.

MOCKAGE, " half in mockage " (25*c*), mocking. " But
all this perchaunce ye were I speake half in moccage."
—Sir Thos. Chaloner, *Moriæ Enc.* (1549), M 3.

MOIL, " moils of velvet . . . moil men—to see asses
go on moils " (292*d*), moil=(*a*) a sort of high shoe,
formerly worn by persons of quality ; (*b*) a lawyer
of eminence : judges and sergeants, says Nares, rode
to Westminster Hall on mules ; (*c*) a mule—the following examples illustrate the different senses.

" They drewe owt of dromondaries dyverse lordes,
Moyllez mylke whitte, and mervaillous bestez."—
Morte Arthure, MS. Lincoln, f. 77. " Well, make
much of him ; I see he was never born to ride upon
a moyle."—Jonson, *Every M. out of H.* (1599), ii. 3.

MOLT, " my heart for woe molt " (91a), melted : an old
form.

MONEY, see Merchant.

MONK, " like a bean in a monk's hood " (76c ; 204a),
lost, like a nonentity : *bean*=a low standard of value.

MONTH, " better is one month's cheer than a churl's
whole life " (84a) : cf. Tennyson's " better fifty years
of Europe than a cycle of Cathay."

MOON, (a) " to cast beyond the moon " (11c ; 207c and
d), to calculate deeply ; make an extravagant conjecture ; be ambitious ; to attempt impossibilities. " But
oh, I talk of things impossible And cast beyond the
moon."—T. Heywood, *A Woman Kill'd with Kindness* (c. 1603).

(b) " to make me believe . . . that the moon is
made of a green cheese " (84d), to hoax, quiz, " chaff."
" Whilst they tell for truthe Luther his lowde lyes,
so that they may make theyr blinde brotherhode and
the ignorant sort beleve that the mone is made of
grene chese."—Shacklock, *Hatchet of Heresies* (1565).

MOONSHINE, " moonshine in the water " (44c ; 220d),
an illusive shadow.

MOP, see Cony mop.

MORE, " for little more or less no debate make " (68d),
trouble not about trifles ; seek not to enforce a difference between Tweedledum and Tweedledee.

MORNINGS, " cloudy mornings turn to clear afternoons "
(98c).

MORTIMER, see Backare.

MOSS, see Rolling stone.

MOTE, (a) " ye can see a mote in another man's eye,
but ye cannot see a balk in your own " (81a),
balk=beam, rafter.

(b) " so mote I thee " (137d), *i.e.* " so may I
thrive."

MOTHER, " your mother bid till ye were born " (98*a*).

MOUSE, (*a*) "as sure as . . . a mouse tied with a thread " (86*c*).

    (*b*) " a mouse in time may bite a-two a cable " (82*b*).

    (*c*) " it had need to be a wily mouse that should breed in the cat's ear " (71*d*).

    (*d*) see Cat.

MOUTH, (*a*) " that shall not stop my mouth " (64*c*; 213*b*), silence me.

    (*b*) " to make up my mouth " (43*c*), *i.e.* to give cause for arranging the features to produce a particular expression ; cf. " make up a face," " make up a lip," &c. ; thus to induce a grimace or wry face : now American by survival. " Make up your face [to a weeping person] quickly."—Brome, *Jovial Crew* (1641), iv. 1.

    (*c*) " ye speak now as ye would creep into my mouth " (94*c*).

    (*d*) " till meat fall in your mouth will ye lie in bed " (21*c*).

    (*e*) see Butter, Horse.

MUCH, " she made much of him and he mocked much of her " (53*c*), see Mocked.

MUCK, " muck of the world " (44*c*), money. " For to pinche, and for to spare, Of worlds mucke to gette encres."—Gower, *Confessio Amantis*, v.

MUM, " I will say nought but mum, and mum is counsel " (65*b* ; 213*b* ; 214*c*), *mum*=a warning to silence.

MUST, see Blab.

MUSTARD, " he will kill a man for a mess of mustard " (211*a*).

NAIL, (*a*) " one nail driveth out another " (188*b*).

    (*b*) " this hitteth the nail on the head " (101*d*), to get at the bottom of a matter, to succeed, to come to the point. In *Sir Thomas More* (*c.* 1590), " my lord Cardinal's players, in answer to the question as to what pieces compose their repertory, reply :—Divers, my Lord, *The Cradle of Security, Hit Nail o' th' Head, Impatient Poverty, The Play of Four P's,*

Dives and Lazarus, Lusty Juventus, and the *Marriage of Wit and Wisdom."*

(*c*) see Paring.

NAKED BOY (299*d*), the minute reflection of one gazing into another's eye : hence *to look a naked boy* (or *babies*) *in the eyes*=to look amorously. "But O, see, see we need enquire no further, Upon your lips the scarlet drops are found, And in your eye the boy that did the murder. . . . See where little Cupid lies Looking babies in the eyes."—Drayton, *Idea* (1594), 2. "In each of her two crystal eyes Smileth a naked boy ; It would you all in heart suffice To see that lamp of joy."—Ellis, *Specimen Eng. Romances,* 7. "Joy had the like conception in our eyes, And, at that instant, like a babe sprung up."— Shakspeare, *Timon of Athens* (1609), i. 2.

NAT (148*b, et passim*), not : note the rhymes.

NAY, (*a*) " say nay and take it " (214*a* and *b*) : another version is, " Maids say ' No ' and mean ' Yes.' "
(*b*) " ye may mend three nays with one yea " (35*d*).
(*c*) see Will.

NE (*passim*), not, nor : frequently in M.E. joined with the verbs " to have," " to be," and " to will " : thus, *nam=ne am=am* not, *nis=is* not, *nill=ne will=*will not, *nadde=ne hadde=*had not, &c.

NEAR, " near is my smock " (28*d*), nearer. " Of friends, of foes, behold my foule expence, And never the neere."—*Mirror for Mag.* (1559), 364.

NEARER, see Church.

NEED, (*a*) " need hath no law " (25*b* and 170*c*), in modern phrase : " Needs must where the devil drives."
(*b*) " need maketh the old wife trot " (99*d* ; 183*d*), Fr. " besoin fait vieille trotter " (Roman de Trubert, *c.* 1300).
(*c*) see Devil, Friend, True.

NEIGHBOURHOOD, " which neighbourhood in thee appears " (125*a*), *neighbourhood=*the state or quality of being neighbours, situate near to.

NESH, " 'tis too nesh " (149*d*), soft. " He was to nesshe and she to harde."—Gower, *Confessio Amantis* (1393), v.

NEST, see Bird.

NET, (*a*) " the rough net is not the best catcher of birds " (22*b*).
 (*b*) see Fish, Fishing.
 (*c*) " set thee out net " (244*d*), neat : note the rhyme.
 (*d*) " all is fish that cometh to net " (39*c*), nothing comes amiss. " But now (aye me) the glasing christal glasse Doth make us thinke that realmes and townes are rych, Where favor sways the sentence of the law, Where al is fishe that cometh to net."— Gascoigne, *Steele Glas* (1571).

NETTLE, (*a*) " she had pissed on a nettle " (99*c*), was peevish, out of temper.
 (*b*) see Dock.

NEVER, see Climbed, Late.

NEW BROOM, see Broom.

NEW MAN, " showing himself a new man " (89*c*), through having reformed.

NEWER, " newer is truer " (63*a*).

NEXT, see Hekst.

NIGH, see Far.

NINE, see Cat, Wonder.

NINTH, " to the ninth degree " (287*a*), completely, perfectly, utterly : in modern phrase " up (or down) to the nines." Probably from the mathematical formula.

NOBLE, " a bag of . . . nobles " (97*a*), *noble*=a gold coin struck by Edward III., and originally of the value of 6s. 8d. In the reigns of Henry VI. and Edward IV., the value of the noble having risen to 10s., another gold coin of the same value as the original noble was issued called an angel (*q.v.*). Half-nobles and quarter-nobles were also current.

NODDIES (261*d*), simpletons, fools. " Ere you came thither, poor I was somebody ; The King delighteth in me, now I am but a noddy."—Edwards, *Damon and Pithias* (1567), *Works* (E.E.D.S.).

NOON, (*a*) " go to bed at noon " (85*a*), betimes, unconscionably early.
(*b*) " the longer forenoon the shorter afternoon " (50*b*).

NOPPY, " some noppy ale " (45*b*), usually *nappy* = strong, " heady." " Nappy liquor will lullaby thy fine wittes."—*New Letter* (1593).

NOSE, (*a*) " thou canst hold my nose to the grindstone " (13*b* and 173*a*), oppress, harass, punish, hold at a disadvantage. " A shame and . . . vilanie for you . . . hable to hold their nose to the grindstone, nowe . . . to be their pezantes, whose lordes your auncestors were."—Aylmer, *Harborough*, &c., 1559 (*Maitland on Ref.*, 220). " They might be ashamed, for lack of courage, to suffer the Lacedæmonians to hold their noses to the grindstone."—North, *Plutarch* (1578), 241.
(*b*) " your nose drops . . . I will eat no browesse sops " (87*d*), *brose* in O.E. = bread and fat meat (Huloet). " That tendre browyce made with a maryboon."—Lydgate, *Order of Fooles* (*d.* 1460).
(*c*) [I shall] " wipe your nose upon your sleeve " (97*c*), affront. " There is one Sophos, a brave gentleman ; he'll wipe your son Peter's nose of Mistress Lelia."—*Wily Beguiled* (1606) [Dodsley, *Old Plays* (1874), ix. 242].
(*d*) see Hunger, Pepper.

NOTHER (*passim*), neither.

NOTHING, (*a*) " nothing hath no savour " (20*b* ; 181*a*), there is no savour in want.
(*b*) " where as nothing is the king must lose his right " (47*d* ; 218*c*), even the king can get nothing from nothing.
(*c*) " where nothing is a little thing doth ease " (29*b* ; 184*a*).
(*d*) see Something.

NOUGHT, (a) " nought venture, nought have " (38c ; 181b).

    (b) " nought lay down, nought take up " (41c ; 227b).

    (c) " a thing of nought " (43c).

    (d) " whom I made of nought " (65c)—" bring to nought " (65d).

    (e) see Mum, Play.

    (f) " all have and nought forgo " (223c).

    (g) " as good seek nought . . . as seek and find nought " (38c).

    (h) " nought won by the tone, nought won by the tother " (41c).

NUN, " as nice as a nun's hen " (52c), see Hen.

NURSE, " God send that head a better nurse " (85d).

NUT, " knack me that nut " (80c), solve me that problem, explain that, overcome this difficulty : *knack* =crack.

NYCEBECETUR, " your ginifinee nycebecetur " (32d), apparently a term of contempt : Heywood uses it again in *Play of the Weather* (E.E.D.S., *Works*, I. 123), " such nycebyceturs as she is." The word has puzzled all editors so far ; all that seems clear is that Heywood in each case employs the word in contempt of a woman. A somewhat exhaustive enquiry on the phrase is summed up in Heywood's *Works* (E.E.D.S.), III. Notebook *s.v.* Nicebecetur : see also Udall's *Works* (E.E.D.S.), pp. 138–9.

OAR, " she (or he) must have an oar in every man's barge " (24b ; 207a), meddle in the business or affairs of others : somewhat earlier, the proverb occurs in a ballad entitled " Long have I bene a singing man," by John Redford (c. 1540). " In each mannes bote would he have an ore."—Udall, *Apop.* (c. 1543), II. 180.

OCCUPY (289c), use, with an eye in the Epigram on the obscene sense of the word. " Inke made of soote, such as printers occupie."—*Nomenclator* (1585). " These villains will make the word captain as odious as the word occupy."—Shakspeare, 2 *Hen. IV.* (1598), ii. 4.

OFFERING, " long standing and small offering maketh poor parsons " (226c).

HEY. II.   E E

OFFICE, see Jack.

OLD, see Children, Devil, Dog, Fool, Need, Saint, Shoe.

ONE, see Cometh.

ONY, " had I ony " (96*b*), any.

OR (*passim*), ere, before, lest, than.

OROLOGE, see Devil.

OSTE, " ye would now here oste " (34*c*), dwell, remain : *i.e.* host.

OTHER, " other thou art a fool or . . . I am one " (144*b*), either.

O'THING, " this o'thing " (29*c*), one thing : *O* = numeral adjective, a reduced form of ôn, oon : cf. nothing. " O flessh they been, and o flessh as I gesse Hath but oon herte, in wele and in distresse."—Chaucer, *Merch. T.* (*c*. 1386), 91. " Ill huswiferie othing or other must craue."—Tusser, *Husb.* (1573), 184 (1878). Also in *Epigrams* (172*b*), " I grant this othing."

OUT, (*a*) " out of sight, out of mind " (8*d*).
(*b*) see Smelled, Way.

OUT ILES (41*d*), properly islands away from the mainland : here figuratively for an outlandish district, up-country, away from a centre of population.

OVEN, " no man will another in the oven seek, except that himself have been there before " (84*b*), the commonest version is, " no woman will her daughter seek in the oven," &c. " A hackney proverb in men's mouths ever since King Lud was a little boy, or Belinus, Brennus' brother, for the love hee bare to oysters, built Billingsgate."—Nash, *Have with you to Saffron Waldon* (1596), 157.

OVERBLOW, see Wind.

OVERCOMETH, see Might.

OVERTHWART, " overthwart the shins " (24*c*), across.

OWL, " keep corners, or hollow trees with th' owl " (71*c*).

OWN, " alway own is own at the reckoning's end "
(64*d* ; 214*d* ; 215*a*).

OX, see Black ox.

PAD, " it will breed a pad in the straw " (63*d* ; 226*b*), a
lurking or hidden danger. " Though they make
never so fayre a face, yet there is a padde in the
strawe."—Palsgrave, &c. (1530), 595, 1.

PADDOCK, see Haddock, Weather.

PAIN, (*a*) " change from ill pain to worse is worth small
hire " (72*c*).
 (*b*) " plant your own pain " (69*b*).
 (*c*) " I have wrought mine own pain " (26*a*).
 (*d*) " take a pain for a pleasure all wise men can "
(13*d*).

PAINTED SHEATH, see Sheath.

PAIR, see Mend.

PAN, see Cat.

PANNIER, see Pig.

PARING, " she will not part with the paring of her nails "
(40*a*).

PARISH PRIEST, " the parish priest forgetteth that ever
he hath been holy water clerk " (38*b* ; 174*d*).

PARS VERS, " tell him he's pars vers " (59*c*), perverse.

PARSONS, " long standing and small offering maketh
poor parsons " (98*a* ; 226*c*).

PARSON'S LEMAN, see Leman.

PART, see Paring, Poverty.

PAST, " let all things past, pass " (90*b*), let bygones be
bygones ; let sleeping dogs lie.

PASTURE, see Calves.

PATERNOSTER, (*a*) " he may be in my paternoster . . but
. . he shall never come in my creed (96*c* ; 189*c*).
" I trust yee remember your jugling at Newington
with a christall stone, your knaveries in the wood by
Wanstead, the wondrous treasure you would discover
in the Isle of Wight, al your villanies about that
peece of service, as perfectly known to some of my

friends yet living as their Paster-noster, who curse the time you ever came into their creed."—Chettle, *Kind-Heart's Dream* (1592).

(*b*) " no penny, no paternoster " (96*c*), no pay, no prayers. "The Pater-noster, which was wont to fill a sheet of paper, is written in the compasse of a penny ; whereupon one merrily assumed that proverbe to be derived, No penny no pater-noster. Which their nice curtayling putteth mee in minde of the custome of the Scythians, who, if they had beene at any time distressed with famine, tooke in their girdles shorter." —Greene, *Arcadia* (1587).

(*c*) " pattering the devil's paternoster to himself " (39*b*), grumbling, muttering imprecations. "Yet wol they seyn harm and grucche and murmure priuely for verray despit, whiche wordes men clepen the deueles Pater noster."—Chaucer, *Pars. T. (c.* 1386), 434.

PATIENCE, " let patience grow in your garden alway " (44*d*).

PATTEN, " her tongue was clapping like a patten " (135*b*), *i.e.*, click-clack like a pair of pattens ; " nineteen to the dozen " : see Tongue.

PAUL, see Peter.

PAUL'S WEATHERCOCK, (115*d*) ; frequently referred to in old writers. "I am as very a turncote as the wethercoke of Poles."—*Mariage of Witt and Wisdome* (E.E.D.S. *Anon. Pl.* 4 Ser.).

PAY, see Peter, Shot.

PAYMENT, " misreckoning is no payment " (64*d* ; 212*d*).

PEAL, see Ringeth.

PEAS, " who hath many peas may put the more in the pot " (12*c*).

PENNY, (*a*) " a penny for your thought " (61*b*), a call to persons in a " brown study." "Come, friar, I will shake him from his dumps. How cheer you, sir? a penny for your thought."—Greene, *Friar Bacon* (1588), 161.

(*b*) " to turn the penny " (92*b*), earn money : the phrase occurs (1510) in Foxe's *Acts and Monuments,* iv. " His wyfe made hym so wyse, That he wolde tourne a peny twyse, And then he called it a ferthynge."—*Maid Emlyn* (*c.* 1520) [Hazlitt, *Early Pop. Poet.* iv. 85].

(*c*) " not one penny to bliss him " (89*a*), very poor.

PENNY FATHER, (123*c*), miser, niggard. " Alas, this re-confirms what I said rather, Cosmus has ever been a penny-father.—Harington, *Epigrams* (*d.* 1612), ii. 21.

PEPPER, (*a*) " pepper in the nose " (64*c* ; 212*a*), quick at offence, testy : Fr., *moutarde au nez.* " There are ful proude-herted men paciente of tonge, And boxome as of berynge to burgeys and to lordes, And to pore peple hav peper in the nose."—Langland, *Piers Plowman* (1362), xv. 197.

(*b*) " pepper is black and hath a good smack " (62*d*).

PERSEVER, " doth persever " (143*d*), note the rhyme with "ever."

PESCOD ALE, (189*b*), *pescod*=pea-pod : much rustic folk-lore was formerly attached to pea-time, of which not a little found survival in New England. In *As You Like It* (ii. 4) Touchstone says to Rosalind, " I remember the wooing of a peascod instead of her," which perhaps is the most fitly paralleled in the following passage from Browne's *Brit. Past.* (p. 71) : " The peascod greene oft with no little toyle Hee'd seeke for in the fattest fertil'st soile, And rend it from the stalke to bring it to her, And in her bosome for acceptance wooe her." Both Nares and Halliwell may be consulted in this respect. *Pescod-ale* is doubtless the brew made for " pescod-time." " In pescod time, when hound and horne, Gives ear till buck be kill'd."—*England's Helicon.*

PETER, " rob Peter and pay Paul " (31*c* ; 170*c*), take of one to give to another. The proverb pretty certainly derives its origin from the fact that in the reign of Edward VI. the lands of St. Peter at Westminster were appropriated to raise money for the repair of St. Paul's in London. John Thirlby, the first and only Bishop of Westminster (1541-50), " having wasted the patrimony allotted by the King (Hen. VIII.) for the support of the see, was translated to Norwich, and with him ended the bishopric of Westminster " (Haydn, *Dignities*). Heylin (*Hist. Ref.* i. 256, 1661) says that the lands at Westminster were so dilapidated by Bishop Thirlby that there was almost nothing to support the dignity. . . . Most of the lands invaded by the great men of the Court, the rest laid out for reparation to the Church of St. Paul, pared almost to the very quick in those days of rapine. From hence, he says, came first that significant byword (as is said by some) of robbing Peter to pay Paul. The French form of the proverb, " découvrir saint Pierre pour couvrir saint Paul " gives additional colouring to the statement, and is supported by Barclay in his *Eclogues* (Percy Soc. xxiii. xvii.), " They robbe St. Peter to cloth St. Paul."

PICKPURSE (31*c*), pickpocket.

PICKTHANK (23*d*), toady : also as verb. " There be two tythes, rude and ranke, Symkyn Tytyuell and Pers Pykthanke."—Skelton, *Works* (1513-25), ii. 60 (Dyce). " Smiling pickthanks and base newsmongers."— Shakspeare, 1 *Henry IV.* (1598), iii. 2.

PIE, (*a*) " merry as a pie " (60*a*).
  (*b*) see High.

PIECE, " this maid, the piece peerless in mine eye " (10*c*), *piece*=a person, male or female : often in contempt. " His princess say you? . . . Ay, the most peerless piece."—Shakspeare, *Winter's Tale* (1604), v. 1.

PIG, (*a*) " a pig of mine own sow " (78*c* ; 204*b*).
  (*b*) " buy the pig in the poke " (97*d* ; 182*b*), of a blind bargain. " And in the floor, with nose and mouth to broke, They walwe as doon two pigges in a poke."— Chaucer, *Reeves Tale* (*c.* 1386), 358.
  (*c*) " yet snatch ye at the poke that the pig is in, not for the poke, but the pig good cheap to win " (97*d*).
  (*d*) " when the pig is proffered . . . hold up the poke " (8*c*), " never refuse a good bargain." " When me profereth the pigge, open the poghe."—*Douce MS.* (*c.* 1400), 52.
  (*e*) " bid me welcome, pig ; I pray thee kiss me " (79*d*).
  (*f*) " a pig of the worse panier " (102*c*).

PIKE, " one good lesson . . . I pike " (8c, 11a, 72b), mark, note, learn, pick out.

PIKED, " a pretty piked matter " (44c), cf. " a pretty kettle of fish "; *piked* = marked.

PILATE'S VOICE (25a), a loud, ranting voice. " In Pilate voys he gan to cry, And swor by armes, and by blood and bones."—Chaucer, *Cant. Tales* (c. 1386), 3126.

PILLAR, see Post.

PINCHPENNY, " that benchwhistler is a pinchpenny " (37c), a niggard in food, dress, or money : it early occurs in Occleve (1412), *De Reg. Princip.* " They accompt one . . . a pynch penny if he be not prodygall."—Lyly, *Euphues, Anat. of Wit* (1579), 109.

PINSONS, " pinching pinsons " (263a), pincers. " Two crosse forkes of tonges which come from it one both sides, in the toppes whereof are little thinges like pynsons, to detaine and hold fast."—Topsell, *Hist. Serp.* (1608), 224.

PIPE, (a) " who that leaveth surety and leaneth unto chance when fools pipe, by authority he may dance " (101d).
   (b) " to dance after her pipe " (75b).
   (c) " he can ill pipe that lacketh his upper lip " (94c).

PISS, see Fart, Nettle.

PITCHERS, " small pitchers have wide ears " (65c), usually of children : what children hear at home soon flies abroad. " *Q. Elizabeth.* A parlous boy ; go to, you are too shrewd. *Archbishop.* Good madam, be not angry with the child. *Q. Elizabeth.* Pitchers have ears."—Shakspeare, *Richard III.* (1597), ii. 4.

PLAIN, (a) " plain without pleats " (69b), in the *Epigrams on Proverbs* (210a) it is thus amplified, " the plain fashion is best . . . plain without pleats."
   (b) see Best.

PLAT, " in any place or plat " (257b), situation, place, locality.

PLAY, " as good play for nought as work for nought " (44b ; 180b).

PLAYETH, see Win.

PLEASURE, (a) " who will, in time present, pleasure refrain, shall in time to come more pleasure obtain "
(32d).
  (b) " follow pleasure and then will pleasure flee :
flee pleasure and pleasure will follow thee " (32d).

PLENTY, " plenty is no dainty " (62b).

POKE, see Pig.

POLL, POUL (passim), rob, plunder, pillage : a play on
poll=shave frequently occurs (see 259d).

POMPOUS PROVISION, " pompous provision cometh not all
alway of gluttony but of pride some time " (81d).

POOR, see Offering, Souls.

POST, (a) " from post to pillar . . . tost " (55c ; 218d),
hither and thither, with aimless effort or action :
literally, from the same to the same—pillar=Lat.
columna=post. Thus in the Ayenbite of Inwit a
good man becomes a post in God's temple. " And,
dainty duke, whose doughty dismal fame From Dis
to Dædalus, from post to pillar, Is blown abroad."—
Shakspeare and Fletcher, Two Noble Kinsmen (c.
1611), iii. 5.
  (b) " in post pace " (51b), with all possible speed
or expedition. " Lord George your brother, Norfolk,
and myself, In haste, post-haste, are come to join with
you."—Shakspeare, 3 Henry VI. (1594), ii. 1.
  (c) " a mill post thwitten to a pudding prick "
(101a), said of unthrifts : twitten=to whittle down ;
pudding prick=the skewer used to fasten a pudding
bag.
  (d) " a post of physic " (55c), probably a posset.

POT, (a) " the weaker goeth to the pot " (68d ; 226c), pot
has been thought to=(a) pit (i.e. of destruction), or (b)
the melting pot of the refiner : the meaning, however,
is clear, and the colloquialism, though ancient, is still
in common use. In the illustration (infra) and in
many monkish references the " pit " or " pot " is
obviously a kind of oubliette, in which refractory
monks or impenitent heretics were immured, suffering
a lingering or speedy death at the will of their
gaolers. " Under a pot he schal be put in a pryvie
chamber."—Piers Plowman, 62. " Not one of them

shall 'scape, but they shall to the pot."—*Jacob and Esau* (E.E.D.S., *Anon. Pl.* 2 Ser. 77a), v. 4 (1568).

(b) "the pot so long to the water goeth, till at the last it cometh home broken" (82b), *i.e.* the inevitable must happen. "So long went the pot to the water, that at last it came broken home, and so long put he his hand into his purse, that at last the empty bottome returned him a writ of *Non est inventus.*"—Greene, *Never too Late* (1590).

(c) "neither pot broken nor water spilt" (227c).

(d) "to see the pot both skimmed for running over and also all the liquor run at rover" (99b), *to run at rover*=to have too much liberty: here=squandered, wasted, dissipated.

(e) "he that cometh last to the pot is soonest wroth" (99b).

(f) "my pot is whole and my water clean" (83a).

(g) "little pot soon hot" (31b), a little suffices; little people (or minds) are soon angered. "Now were I not a little pot, and soon hot, my very lips might freeze to my very teeth, . . . for, considering the weather, a taller man than I will take cold."—Shakspeare, *Taming of the Shrew* (1593), iv. 1.

POTTED, "she was potted thus like a sot" (99b), ruined: see Pot (a).

POULST, (170c), see Poll.

POVERTY, "poverty parteth fellowship" (48d; 218c).

POWDERING TUB (245a), properly a salting tub, but also applied to the salivation bed or cradle, formerly used in the cure of the *lues venerea*.

PERIL, "the peril of prating out of tune by note" (68c).

PRAYERS, "much motion . . . to prayers with . . . little devotion" (96c).

PREASE, "some folk in luck cannot prease" (21b, 34c), press forward, hasten, "crowd in." "No humble suitors prease to speak for right."—Shakspeare, 3 *Henry VI.* (1595), iii. 1.

PRECIOUS STONES, see Hog.

PREFE (in pl. PREVES), "some case . . . showeth prefe " (46d, 27d), proof : also Preef (120b).

PRESSED (220b), ready : Fr. *prêt* or O. Fr. *prest*.

PRICK, (a) "folly it is to spurn against a prick " (68b), in Biblical phrase, "to kick against," &c.

(b) "ye shoot nigh the prick " (15a), in archery the point or mark in the centre of the butts ; or, as we should now say, " the bull's-eye." " Therefore seeing that which is most perfect and best in shootinge, as alwayes to hit the pricke, was never seene nor hard tell on yet amonges men."—Ascham, *Toxoph.* (1544), 123.

PRICKETH, see Provender, Sharp thorn.

PRIDE, (a) " pride will have a fall " (27a).

(b) " pride goeth before and shame cometh after " (27b). " Pryde gothe before and shame cometh be-hynde . . . We may wayle the tyme that ever it came here."—*Treatise of a Gallant* (c. 1510).

PRIEST, " I would do more than the priest spake of on Sunday " (95d).

PRITCHT, " his nostrils so pritcht " (129c), pricked : still dialectical.

PROFACE (79b), " much good may it do you ! " a common welcome at meals : in the *Epigrams* we find (page 267) : " Reader . . . for preface, proface." " The dinner's half done before I say grace, And bid the old knight and his guest proface."—Heywood, *Wise Wom. of Hogsdon* (1638).

PROFFERED, " proffered service stinketh " (61a ; 209a and b).

PROPERTY, " her property preves " (27d), cloak, disguise.

PROPHET, " not to my profit a prophet was I " (91b), the pun still does yeoman service.

PROUD, (a) " I proud and thou proud who shall bear th' ashes out ? " (26d).

(b) see Cock.

PROVE, see Friend.

PROVENDER, " his provender pricketh him " (33d ; 216c and d).

PROVIDE, see Worst.

PUDDING, see Dog.

PUDDING TIME, " this year cometh . . . in pudding time " (97c), in the nick of time, opportunely. " You come in pudding time, or else I had dress'd them."—Tylney, *Locrine* (1594), iii. 3.

PULL, see Crow.

PULPIT, " a proper pulpit piece " (82c), " gospel," something to be received without question because expounded as it were *ex cathedrâ*.

PURSE, (a) " the purse is threadbare " (20b ; 221c).
  (b) " he is purse sick and lacketh a physician " (41b), needy, hard up.
  (c) " ye would buy my purse—give me a purgation " (41a).
  (d) " be it better, be it worse, do ye after him that beareth the purse " (13a).
  (e) see Light.

PUT, see Case.

QUARRELOUS (231a), here = apt to engender contention, fault-finding, complaining. " Goete wepynges and quarrellouse plaintes."—Caxton, *Encydos* (1490), xxii. 80.

QUARTERS, see Four Quarters.

QUEANS, " flearing queans " (66a), wantons, strumpets : primarily *quean* (like queen) = a woman without regard to character or position ; the spelling ultimately differentiated the debased from the reputable meaning, a noteworthy instance occurring in Langland (*Piers Plowman* [1363], ix. 46, " At church in the charnel cheorles aren yuel to knowe Other a knyght fro a knave other a queyne fro a queene."

QUESTION, " this is a question of old enquiring " (91a).

QUICH, " pigs dare not quich there " (293a), quich = stir, move.

QUICK, " quick as a bee " (21d).

QUIGHT (47d), quit.

QUITTANCE, see Sufferance.

RABBIT, " who the devil will change a rabbit for a rat " (86a).

RAIN, see Cloak.

RATE, " rise ye as ye rate " (55d), reckon, fix, decide.

RAVINE, " ruin of one ravine " (93c), *ravine*=an act of rapine. " I sorowed for the provinces misfortunes, wrackt by private ravins and publick taxes."—Q. Eliz. tr. *Boeth.* (1593), I. pr. iv. 9.

REAM, " a ream thence " (200a), realm, kingdom ; here a type of great distance : the usage is unrecorded in the O.E.D.

RECEIVERS, " where be no receivers, there be no thieves " (48c ; 180b). " It is a comon sayinge, ware there no receyver there shoulde be no thefe. So ware there no stewes, there shulde not so many honeste mennes doughters rune awaye from there fathers and playe the whores as dothe."—*A Christen Exhortation unto Customable Swearers* (1575).

RECKONERS, (a) " reckoners without their host must reckon twice " (19d). Fr., " Comptoit sans son hoste." —Rabelais, *Gargantua.*
     (b) " even reckoning maketh long friends " (64d ; 213a).
     (c) " reckoning without thine host thou must reckon twice " (173b).

RECKONING, see Reckoners.

RECUMBENTIBUS (85b), a knock-down blow : cf. " circumbendibus." " He yaff the Kyng Episcropus Suche a recumbentibus, He smot in-two bothe helme and mayle."—*Laud Troy Bk.* (c. 1400), 7400.

RED HERRING, see Fish.

RELEVAVITH, " what shall be his relevavith " (36a), relief. " I see not any greate lightlywod that any good summe will comm in, tyl after Christmas, and then no more than the releuauithes."—*State Papers, Hen. VIII.* (1546), I. ii. 840.

REN, RENNING, " to ren as swiftly " (118d), run : hence (119a), running ; and so forth.

REST, " money . . . thou dost rest so " (255c), lay by, store for use.

RESTY, " resty wealth " (12d): *resty* may be subject to three glosses = (a) indolent, lazy: meaning that wealth obtained by a rich marriage tends thereto; or (b) it may = restive, coy (as hard to get); or (c) = it may be a contemptuous application of *resty* = rancid, thus referring to money as " dross," " muck," &c. " Where the master is too resty or too rich to say his own prayers, or to bless his own table."—Milton, *Iconoclastes* (1649), xxiv.

REVART, " that oath again revart " (128b), take back.

REWETH (78c), rues.

RHYME, " it may rhyme but it accordeth not " (44c; 221a). " It may wele ryme but it accordith nought." —Lydgate, *MS. poem*, " On Inconstancy."

RICHES, " riches bringeth oft harm and ever fear, where poverty passeth without grudge of grief " (46d).

RICHESSE, " beauty without richesse " (14b), riches: properly a singular, but now used as a plural.

RID, see Rock.

RIGHT, see Might, Nothing.

RIGHT SIDE, " you rose on your right side " (62c), a happy augury: the modern usage speaks of the reverse or " wrong side of the bed." " C. What! doth shee keepe house alreadie? D. Alreadie. C. O good God: we rose on the right side to-day."—*Terence in English* (1614).

RIME, see Rhyme.

RING, " I hopping without for a ring of a rush " (9a), see Rush-ring.

RINGETH, " she ringeth a peal, a larum " (78b).

RINGLEADER (24d), originally one who led a ring, as of dancers, &c.

RIPE, " soon ripe soon rotten " (27c): this proverb also occurs in Harman, *Caveat*, &c. (1567).

RISE, see Sit.

RIVELED, " with riveled old face " (142b), wrinkled, shrunk. " Grumbates . . . a man . . . of middle age, and with riveled lims, but carrying with him a brave mind, and ennobled for the ensignes of many goodly victories."—*Ammianus Marcellinus* (1609).

ROAST, (*a*) " rule the roast " (13*a*), to have (or take) the lead (or mastery) : *roast*=roost (probably). " But at the pleasure of me That ruleth the roste alone."— Skelton, *Colyn Cloute* (*c.* 1518).

(*b*) " he looked like one that had beshit the roast " (89*c*).

(*c*) " roast a stone " (56*c*), *i.e.* one may put warmth into but can never get heat out of a stone. " They may garlicke pill Cary sackes to the mil Or pescoddes they may shil Or els go roste a stone."—Skelton, *Why come ye not to Court?* (1520).

ROB, see Peter.

ROBBERY, " change is no robbery " (204*b*), see Change.

ROBIN HOOD, " tales of Robin Hood are good among fools " (94*c*), the story of Robin Hood ultimately grew so misty and traditional that the name became a generic byword for the marvellous that was not believable. Thus Robin Hood, *subs.*=a daring lie; Robin Hood's pennyworth (of things sold under value); " Good even, good Robin Hood " (said of civility extorted by fear) ; " Many talk of Robin Hood that never shot in his bow " (75*a*)=many speak of things of which they have no knowledge ; and " Tales of Robin Hood are good enough for fools." " I write no ieste ne tale of Robin Hood."—Barclay, *Ship of Fooles* (1509), fol. 250 (1570).

ROCK, " thus rid the rock " (92*b* and 186*d*), *i.e.* so was the distaff managed, manipulated : *rock*=the distaff or frame about which flax, wool, &c., was arranged and from which the thread was drawn in spinning. Hence here the meaning is " So managed you your thrift badly." " I'll ride your horse as well as I ride you."—Shakspeare, *Twelfth Night* (1602), iii. 4.

ROD, (*a*) " when haste proveth a rod made for his own tail " (7*a*).

(*b*) " beaten with his own rod " (7*a*). " —— don fust C'on kint sovent est-on batu."—*Roman du Renart* (*c.* 1300).

ROLLING STONE, " the rolling stone never gathereth moss " (31c). " I, thy head is alwaies working; it roles, and it roles, Dondolo, but it gathers no mosse, Dondolo."—Marston, *Fawn* (1606). " Pierre volage ne queult mousse."—*De l'Hermite qui se désespéra pour le Larron qui ala en Paradis avant que lui* (13th century).

ROME, " Rome was not built in one day and yet stood till . . . finished " (36d; 223a). " Hæc tamen vulgaris sententia me aliquantulum recreavit, quæ etsi non auferre, tamen minuere possit dolorem meum, quæ quidem sententia hæc est, Romam uno die non fuisse conditam."—Queen Elizabeth, *Extempore speech before the University of Cambridge* (9th August, 1564).

ROOF, " he is at three words up in the house roof " (66d): nowadays we say " up in the skies."

ROPE, (a) " as meet as a rope for a thief " (24c).
    (b) " he haleth her by the boy rope " (78c), see Boy rope.

ROPE-RIPE (281a), fit for (or deserving) the hangman's rope. " Lord, how you roll in your rope-ripe terms ! " —Chapman, *May Day* (1611), iii.

ROUGH BIT, " I will bridle thee with rough bit " (181d).

ROUTING, " routing like a hog " (30a), *rout*=snore.

ROVERS, " ye pry and ye prowl at rovers " (31c)—" let not your tongue run at rover " (69a)—(also 99b), *at rover* =wild, unrestrained, at random.

ROWLES, " at rowles " (280b), a precinct situated between the cities of London and Westminster, enjoying certain immunities, and hence called the Liberty of the Rolls: the name being derived from the rolls or records deposited in its chapel.

ROYALS (*i.e.* RIAL), " a bag of royals and nobles " (97a), *royal*=an old English gold coin, of varying value, from 10s. in Henry VI.'s time to 15s. in Queen Elizabeth's, whilst in the reign of James I. the rose-rial was worth 30s., and the spur-rial, 15s. : see Noble.

ROYLE, " by your revellous riding on every royle " (81*a*), *royle*=a Flemish horse : this would seem to echo the alleged contempt of Henry VIII. as regards Anne of Cleves, whom he described as " a Flanders mare."

RUB, see Horse.

RUIN, " ruin of one ravin was there none greater " (93*c*), see Ravine.

RULE, " better rule than be ruled " (13*a* ; 185*c*).

RULED, see Dame.

RUN, (*a*) " he may ill run that cannot go " (94*b* ; 189*b*).
(*b*) " ye run to work in haste as nine men held ye " (42*c*).
(*c*) " she thinketh I run over all that I look on " (77*c*), examine, " possess," have to do with.
(*d*) see Cat, Hare.

RUNNETH, (*a*) " he runneth far that never turneth again " (90*b* ; 182*a*).
(*b*) see Tongue.

RUSH, " care not a rush " (95*a*), *rush*=low standard of value. " And yet yeve ye me nevere The worthe of a risshe."—Langland, *Piers Plowman* (1362), 2421.

RUSHES, " green rushes for this stranger, straw here " (59*b*) : it was usual, before the introduction of carpets, to strew rushes on the floors of dwelling-houses ; and on the entrance of a visitor, hospitality required that they should be renewed. " Where is this stranger? Rushes, ladies, rushes : Rushes as green as summer for this stranger."—Beaumont and Fletcher, *Valentinian* (1617), ii. 4.

RUSH-RING, " a ring of a rush " (9*a*), a *rush ring*=a symbol of a mock marriage. " As fit . . . as Tib's rush for Tom's forefinger."—Shakspeare, *All's Well* (1598), ii. 2, 22.

SACK, (*a*) " an old sack axeth much patching " (58*a*).
(*b*) " it is a bad sack that will abide no clouting " (60*d*).

SADDLES, (*a*) " where saddles lack better ride on a pad than on the horse bareback " (29*b*).
(*b*) see Sow.

SAGE, " sage said saws " (7b).

SAID, (a) " sooner said than done " (73b).
(b) " little said soon amended " (202c), the modern form is " least said soonest mended."
(c) " other folks said it but she did it " (99d).

SAINT, (a) " young saint, old devil " (27c; 177a), the reverse was quite as common—" young devil, old saint."

SAINT AUDRY (73d), or Auldrey, meaning Saint Etheldreda, who (by tradition) died of a swelling in her throat, which she considered as a particular judgment for having been in her youth much addicted to wearing fine necklaces (Nich. Harpsfield (1622), *Hist. Eccl. Anglicana*): hence tawdry.

SAINT NEEDS (244a), a play, most likely, on the Huntingdonshire St. Neots.

SAT, " she sat upon thorns " (27c).

SAUCE, see Sweet.

SAVOUR, see Nothing.

SAVOURLY, " very savourly sound " (14b), properly, rightly—as with a good and proper sense.

SAY, (a) " I say little . . . but I think more " (57b).
(b) see Day, Mum, Nay.

SAYING, " saying and doing are two things " (73b; 171c).

SCABB'D, SCALD, see Horse.

SCARBOROUGH WARNING, " Scarborough warning I had " (43b; 223d), no warning at all; a blow before the word. Fuller in his *Worthies* says : " The proverb took its original from Thomas Stafford, who in the reign of Queen Mary, 1557, with a small company seized on Scarborough Castle (utterly destitute of provision for resistance) before the townsmen had the least notice of his approach." " I received a message from my lord chamberlaine . . . that I should preach before him upon Sunday next; which Scarborough warning did not only perplex me, but so puzzel me."—Mayhew, *Letter* (1603, 19th January).

SCRATCHING, see Cat.

HEY. II.

F F

SEALED, see Butter.

SEE, (a) " see me and see me not " (69c ; 211c).
    (b) " I see much, but I say little and do less " (41b).
    (c) see Far, Millstone.
    (d) " seeing that ye never saw " (33a).

SEEK, (a) " to seek for that she was loth to find " (71a)—
" I seek for a thing . . . that I would not find "
(205a). Also see Find and Nought.

SEELD (*passim*), seldom.

SEELED WHEN, " coming seeled when " (44b ; 314a),
seldom.

SEELY, " these seely worms " (131b), silly.

SEEN, (a) " seen of the tone sort and heard of the
tother " (101b).
    (b) see Far.

SEEST, see See.

SEGGING, " the Dutchman saith that segging is good
cope " (94a), *segging*=sedge.

SELDOM, (a) " seldom cometh the better " (11a ; 188b).
" This change is like to the rest of worldly chaunges
. . . from the better to the worse : For as the Proverb
sayth : Seldome coms the better."—*English Courtier
and Country Gentleman* (1586).
    (b) " seldom seen, soon forgotten " (30d).

SELF, " self do, self have " (20a).

SENIOR DE GRAUNDE (13a). " I myself will mounsire
graunde captain undertake."—Udall, *Roister Doister*
(E.E.D.S.), iv. 8, 98b.

SERVICE, " proffered service stinketh " (61a ; 209a and
b), see Proffered.

SET, see Foot, Heart.

SEVEN, see Six.

SEVEN YEAR, see Happeth.

SHALL, " that shall be, shall be " (53b ; 181c), the
modern " we shall see what we shall see " is regarded
as a modern echo of *nous verrons que nous verrons,*
whereas the idiom is apparently of ancient lineage of
native growth.

SHAME, (a) "shame take him that shame thinketh" (21b; 174c), *i.e.* "Honi soit qui mal y pense."

SHAME, see Pride.

SHAMEFUL, "shameful craving . . . must have shameful nay" (35d).

SHARP, "all thing that is sharp is short" (56d).

SHARP THORN, "it pricketh betimes that shall be a sharp thorn" (94a; 187d). "Young it pricketh that will be a thorn."—*Jacob and Esau* (E.E.D.S., *Anon. Pl.* 2 Ser. 11d).

SHEAF, "take as falleth in the sheaf" (64b; 213a).

SHEATH, "she maketh so much of her painted sheath" (26d; 180c).

SHEEP, (a) "as rich as a new shorn sheep" (42d), penniless, "fleeced." "The nexte that came was a coryar And a Cobelar, his brother, As ryche as a new shorne shepe."—*Cocke Lorelles Bote* (*c.* 1510).
     (b) "subtilly like a sheep thought I" (20b).

SHEEP'S EYE, "he cast a sheep's eye at her" (185c), ogled, leered : originally to look modestly and with diffidence but always with longing or affection. "That casting a sheepe's eye at hir, away he goes ; and euer since he lies by himselfe and pines away."—Greene, *Francesco's Fortunes* (1590), *Works*, viii. 191.

SHEEP'S FLESH, "he loveth well sheep's flesh that wets his bread in the wool" (70c) : Sharman thinks this refers to a broth or jelly made from the sheep's head boiled with the wool ; as also witness the following from a poem attributed to Lydgate—" Of the shepe is cast aways no thynge ; . . . Of whoos hede boyled, with wull and all, Tere cometh a gely and an oyntement ryal."—*Treatyse of the Horse, Shepe, and Goos*.

SHIFT, "shift each one for himself as he can" (96d).

SHILLING, "to bring a shilling to ninepence" (66c).

SHINS, see Cast.

SHOD, see Shoemaker's wife.

SHOE, (a) "the shoe will hold with the sole" (67c; 197b).
     (b) "now for good luck cast an old shoe after me" (21d), an old and still intelligible bit of folk-lore :

F F 2

allusions to it are very numerous in old writers. "Captain, your shoes are old, pray put 'em off, And let one fling 'em after us."—Beaumont and Fletcher, *Honest Man's Fortune* (1613).

(c) " myself can tell best where my shoe doth wring me " (69d), the moderns substitute " pinch " for " wring." " I wot best, wher wringeth me my sho."—Chaucer, *Cant. Tales* (1383), 9426.

(d) " who waiteth for dead men's shoes shall go long barefoot " (45a), it is tedious looking forward to inheritances. " You are my maister's sonne, and you looke for his lande; but they that hope for dead men's shoes may hap go barefoote."—*Two Angry Women of Abington* (1599).

(e) see Gosling.

SHOEMAKER'S WIFE, " who is worse shod than the shoe-maker's wife " (39d; 223c), an excuse for lack of something one ought to possess: compare Slipper.

SHOON, " clouted shoon " (145d), *shoon* = shoes: still good Scots.

SHOOT, (a) " ye shoot nigh the prick " (15a), *prick* = point, dot, mark, " bull's-eye."

(b) " he shooteth wide " (205c and d).

(c) " whom ye see out of the way, or shoot wide, over-shoot not yourself any side to hide " (58c).

SHOOTANKER, " her substance is shootanker whereat I shoot " (13d), chief support; *i.e.* the principal attraction as constituting the lady's last chance of marriage.

SHOOTING, " short shooting leseth your game " (97c), a technical term in archery: *i.e.* shooting wide of the mark.

SHORE, " ye lean . . . to the wrong shore " (57b).

SHORN, (a) " as rich as a new shorn sheep " (42d), see Sheep.

(b) see Face.

SHORT, see Cow, Horse.

SHOT, (a) " pay the shot " (45d), *shot* = reckoning, share of expense. " Well at your will ye shall be furnisht. But now a jugling tricke to pay the shot."—Chettle, *Kind Harts Dreame* (1592).

(b) see Coming, Fool.

SHREW, " every man can rule a shrew save he that hath her " (75*a*).

SHREWD COW, see Cow.

SHRIFT, " at shrift " (136*b*).

SIDE, see Bread, Hear.

SIGHT, " out of sight out of mind " (8*d*; 172*d*), a saying which is found in Thomas à Kempis (1450), and earlier in *Prov. of Hendyng* (*c.* 1320)—" Fer from eye, fer from herte, Quoth Hendyng."

SILVER, see Farthing.

SIMPER DE COCKET (52*b*), found as a *subs.* as well as an *adj.* = coquettish, wanton. " I saw you dally with your simper de cocket."—Heywood, *Play of Weather* (*Works*, I. 122*d*). " And gray russet rocket With simper the cocket."—Skelton, *The Tunnyng of Elynoure Rummyng* (1520).

SING, see Thieves.

SINK, (*a*) " sink in thine own sin " (28*c*; 217*c*).
   (*b*) " sink or swim " (92*b*).

SIR JOHN (66*d*), generic for a parish priest : our universities . . . confer the designation of Dominus on those who have taken their first degree of Bachelor of Arts ; the word Dominus was naturally translated Sir, and, as almost every clergyman had taken his first degree, it became customary to apply the term to the lower class of the hierarchy.

SIT, " better sit still than rise and fall " (68*c*; 210*d*). " Oh Cousin, I have heard my father say, that it is better to sit fast than to rise and fall, and a great wise man who knew the world to a hayre, would say, that the meane was sure : better be in the middle roome, then either in the Garret or the Sellor."—Brereton, *Court and Country* (1618).

SIX, " a six and seven " (38*d*; 20*c*), in confusion, at loggerheads. " Alle in sundur hit [a tun] brast in six or in seuyn."—*Avowyne of King Arther* (*c.* 1340), 64 [Camden Soc., *Eng. Meln. Rom.* 89].
   (*b*) " six days in the week beside the market day " (31*a*), always.

SKIN, (a) "a lamb's skin ye will provide . . . to lap her in " (76c), see Lamb's skin.

(b) " it is good sleeping in a whole skin " (69a), this is the title of a play by W. Wager, not now extant.

(c) see Fox.

SKIRTS, " sit on their skirts " (13b), pursue, persecute, " go for." " Touching the said archbishop, he had not stood neutrall as was promised, therefore he had justly set on his skirts."—Howell, *Fam. Lett.* (1650).

SKY, " when the sky falleth we shall have larks " (11c), a retort to a wild hypothesis; " if pigs had wings they would be likely birds." " Si les nues tomboyent esperoyt prendre les alouettes."—Rabelais, *Gargantua.*

SLANDER, " it may be a slander but it is no lie " (84c).

SLEEPING DOG, see Dog.

SLEEVE, (a) " laughed in my sleeve " (71a ; 204d), derided or exulted in secret.

(b) " flattering knaves and flearing queans . . . hang on his sleeve " (66a), lickspittle, cadge from, are dependent on.

(c) " a broken sleeve holdeth th' arm back " (21b). " It is a terme with John and Jacke, Broken sleeve draweth arme a backe."—*Parliament of Byrdes* (1550).

(d) " she lacketh but even a new pair of sleeves " (28a).

(e) see Dagger.

SLEEVELESS ERRAND (17d), the origin of " sleeveless " is a matter of conjecture, though its meaning is tolerably clear : thus " a sleeveless (=inadequate) reason " (*Relig, Antiq.*); " a sleeveless (=trifling) excuse " (Lyly); " sleeveless (=aimless) rhymes " (Hall); " a sleeveless (=objectless, wanting cover or excuse, fruitless, fool's) errand " (Chaucer, Shakspeare, &c.). Sharman suggests the mediæval custom of favoured knights wearing the sleeve of their mistress as a mark of favour, aspirants failing to obtain the badge being dubbed " sleeveless "—" Sir Launcelot wore the sleive of the faire maide of Asteloth in a tourney, whereat queene Guenever was much displeased " (Spenser).

SLIPPER, " let not the cobbler wade above his slipper " (*Epigrams*). " Heere are the tenne precepts to be observed in the art of scolding : therefore let not the cobler wade above his slipper. The cobler above his slipper, said Chubb, hee is a knave that made that proverb."—Simon Snel-knave, *Fearefull and Lamentable Effects of Two Dangerous Comets* (1591).

SLIPSTRING, " a waghalter slipstring " (86*d*), a gallows-bird, one rope-ripe but who has cheated the gallows. " Thow art a slipstring I'le warrant."—Lyly, *Mother Bombie* (1594), ii. 1.

SLOPS, " his slops are . . ." (259*a*), a linen outer garment.

SLOTH, " sloth must breed a scab " (9*b*).

SLUGGING, " slugging in bed " (58*a*), lazing. " All night slugging in a cabin."—Spenser, *State of Ireland*.

SMALL, (*a*) " many small make a great " (37*b* ; 216*b*), mod. " many a mickle makes a muckle." " The proverbe saith that many a small makith a grete."—Chaucer, *Parson's Tale* (1383).
  (*b*) see Offering, Pitchers.

SMELLED, " I smelled her out " (39*c* ; 227*b*), discovered, " nosed," found. " Can you smell him out by that? " —Shakspeare, *Much Ado* (1600), iii. 2.

SNAIL, " in haste like a snail " (21*d*).

SNEAKBILL, " such a sneakbill " (88*c*), a generic term of contempt. " A checheface, mecher, sneakebill, wretched fellow, one out of whose nose hunger drops." —Cotgrave, *Did.* (1611).

SNOW, " snow is white and lyeth in the dike and every man lets it lie " (62*d*).

SNOWERING, " lowering and snowering " (286*b*).

SNUDGE, " pinch like a snudge " (83*b*), *snudge*=miser. " Your husbandry . . . is more like the life of a covetous snudge that ofte very evill proves."—Ascham, *Toxoph.* (1544), i.

SOCKET, see Candle.

SOFT, see Fire.

SOLARUM, see Familorum.

SOLD, (*a*) " better sold than bought " (27*a*).
(*b*) " like one to be sold she set out herself in fine apparel " (52*a*).

SOLE, see Shoe.

SOME, " here some and there some " (217*a*).

SOMETHING, " something is better than nothing " (172*b* and 29*c*, with " somewhat " for " something ").

SOOL, " a thing by itself sool " (148*c*), by itself, alone.

SOON, (*a*) " till soon fare ye well " (74*a*), this may = till some future time not far distant, or *soon* = evening, a provincialism.
(*b*) see Hot, Said.

SOOTH, (*a*) " ye say sooth " (131*d*), truth. " If thy speech be sooth, I care not if thou dost for me as much."—Shakspeare, *Macbeth* (1606), v. 5.
(*b*) see Bourd.

SORE, (*a*) " present salve for this present sore " (20*d*).
(*b*) see Flies, Store.

SORROW, (*a*) " I had sorrow to my sops " (87*d*).
(*b*) " make not two sorrows of one " (72*d* ; 173*d*).
(*c*) " to bring her solace that bringeth me sorrow " (88*c*).

SOT, " he is a sot " (238*c et passim*), fool : see Heywood, *Works* (E.E.D.S.), I, 267*a*.

SOULS, " poor men have no souls " (201*d* ; 202*a*).

SOUR, see Sweet.

SOUSE HEAD, " like a souse head " (136*a*), fool, simpleton, sillikins : also souse-crown.

SOW, (*a*) " meet as a sow to bear a saddle " (52*c* ; 226*a*).
(*b*) " the still sow eats up the draff " (27*c* ; 196*d*), *still sow* = a generic reproach, a sly lurking fellow ; *draff* = anything unfit for human food. " We do not act, that often jest and laugh ; 'Tis old but true, still swine eat all the draff."—Shakspeare, *Merry Wives of Windsor* (1596), iv. 2.
(*c*) " grease the fat sow on th' arse (or tail) " (39*a*), be insensible to kindness : see *Scogin's Jests*.
(*d*) " the sow will no more so deep root " (58*c*).

SUMM'D, SUMMING, " wings full summ'd " (224*a*), full feathered : a falconry term. " The muse from Cambria comes, with pinions summ'd and sourd."— Drayton, *Polyolb.* (1613), xi. 859.

SUMMER, see Swallow.

SUN, " when the sun shineth make hay " (8*c*), seize your chance or opportunity.

SURE, see Butter.

SURGEON, " I am like the ill surgeon (said I) without store of good plasters " (20*d*).

SWALLOW, " one swallow maketh not summer " (70*a*). " One swallowe prouveth not that summer is neare." —Northbrooke, *Treatise against Dauncing* (1577).

SWEEPETH, see Broom.

SWEET, (*a*) " sweet meat will have sour sauce " (19*d* ; 208*d* ; 209*a*).
    (*b*) " take the sweet with the sour " (62*c*).
    (*c*) " sweet sauce began to wax sour " (54*b*).
    (*d*) " sweet beauty with sour beggary " (49*b*).
    (*e*) see Fire.

SWIM, " he must needs swim that is hold up by the chin " (12*d*), see *Scogin's Jests* (1565).

SWORD, (*a*) " he that striketh with the sword shall be stricken with the scabbard " (77*d*), see *Revelation,* xiii. 10. " *Nich.* Blessed be the peace-makers ; they that strike with the sword shall be beaten with the scabbard. *Phil.* Well said, proverbs, nere another to that purpose? *Nich.* Yes, I could have said to you, syr, Take heede is a good reede."—Haughton, *Two Angry Women of Abington* (1599).
    (*b*) " it is ill putting a naked sword in a mad man's hand " (87*c*).

TABER, see Hare.

TABLES, " play at tables " (138*b*), backgammon. " This is the ape of form, monsieur the nice, That, when he plays at tables, chides the dice."—Shakspeare, *Love's L. L.* (1594), v. 2.

TAIL, see Stools, Worm.

TAKE, see Inn, Give, Heart, Nay, Pepper, Sheaf, Time.

TALE, (a) " tale of a tub " (94c ; 189b), nonsense, fooling, absurdity. " Ye say they follow your law, And vary not a straw, Which is a tale of a tub."—Bale, *Three Laws* (1538), *Works* (E.E.D.S.).

　　(b) " a good tale ill told in the telling is marred " (82c), see *infra*.

　　(c) " good tales well told and ill heard . . . are marred " (82c), see *supra*.

　　(d) " to tell tales out of school " (23d), to romance, play the informer (Tyndale, d. 1536).

　　(e) " by told tales " (27c), *tale*=incredible story, marvellous narration ; also words of wisdom : thus the acme of truth or falsehood. " Telle no talys."—*Cov. Myst.* (1469).

　　(f) " thy tales all taste of ale " (189b), *i.e.* are pot-house yarns.

TALLOW, " plainness is most tallow " (248c).

TARRIER, " let him be no longer tarrier " (35d), a dawdler, a " slowcoach." " And for that cause he is often times called of them Fabius cunctator, that is to say, the tarier or delayer."—Elyot, *Governour* (1531), bk. i., ch. xxiii.

TASTE, see Ale, Tale.

TATCH, see Colt.

TAUGHT, see Fed.

TAUNT TIVET (87d), primarily a hunting call, a note on the horn : here an exclamatory salutation.

TEETH, " to cast in my teeth checks and choking oysters " (43c), see Checks and Choking oysters.

TELL, see Cards.

TEN, see Bird.

TENDER, see Leman.

TERMS, " in plain terms plain truth . . . to utter " (54c).

THAMES, (a) " to cast water in Thames " (39b), a simile of useless or thankless labour ; a work of supereroga-tion.

(*b*) " bearing no more rule than a goose turd in Thames " (76*c*).

THAN (*passim*), then.

THANK, " I can thee good thank " (141*b*), *can*= able to give ; *thank* is singular=thanks.

THANKLESS, " a thankless office " (58*d*).

THARE (238*d*), there : note the rhyme.

THERE, see Some.

THIEF, " to ax my fellow whether I be a thief " (72*b* ; 177*d*).

THIEVES, (*a*) " when thieves fall out true men come to their good " (93*b* ; 198*d*), or (modern) " when thieves fall out honest men come by their own " : *good*=belongings, possessions.
   (*b*) " beggars may sing before thieves and weep before true men " (47*a* ; 180*d*).
   (*c*) see Receivers.

THING, (*a*) " too much of one thing is not good " (64*d*), this we now shorten to " too much of a good thing."
   (*b*) see Call, Gosling, Nothing, Seek.
   (*c*) " a wonder thing what things these old things tell " (33*c*).

THINK, " even as ye think now so come to you " (60*b*).

THINKETH, see Farthing, Shame.

THONG, see Buckle.

THORN, see Sat, Sharp thorn.

THOUGHT, (*a*) " thought is free " (57*b*). " Since thought is free, thinke what thou will."—James I., MS. Add. 24,195.
   (*b*) " my thought . . . is a goodly dish " (61*c*).

THREAD, " you spin a fair thread " (68*c*), with which compare " this thread finer to spin " (12*d* ; 215*b*).

THREADBARE, see Purse.

THREATING, " in brawling and threating " (167*c*), threatening. " The face of warre would looke so sterne and great. As it might threat to heave him from his sea."—Drayton, *Poems* (1637), p. 18.

THREE, (*a*) " three may a-keep counsel if two be away " (65*b* ; 222*d*). " Three may keep a counsel if twain

be away."—Chaucer, *Ten Commandments of Love.*
" The empress, the midwife, and yourself : Two may
keep counsel, when the third's away."—Shakspeare,
Titus Andronicus (1593), iv. 2.

(b) " frenzy, heresy, and jealousy are three that . . .
never cured be " (77c).

THREE TREES, " frame of three trees " (247c), the gallows : variants of like kidney are numerous—*e.g.*
Two-legged mare, Three-legged stool, Three-cornered
tree, Mare with three legs, Tyburn tree, Triple tree,
&c., &c.

THRIFT, (a) " when thrift is in the town ye be in the
field, &c." (92a).

(b) " I will now begin thrift when thrift seemeth
gone " (93d).

(c) " now thrift is gone now would ye thrive in all
haste " (95b).

(d) " thou art past thrift before thrift begin " (35a).

(e) " when thrift and you fell first at a fray you
played the man, for ye made thrift run away " (42d).

THRIVE, (a) " he that will thrive must ask leave of his
wife " (34d), another form of which occurs in Thynn's
Deb. betw. Pride and Lowliness (1570) :—" He had a
sonne or twaine he would advaunce, And sayd they
should take paines untyll it fell ; He that wyll thrive
(quod he) must tary chaunce."

(b) see Weddeth.

THROW, see Gift.

THUMB, (a) " ye taunt me tit over thumb " (64a).

(b) " she hitteth me on the thumbs " (64a).

(c) " this biteth the mare by the thumb " (76c).

TICKING, " their ticking might have taught any young
couple their love ticks to have wrought " (53d)—
" leave lewd ticking " (70d)—" to tick and laugh with
me he hath lawful leave " (71a), *tick* =to dally, wanton : frequently " tick and toy." " Such ticking, such
toying, such smiling, such winking, and such manning
them home when the sports are ended."—Gosson,
School of Abuse (1579).

TICKLE, (a) " my tongue must oft tickle " (15b), itch to
be wagging (Udall, *Apoph.* 381).

(b) see Time.

TIDE, " the tide tarrieth no man " (8*c* ; 202*c*). " Hoist saile while gale doth last, Tide and wind stay no man's pleasure."—Southwell, *St. Peter's Complaint* (1595).

TILL, " thou consentest not till " (126*d*), *till* = to.

TIME, (*a*) " take time when time cometh, lest time steal away " (8*c* ; 225*a* to *c*).
    (*b*) " let time try " (72*c*).
    (*c*) " time trieth truth " (72*c*).
    (*d*) " time is tickle " (8*d* ; 207*b* and *c*), uncertain.
    (*e*) " time lost again we cannot win " (51*d*).

TIPPETS, " so turned they their tippets " (54*c*), changed right about : cf. " turncoat "; frequently of girls on marriage. " Another Bridget; one that for a face Would put down Vesta; You to turn tippet ! "—Jonson, *Case is Altered* (1609). Also *Epigrams* (178*b* to 180*a*).

TIT, (*a*) " tit for tat " (64*a*), blow for blow, an equivalent, as good one side as the other : *i.e.* Fr. *tant pour tant.*
    (*b*) " little tit, all tail " (24*c*), *tit* originally = anything very small or diminutive.

TITIFILS, " no mo such titifils " (24*a*), a knave, a jade : a generic reproach. " The devill hymself . . . did apparell certain catchepoules and parasites, commonly called titivils and tale tellers, to sowe discord and dissencion."—Hall, *Henry VI.* (1542), f. 43.

TOAD, " she swelled like a toad " (39*b*).

TOAST, " hot as a toast " (54*b*).

TOLLETH, " the milner tolleth corn " (149*b*), takes a portion of grain as compensation for grinding.

TOMB, see Dead.

TONE (*passim*), the one : see Tother.

TONGUE, (*a*) " her tongue runneth on pattens " (78*a*), see Pattens.
    (*b*) " let not your tongue run at rover " (69*a*), see Rovers.
    (*c*) " thy tongue runneth before thy wit " (64*a* ; 214*d*).

(*d*) " biteth not with teeth but with her tongue " (75*b*).

(*e*) " her tongue is no edge tool but yet it will cut " (24*b*).

(*f*) " tongue breaketh bone, itself having none " (68*c*; 206*b* to *d*). " Tonge breketh bon, Ant nad hire selve non."—*Proverbs of Hendyng, MS.* (*c.* 1320).

(*g*) " when your tongue tickleth, at will let it walk " (15*d*).

(*h*) " my tongue must oft tickle " (15*b*), itch to be wagging.

(*i*) " it hurteth not the tongue to give fair words " (22*b*). " O, madam, faire words never hurt the tongue."—Jonson, &c., *Eastward Hoe* (1605).

(*j*) " he may show wisdom at will that with angry heart can hold his tongue still " (44*d*).

(*k*) " I would thy tongue were cooled to make thy tales more cold " (85*c*).

(*l*) " my tongue is a limb to match and to vex every vein of him " (68*b*).

(*m*) " think ye . . . I will be tongued-tied " (69*c*).

Tools, see Workman.

Tooted, " cards be tooted on but on the tone side " (231*b*), looked at, examined.

Tooting, " on my maids he is ever tooting " (70*b*), casting " sheep's eyes," leering.

Top, " as soon drive a top over a tiled house " (71*c*).

Tossed, see Post.

Tother (*passim*), the other : see Tone.

Tott'n'am, " Tott'n'am was turned French " (17*d*), said of great alterations and changed conditions : from the migration of a number of French workmen to this locality early in the reign of Henry VIII., their competition provoking the jealousy of English mechanics, and resulting in disturbances in the streets of London on May-day, 1517.

Tow, " more tow on their distaves than they can well spin " (73*c*), more in hand than can be well undertaken. " I have more tow on my dystaffe than I can well spyn."—Heywood, *Works* (E.E.D.S.), I. 25*c*.

Toy, (a) " every trifling toy age cannot laugh at " (88a), *toy* = whim, fancy, jest, &c.

(b) " such toys in her head " (75b), see *supra*.

(c) " their faces told toys " (17d), see Face.

Tract, " tract of time " (8a), process, length, continued duration. " This in tracte of tyme made hym welthy." —Fabyan, *Chronicle*, ch. lvi.

Trade, " yourself . . . taketh direct trade " (14c), way, means, course. " The Jewes, emong whom alone and no moe, God hitherto semed for to reigne, by reason of their knowledge of the law, and of the autoritee of being in the right trade of religion."—Udall, *Luke* xix.

Tread, (a) see Worm.

(b) " my wife doth . . . tread her shoe awry " (278a), play the whore; and (in a weaker sense) play fast and loose. " A woman to play false, enter a man more than she ought, or tread her shooe awry."—Cotgrave, *Dict.* (1611).

Treason, " in trust is treason " (67c).

Tree, (a) " it were a folly for me to put my hand between the bark and the tree " (57d), to meddle in family matters.

(b) " timely crooketh the tree that would a cammock be " (94a), see Cammock.

(c) " you cannot see the wood for trees " (62b), see Wood.

(d) see Three trees.

Triacle (191d), a medicine, an antidote. " Is there no triacle in Gilead? "—Wycliffe, *Jer.* viii. 22.

Trick, " so deep and so trick " (257d), smart, trig.

Trip, " take me in any trip " (59d).

Trod, see Black ox.

Trot, see Need.

True, (a) " it must needs be true that every man sayeth " (38a ; 200a and b).

(b) see Thieves.

Trust, see Treason.

TRUTH, (a) " tell truth without sin " (28a).
  (b) " deem the best till time hath tried the truth out " (72d), see Time.

TUB, see Tale.

TUN, " as full as a tun " (45b ; 208a), *tun* = a large cask. " And ever sith hath so the tappe yronne, Til that almost all empty is the tonne. "—Chaucer, *Cant. Tales* (1383), 3,891.

TUNE, (a) " out of tune by note " (68c).
  (b) " no tale could tune you in time to take heed " (90c).

TURD, (a) " one crop of a turd marreth a pot of potage " (76d).
  (b) " the more we stir a turd, the more it will stink " (76d).

TURN, (a) " one good turn asketh another " (41c): we now say " deserves."
  (b) " he is cast in his own turn " (213c).
  (c) see Cat.

TURNETH, see Runneth.

TWAIN, (a) " we twain are one too many " (65b).
  (b) see Three.

TWO, see Faces, Sorrow, Stools.

UNBORN, " better unborn than untaught " (25a ; 197d). " Old men yn proverbe sayde by old tyme, ' A chyld were beter to be unbore, Than to be untaught.' "— Symon, *Lessons of Wysedome for all Maner Chyldryn* (c. 1450).

UNKISSED, (a) " farewell, unkissed " (29d), of a not over-friendly parting : see next entry.
  (b) " unknown, unkissed " (38c ; 194b and c).

UNMINDED, " unminded, unmoaned " (21c).

UNTAUGHT, see Unborn.

URE, see Pig.

USE, " use maketh maistry " (55d ; 219a), *maistry* = mastery, perfection.

VARIORUM READINGS AND ERRATA. These, except where
otherwise stated, are those of the edition of 1566 as
compared with that of the original published in 1562.
Anno christi (Title *d*), omitted; to *make* out of hand
(5*c*), *take*; Since *that, that one* will not (8*d*), Since
that one will not; my tail *go to ground* (9*b*), *go to
the ground*; may *win my* heart (11*d*), *my* omitted;
Chapter V. (12*a*), erroneously given in both editions
(and in the Spenser Soc. reprint without a note) as
Chapter VI.; *to be* led (14*b*), *to be* is duplicated;
Chapter VII. (16*a*), throughout the present text the
Chapter headings have been modernised: in the
original editions these usually read *The. i chapiter,*
and so forth; in the present instance the reading of
the 1562 edition is *The seventh chapiter*, but in the
1566 edition it follows the regular rule, having been
corrected in the press; thought *this the best way* to
be (23*a*), *the* and *way* are omitted; cometh *a* good
end (25*d*), *a* is omitted; no scratching *will* forbear
(28*c*), *will* is omitted; ye *pry and ye prowl* (31*c*), *pry
and prowl*; *may* prove well (33*b*), *may* is omitted;
mine own *said* brother (33*d*), *said* is omitted; at
mangy *hackney's* hire (40*b*), *hackney*; by'r lady
friend (41*c*), in 1562 ed. freed, *freend* in 1566 issue;
one draught of drink (41*d*), *a* draught; beggarly
beauty and *rivalled* riches (50*a*), *rivalled* is a misprint in the present text for *rivelled* (=wrinkled,
shrunken): in the original 1562 ed. it is *riueld* and
reueld in the 1566; the choice is between a poor
beauty and a rich, but foundered, old woman; *he might
have*; his wife was set (53*c*), *he might have* omitted;
her biggest bags (54*b*), a curious misprint occurs in
the 1566 edition, the *biggest baggs* of the original
reading *beggs baggest*; two *days* past (58*c*), *days*
omitted; Well amended (*thought I*) (59*c*), *quoth I*;
ye *shall* first jet (60*d*), *shall* omitted; this *fair* young
wife (61*b*), *fair* omitted; *ye* cannot see (62*b*), *you*
cannot; as alike *to* compare (63*c*), *to* omitted; than
be *too* bold (64*b*), *too* omitted; may a-keep counsel
(65*b*), *keep*; in *the* fields (70*b*), *the* omitted; look on
a king (70*c*), *a* omitted; head *fast* under (71*b*), *fast*
omitted; stand at *receipt* (72*b*), in original *receite*,
but changed in 1566 to *recite* as though=recital: a
rare form, and one which the O.E.D. does not gloss

until 1685; your maid *examined* (72*b*), *examine*; proof
to his *reproof* (73*a*), *proof*; *then* to deprave (75*c*),
then omitted; she is *so* far gone (77*c*), *so* omitted;
that *striketh* with the sword (77*d*), *strike*; reporteth
it for a truth (77*d*), *it* omitted; the heart *reweth* not
(78*c*), *reneweth*; see a *balk* (81*a*), *block*; to end *of*
all things (82*b*), *of* omitted; thou art so *wood* (86*c*),
good; *whereby* each man (87*b*), *where* each man; *in*
ought that mirth (88*a*), *in* omitted; the fletcher *mends*
(91*a*), *mend*; to *some* tell this tale (92*a*), *some*
omitted; leapt *over* a block (92*b*), in original *ever*,
but *ouer* in ed. 1566; *with* one bush (95*a*), *with* is
duplicated in error; *liked* then (95*b*), *like*; hundred
pound (95*d*), misprinted *pround* in original and set
right in ed. 1566; wellnigh *tryeth* me (97*b*), *tyreth*;
Fond wedding (102*d*), *found*; For unhonest . . .
sounds (107*d*), included in parentheses; A Louse and
a Flea (110*c*), *a* omitted; A Hearer of *a* Sermon
(111*a*), *a* omitted; Thick ears and *thick* wits be plenty
(115*a*), so in original, the 1566 reading being *thin*;
did die for lack of wind (115*d*), *died*; so feat *a*
reason (116*a*), *a* omitted; and *yonder* weathercock
(116*b*), *yonde*, in a field (118*b*), *the*; I *heard* of truth
(120*c*), *hear*; as for *the* holy day (126*d*), *the* omitted;
too shrewd a wit in desire to dwell (127*d*), *a shrewd
wit in desire*; in *God's* precepts (127*d*), *God's*
omitted; which *were best* choice (130*c*), *were the best*
choice; Made I *any* lie (132*d*), *a*; A Louse and *a*
Flea (135*b*), *a* omitted; Of *this* Word, Enough
(137*c*), *the*; strike and chime *twelve* (141*a*), in
original "xij." and "12." in ed. 1566; smart, *or*
tickle (142*b*), *or* omitted; *(think* I) (144*d*), *(quoth* I);
as *I wot thou art* (151*d*), *as thou I wot art*; Of
treading *on* a worm (157*d*), *of*; Of mirth *with* wisdom
(128*a*), *and*; Of the *Fox's* preaching (161*d*), *fox*;
better take *twenty* pounds (169*b*), the roman numerals
of the original are, as before, replaced by Arabic
figures in the edition of 1566; *better for birders but
for birds* not so good (173*d*), *better for birds but for
birders, &c.*; "*too* far past shame" (174*c*), *too*
omitted; store may be *a* sore (176*d*), *a* omitted;
mo of *womankind* (177*a*), *womenkind*; as *to* work
for nought (180*b*), *to* omitted; Of *a* painted
sheath (180*c*), *a* omitted; venturing is *now* such

(181*b*), *no* ; good *horse* (186*c*), *horses* ; Measure is *a merry mean In volumes*, &c. (192*c*), *a* omitted in original : here as in ed. 1566 ; *how . . . sure that malkin one* (200*b*), *is one* ; *scalded* squire (200*c*), *scabbed* ; say *so a long* space (203*c*), *so long a* ; *each will other* disdain (204*a*), *each other will* ; 234 (216*a*), in original misnumbered 233 ; 235 (216*b*), in the original misnumbered 234 ; in both cases put right in the 1566 copy ; few *good* doles (224*d*), *good* omitted ; 291 (226*b*), misnumbered 281 in original, but correctly in 1566 copy ; Of *smellings* (227*a*), *smelling* ; Of *least* tittle (231*b*), of *the least* tittle ; Of *a* disagreement (233*c*), *a* omitted ; Of loving of a *goose* (234*b*), *geese* ; Between dogs and *a* deer (234*c*), *a* omitted ; *An* advice against mocking (238*b*), *Of* ; Of *a* horse (238*d*), *a* omitted ; I would *be, both* for (239*d*), *be in both* ; gable ends, *cambers* (239*d*), *chambers* ; the leg *is* itching (240*a*), *is* omitted ; may *seem your* wife's father (243*a*), *seem you,* your ; whence come *their* glittering spangs (243*d*), *these* ; *corned* crooked toes (243*d*), *corn* ; like a *now* hunted sow (245*d*), *new* ; Of *a* Cutter of Purslane (246*b*), *the* ; standeth in *no* man's else (246*c*), *no* omitted ; 41 (248*d*), erroneously in original 40 ; choice of one *of* two things (250*d*), *of* omitted ; *is chief* part (251*b*), *is the chief part* ; so *courteous* (255*a*), original has *curtusie* ; and *one* on each side (258*d*), *one* omitted ; March hare's *mad* property (274*d*), *made* ; Of *a* lanthorn and Light (279*c*), *a* omitted ; *lost'st* a mark (279*c*), losest (lostest—losist) ; at *the* tale's end (280*a*), *thy* ; bring both *these* about (280*d*), *these* omitted ; *axt* (283*c*), *axe* ; *Smart's* Key (284*a*), *Smarris* ; Carter Lane? *nay, nay* (284*a*), one *nay* is omitted ; in *thy* head (284*b*), *the* ; to *scratch* (285*b*), *scart* ; Hast *any* marjorum, gentle (288*a*), hast *thou* any : in present text delete the comma before " gentle " ; Of *Pineapple* (288*d*), " Of a pine *tppell* " ; Epigram 76 (289*c*), in original *lettuce* is spelt *lettes* in the text, and *lettis* in the title of the Epigram—in modernising the spelling, the *es* of the former is represented by *uce* : the pun, such as it is, is thus preserved, its modern guise being *let us* ; when *ye* list (293*c*), *he* list ; is *now* assigned (294*a*), *now* is omitted ; walk *plainly* (295*c*), *blainly* ; turned *to merry* scoff

(297c), *to a merry*; *If* all the world (299), *of* in MS. copy. See Errata, page 466.

VENGEABLY, " vengeably strait-laced " (129d, *et passim*), very, exceedingly : an intensive.

VENOM, " spit her venom " (24d).

VENTURE, see Nought.

VIAGE, " this viage make " (21c), *voyage*=a journey by land or sea.

WADE, " for what should I further wade " (43a).

WAG, see Merry.

WAGHALTER, " waghalter slipstring " (86d), *waghalter* =a rogue, gallowsbird, crackrope : see Slipstring.

WAKING, " might have been asleep for ought they in waking . . . would do " (30b).
  (b) see Dog.

WALK, (a) " walk, drab, walk ! " (63c).
  (b) " walk, knave, walk ! " (63c).
  (c) see Waster.

WALKING-STAFF, " the walking-staff hath caught warmth in your hand " (26c).

WALL, (a) " to winch . . . against the hard wall " (68b ; 219b and c), *winch* (or *wince*)=kick. " Paul, whom the Lord hadde chosun, long tyme wynside agen the pricke."—Wycliffe, *Prolog on the Dedes of Apostles*.
  (b) " further than the wall he cannot go " (71b ; 192d).
  (c) " drive him to the wall " (71b), urge to extremities, " corner."
  (d) " I shall pike out no more than out of the stone wall " (72b), *pike*=pick, find out, learn, mark.
  (e) " as in frost a mud wall . . . cracketh and crummeth . . . so melteth his money " (79a).

WALTHAM, " as wise as Waltham's calf " (58d), the allusion is lost though the meaning is clear and examples are many, the earliest I have found occurring in Skelton's *Colin Clout* (1520), where a rascal priest is described " As wyse as Waltom's calfe . . . he can nothyng smatter Of logyke nor scole matter."

" Some running and gadding calves, wiser than Waltham's calfe that ranne nine miles to sucke a bull."—*Disclosing of the great Bull* [*Harl. Misc.* (1567), vii. 535].

WAN, " I wan them " (42*a*; 118*c*), won.

WARE, see Merchant.

WARELY, " Being fled warely " (140*c*), warily : note the rhyme with " barely " and " charely " (=charily).

WARLING, see Darling.

WARM, see God's blessing, Wise.

WARS, " we do much wars " (39*a*), worse : note the rhyme.

WASH, " as sober as she seemeth, five days come about but she will once wash her face in an ale clout " (26*d*) : see Ale-clout.

WASP, " angry as a wasp " (31*b*).

WASTE, see Haste.

WASTER, " walked with a waster " (148*a*), beaten : walk=beat ; *waster*=cudgel.

WAT, " thy head . . . sheweth thee a wat " (141*c*), *wat*=hare : a type of light or empty headedness, as in " hare-brained."

WATER, (*a*) " the trial thereof we will lay a water " (10*a*)—" my matter is laid a water " (191*a*), put aside, defer judgment, render nugatory : see Lay.

(*b*) " you come to look in my water " (41*a*), physicians once diagnosed complaints by " casting the water of a patient." " If thou could'st, doctor, cast The water of my land, find her disease."—Shakspeare, *Macbeth* (1606), v. 3.

(*c*) " no more water than the ship drew " (89*a*).

(*d*) see Horse, Moonshine, Pot.

WATER-DRINKER, " a falser water-drinker there liveth not " (72*a*).

WAX, " she should have wrought like wax " (75*a*).

WAY, (a) " if ye haul this way I will another way draw " (63d).

    (b) see Wood.

    (c) " it is out of my way " (220d).

WEAKER, (a) " the weaker hath the worse " (23b ; 199d).

    (b) see Pot.

WEALTH, (a) " both for wealth and woe " (17a), *wealth* =(originally) good, weal, prosperity. " Let no man seek his own, but every man another's wealth."— 1 *Corinth. (Auth. Ver.,* 1611), x. 24.

    (b) " all thing may be suffered saving wealth " (62b).

WEAR, see Breech.

WEATHER, (a) " when all shrews have dined, change from foul weather to fair is oft inclined " (50c).

    (b) " weather meet to set paddocks abrod in " (50b), see Clouds, Curryfavel, Paddock.

WEATHERCOCK, " like a weathercock " (102a).

WED, " where nought is to wed with wise men flee the clog " (32a).

WEDDED, " I was wedded unto my will . . . I will be divorced and be wed to my wit " (102c).

WEDDETH, " who weddeth or he be wise shall die or he thrive " (19b ; 172b).

WEDDING (TERMS OF), (a) " wooing for woeing, banna for banning, the banns for my bane, marrying marring, a woman, as who saith, woe to the man " (83c).

    (b) " wedding and hanging are destiny " (9c ; 168b), an earlier mention, " Hanging and wiving go by destiny," is found in the *Schole-hous for Women* (1541). In 1558 a ballad was licensed with the title " The Proverbe is true yᵗ Weddynge is destinyē."

    (c) " they went (witless) to wedding whereby at last they both went a-begging " (33d).

    (d) " quick wedding may bring good speed " (10a).

WEED, (a) " ill weed groweth apace " (27d ; 217b).
" Ewyl weed ys sone y-growe."—*M.S. Harleian*
(c. 1490).
  (b) " the weed overgroweth the corn " (27d).

WEEK, " in by the week " (84b ; 176d).

WEEP, " better children weep than old men " (175c),
see Children.

WEET (220a), wet.

WELCOME, " welcome when thou goest " (79d).

WELL, (a) " all is well that ends well " (25c ; 202d).
  (b) " believe well and have well " (90d).
  (c) " do well and have well " (90d).
  (d) see Bag.
  (e) " many wells, many buckets " (85b), with which
compare the modern retort, " How many wells make
a river ? "

WET, see Cat.

WET FINGER, " with a wet finger " (95c), easily, readily :
as easy as turning over the leaf of a book, rubbing
out writing on a slate, or tracing a lady's name on
the table with spilt wine—the last may well be the
origin of the phrase : cf. " Verba leges digitis, verba
notata mero " (Ovid, *Amor.* i. 4. 20). So also Tibullus,
lib. i. el. 6 :—" Neu te decipiat nutu, digitoque
liquorem Ne trahat, et mensæ ducat in orbe notas."
" What gentlewomen or citizens' wives you can with
a wet finger have at any time to sup with you."—
Dekker, *The Gull's Hornbook* (1602).

WHAT'S O'CLOCK, see Clock.

WHELP, " as a whelp for wantonness in and out whips "
(17c).

WHIP, " at a whip " (118d), at a bound, as if in re-
sponse to a slash of a whip.

WHISTERS, " this lesson he whisters " (122c), tells
softly, whispers : note the rhyme.

WHIT, " as good never a whit as never the better "
(102b).

WHITE, see Crow.

WHITE LIVERED (69c), cowardly, mean: an old notion
was that cowards had bloodless livers. "White
liver'd runagate."—Shakspeare, *Richard III.* (1597),
iv. 1.

WHITENESS, "that all her whiteness lieth in her white
hairs" (4c), *whiteness*=chastity. "The purity and
whiteness of my sheets."—Shakspeare, *Winter's Tale*
(1604), i. 2.

WHITING, "there leaped a whiting" (78d), there was
an opportunity missed.

WHOLE, (a) "if ye lack that away ye must wind with
your whole errand and half th' answer behind" (51c).
(b) "hear the whole, the whole wholly to try"
(50a).

WHORE, "hop whore, pipe thief" (86d).

WIDE, (a) see Shoot.
(b) "wide a bow of Bridewell" (243b), beyond a
bow shot."

WIFE, (a) "he that will thrive must ask leave of his
wife" (34d): a variant is "it is hard to wive and
thrive Both in a year" (34d). "A man may not
wyfe And also thryfe And alle in a yere."—*Towneley
Mysteries* (c. 1420).
(b) "the best or worst thing to man for this life
is good or ill choosing his good or ill wife" (6b).
(c) "a good wife maketh a good husband" (88c).
(d) see Shoemaker's wife.

WIGHT, "as wight as the hound" (180c), *wight*=
nimble, active. "He was so nimble and so wight."
—Spenser, *Shepheards Calendar*, March.

WILL, (a) "he that will not when he may, when he
would, he shall have nay" (8a; 168c), compare "who
that may not as they would, will as they may" (68a).
(b) "when we would, ye would not . . . wherefore
now when ye would, now will not we" (28b).

(c) " that one will not, another will " (8*d*).

(d) " will will have will, though will woe win " (35*a*).

(e) " will is a good son and will is a shrewd boy and wilful shrewd will hath wrought thee this toy " (35*a*).

(f) see Wax, Wedded, Win.

WILLING, " nothing is impossible to a willing heart " (11*c*).

WIN, (a) " will may win my heart " (11*d*).

(b) " although I nought win yet shall I nought lose " (102*a*).

(c) " ye can nought win by any wayward mean " (68*d*).

(d) " he playeth best that wins " (215*c*), see Laugh.

WINCH, see Wall (*a*).

WIND, (a) " an ill wind that bloweth no man to good " (93*c*; 183*a*). " *Falstaff.* What wind blew you hither? *Pistol.* Not the ill wind which blows no man to good." —Shakspeare, 2 *Henry IV.* (1598), v. 3.

(b) " let this wind overblow " (36*c*; 215*d*).

(c) " every wind bloweth not down the corn " (93*d*)

(d) " all this wind shakes no corn " (36*c*).

(e) " he smelled her out and had her straight in the wind " (39*c*), had at an advantage; understood her.

(f) " I have him in the wind " (223*b*), see *supra.*

(g) " what wind bloweth ye hither? " (25*a*).

(h) " to take wind and tide with me " (36*c*).

(i) " if the wind stand in that door, it standeth awry " (68*c*). " It is even so? is the winde in that doore? "—Gascoigne, *Supposes* (1566).

(j) " your meddling . . . may bring the wind calm between us " (59*d*).

(k) " I will . . . ill winds to sway, spend some wind . . . though I waste wind in vain " (60*a*), *wind* =breath is ancient. " Woman thy wordis and thy wynde thou not waste."—*York Plays* (*c.* 1362), 258.

(*l*) " knew which way the wind blew " (91*b*), aware of the position of matters, state of affairs.

(*m*) " wavering as the wind " (54*d*).

WINDFALL, " to win some windfall " (38*d*).

WINE, " ye praise the wine before ye taste of the grape " (27*d*).

WING, " keep your bill under wing mute " (69*a*).

WINK, see Cat.

WINNETH, " he laugheth that winneth " (12*d*; 215*b*), see Laugh.

WINS, see Win.

WISE, (*a*) " ye are wise enough if ye keep ye warm " (56*c*; 193*c*).

(*b*) " better to be happy than wise " (75*c*; 190*b*).

(*c*) " as ye can seem wise in words be wise in deed " (73*b*).

(*d*) " every wise man staggers in earnest or boord to be busy or bold with his biggers or betters " (47*d*).

(*e*) see Merry, Weddeth.

WISEST MEN, see Clerks.

WISH, " better have than wish " (61*c*; 222*b* and *c*).

WISHERS, " wishers and woulders be no good house-holders " (32*b*). " Wysshers and wolders ben smal housholders."—*Vulg. Stambrigi* (1510). " He . . . resolved rather to live by his wit, then any way to be pinched with want, thinking this old sentence to be true, the wishers and woulders were never good house-holders."—Green, *Never too Late* (1590).

WIST, (*a*) " beware of Had I wist " (6*c*; 219*d*), an exclamation of regret. " Be welle war of wedyng, and thynk in youre thought ' Had I wist ' is a thyng it servys of nought."—*Towneley Myst.* (*c.* 1420).

(*b*) see Blab.

WIT, (*a*) " wit is never good till bought " (18*d*; 169*c* and *d*), *wit* = wisdom, knowledge. " Stationers could not live, if men did not beleeve the old saying, that Wit bought is better than Wit taught."—*Conceits, Clinches, Flashes and Whimzies* (1639).

(*b*) " to leave my wit before it leave me " (55*c*).

(*c*) " at our wit's end " (18*d* ; 169*c*).

(*d*) " one good forewit worth is two afterwits " (19*a*).

(*e*) see Ale, Head, Tongue, Wedded.

WOE, (*a*) " she hath wrought her own woe " (25*d*).

(*b*) " woe worth all crafty inventions " (116*b* ; 304*a*), worth=to become, to be : here in imperative with the noun in the dative, and meaning " Woe be to," &c.

(*c*) see Hasty.

WOLF, (*a*) " to keep the wolf from the door " (83*b*).

(*b*) " a wolf in a lamb's skin " (28*a*).

WOMAN, see Cat.

WON, see Cards, Nought.

WONDER, " this wonder lasted nine days " (53*b* ; 196*b*). " Eke wonder last but nine deies never in town."— Chaucer, *Troilus and Creseide*. " A book on any subject by a peasant, or a peer, is no longer so much as a nine-days wonder."—Ascham, *Schoole-master* (1570).

WONDERED, " he that doeth as most men do, shall be least wondered on " (56*a*).

WONDERFOOL, " wonderfool well " (243*a*), a play on " fool " and " full."

WOOD, (*a*) " there be mo ways to the wood than one " (93*d* ; 187*b*).

(*b*) " thou art so wood " (31*b* ; 86*c*)—" horn wood " (99*c*), mad, furious, frantic, raging. " Flemynges, lyke wood tygres."—Fabyan, *Cronycle* (an. 1299). See Horn wood.

(*c*) " ye cannot see the wood for trees " (62*b*). " From him who sees no wood for trees And yet is busie as the bees . . . Libera nos."—*A Letany for S. Omers* (1682).

(d) " ye took the wrong way to wood " (91d).

(e) see Bird, Cow, Crow, Eyes, Woodness.

WOODCOCK (242d), simpleton, fool. " O this wood-cock! what an ass it is! "—Shakspeare, *Taming of the Shrew* (1593), i. 2.

WOODNESS, " worse than woodness " (193a), *wood=* mad, furious, frantic, raging : see other volumes of this series.

WOOL, (a) " what should your face thus again the wool be shorn? " (36c).

(b) " thy face is shorn against the wool, very deep " (198d).

(c) see Sheep's flesh.

WORD, (a) " not afford you one good word " (93b).

(b) " one ill word axeth another " (22a).

(c) " many words, many buffets " (85b).

(d) " good words bring not ever of good deeds good hope " (94a).

(e) " this doth sound . . . on your side in words, but on my side in deed " (83d).

(f) " few words to the wise suffice " (82c).

(g) see Losers, Tongue, Wood.

WORK, see Hands, Play.

WORKMAN, " what is a workman without his tools? " (94c; 189b).

WORLD, (a) " the world runneth on wheels " (78b), runs easily, expeditiously.

(b) " let the world wag " (12d), let go, let things take care of themselves. " Y'are a baggage; the Slies are no rogues; Look in the chronicles, we came in with Richard Conqueror. Therefore, paucas palla-bris; let the world slide."—Shakspeare, *Taming of the Shrew*, Induction, i. 6.

(*c*) " he brought the world so about " (98*d*).

WORM, " tread a worm on the tail and it must turn again " (64*c*; 171*c*). " The .. worm will turn, being trodden on; And doves will peck in safe-guard of their brood."—Shakspeare, 3 *Henry VI.* (1595), ii. 2.

WORSE, (*a*) " all thing is the worse for the wearing " (54*a*).

(*b*) see Lady, Lord, Shoemaker's wife, Weaker.

WORST, (*a*) " provide for the worst, while the best itself save " (12*d*; 220*b*).

(*b*) " the worst is behind, we come not where it grew " (57*c*; 195*d*; 196*a* and *b*).

(*c*) " if the worst fell, we could have but a nay " (44*c*).

(*d*) see Candle.

WOT, " I wot what I wot " (84*d*).

WOULD, see Will.

WRESTLING, see Weaker.

WRINGER, " your wealth's wringer " (280*c*), *i.e.* the thumb and finger as the instruments of the payment away, or the dissipation of money.

WRITE, see Friends, Health.

WRONG, (*a*) " thou beggest at wrong door " (181*a*)—" ye beg at a wrong man's door " (20*c*).

(*b*) see Sow.

WROTING, " the wroting hog " (172*c*), grubbing, rooting.

WULL (75*d*), will : note the rhyme.

HEY. II.   H H

YEAR, (a) " I am too old a year " (90c).
    (b) see Dear, Fair, Happeth, Stake.

YESTERDAY, (a) "·it is too late to call again yesterday "
(90b).
    (b) " the offence of yesterday I may redeem " (90b).

YIELD, " in case as ye shall yield me as ye cost me, so
shall ye cost me as ye yield me " (43c).

YIS (282d; 291b), yes: note the rhyme and compare
with the modern Cockney vulgarism.

YIT (82a), yet : note the rhyme.

YOUNG, (a) " ye be young enough to mend . . . but I
am . . . too old to see it " (90c).
    (b) see Saint, Devil.

YOUNGER, " ye shall never labour younger " (21c), see
Labour.

YOW (*passim*), you.

ERRATA.

PAGE
8d, Blame me not to haste *read* too.
20a, day after fair *read* after the fair.
33a, in saying that *read* in seeing that.
33c, like to the fire *read* like to the sire.
51b, Diners *read* Dinners.
84d, good children *read* godchildren.
242a, Yes, Clim *read* Yes, clim.
244d, nett *read* net.